Ambush Marketing

Ambush Marketing
Game within a Game

Arul George Scaria

OXFORD
UNIVERSITY PRESS

YMCA Library Building, Jai Singh Road, New Delhi 110001

Oxford University Press is a department of the University of Oxford. It furthers the University's objective of excellence in research, scholarship, and education by publishing worldwide in

Oxford New York
Auckland Cape Town Dar es Salaam Hong Kong Karachi
Kuala Lumpur Madrid Melbourne Mexico City Nairobi
New Delhi Shanghai Taipei Toronto

With offices in
Argentina Austria Brazil Chile Czech Republic France Greece
Guatemala Hungary Italy Japan Poland Portugal Singapore
South Korea Switzerland Thailand Turkey Ukraine Vietnam

Published in India
by Oxford University Press, New Delhi

First published 2008

ISBN-13: 978-0-19-569307-2
ISBN-10: 0-19-569307-8

Typeset in Giovanni 10.5/13.6
By Jojy Philip New Delhi 110 015
Printed in India by Rajshree Photolithographers, Delhi 110 032
Published by Oxford University Press
YMCA Library Building, Jai Singh Road, New Delhi 110 001

Dedicated to
Achachan and Amma,
Who made me what I am!

Contents

Abbreviations

AIR	All India Reporter
B.U. L. Rev.	Boston University Law Review
BOCOG	Beijing Organizing Committee for the Games of the XXIX Olympiad
Cardozo Arts & Ent. L.J.	Cardozo Arts and Entertainment Law Journal
Colum. L. Rev.	Columbia Law Review
Columbia Bus. L. Rev.	Columbia Business Law Review
Duke L.J.	Duke Law Journal
EIPR	European Intellectual Property Review
EC	European Commission
ECJ	European Court of Justice
Ent. & Sports Law.	Entertainment and Sports Lawyer
Ent. L.R.	Entertainment Law Review
FDA	Food and Drug Administration
FIFA	Federation Internationale De Football Association
Fordham Intell. Prop. Media & Ent. L.J.	Fordham Intellectual Property, Media and Entertainment Law Journal

Harv. L.Rev.	Hardvard Law Review
HMRC	Her Majesty's Revenue and Customs
ICC	International Cricket Council
IOC	International Olympic Committee
Intell. Prop. Strategist	Intellectual Property Strategist
J. Contemp. Legal Issues	Journal of Contemporary Legal Issues
J. Intell. Prop. L.	Journal of Intellectual Property Law
J. Legal Aspects Sport	Journal of Legal Aspects of Sport
J.C. & U.L.	Journal of College and University Law
LOCOG	London Organising Committee of the Olympic Games
Loy. L. A. Int'l & Comp. L. Rev.	Loyola of Los Angeles International and Comparative Law Review
Loy. L.A. Ent. L. Rev.	Loyola of Los Angeles Entertainment Law Review
Marq. Sports L.J.	Marquette Sports Law Journal
NHL	National Hockey League
Nw. J. Tech. & Intell. Prop.	Northwestern Journal of Technology and Intellectual Property
ODA	Olympics Development Authority
OSPA	Olympic Symbol (Protection) Act 1995
SC	Supreme Court
SLOC	Salt Lake Organizing Committee
Seton Hall J. Sport L.	Seton Hall Journal of Sport Law
Tex. Rev. Ent. & Sports L.	Texas Review of Entertainment and Sports Law
TOP	The Olympic Partnernship
Trademark Rep.	The Trademark Reporter
U. Toronto Fac. L. Rev.	University of Toronto Faculty of Law Review

U.S. Dep't of Justice & Fed. Trade Comm'n	U.S. Department of Justice and the Federal Trade Commission
USOC	United States Olympic Committee
Vill. Sports & Ent. L.J.	Villanova Sports and Entertainment Law Journal

Cases

Preface

An ambush marketer is an uninvited guest to a sponsored event. As the very term indicates, ambush marketing is a type of marketing wherein non-sponsors make startling appearances in a sponsored event to give an impression of involvement, without formally associating with the event and committing to the financial liabilities involved in it. Needless to say, such apparent involvement and the fallacious impression created by it can have devastating consequences, not only for the sponsors but also for the event organizers. Sponsorship is one of the most important sources of income for event organizers across the world and for the corporate world it is a befitting conduit for promoting their brands. However, it is certain that the sponsorship potential will dwindle if the exclusivity of association with an event is not suitably protected.

Most of the event organizers today are threatened by ambush marketing practices and many have found themselves entangled in unpleasant litigations. Often, event organizers have been forced to return at least a part of the sponsorship money for failing to protect the legitimate exclusivity rights of the sponsors. As many studies have pointed out, ambush marketing occurrences can tone down the sponsorship value of such events and needless to say, inadequate sponsorships would be a severe dint in conducting massive events like the World Cup and the Olympics in future.

The issue of ambush marketing is taken up in this work for discussion from the point of view of intellectual property law. The question of legitimacy or illegitimacy is particularly significant in the current context of escalating ambush marketing incidents. As the area has hardly attracted the serious attention of the academia, the present exercise attempts to break new ground in an exciting interdisciplinary sphere of knowledge. It is my earnest belief that only meaningful debates can help us arrive at feasible legal mechanisms to counter ambush marketing. It is also important that such answers do not disregard existing democratic values and overlook larger public interests. How do intellectual property laws perceive and tackle the issues of ambush marketing? How do traditional legal regimes attempt to counter it? What are the viable resolutions one can possibly arrive at? How far are event-specific anti-ambush marketing legislations effective in checking the menace? What are the incidental effects of the event-specific anti- ambush marketing legislations from the angle of constitutional and competition law? How can public opinion be accommodated in measures aimed at curbing ambush marketing? These questions are problematized in detail and viewed from a multiplicity of angles in the pages to follow. The attempt is not to provide conclusive answers to the problem but rather, to throw light upon a relatively unexplored area, and to bring it to the gaze of academics, jurists, managers, and the public for generating profitable discussions that can pave the way to better solutions.

This work has been in the making for sometime now and I have benefited immensely out of the resourceful inputs from various quarters. It was V.K. Unni, Assistant Professor, NALSAR University of Law, Hyderabad, who encouraged me to explore the issues related to intellectual property rights in this area and it is his valuable guidance that has kept me moving at every stage of this study. V. Balakista Reddy, Associate Professor, NALSAR University of Law, Hyderabad, has been an inspiring guide with profound insights throughout. V.J. Varghese, Lecturer, Centre for Development Studies, Thiruvananthapuram, has been on my side from the very beginning with his considered interventions and musings.

I am indebted to Ramakrishna, National Law School of India University, Bangalore, for sparing his precious time for the fruitful discussion on the subject and to N. S. Gopalakrishnan, Director, School of Legal Studies, Cochin University of Science and Technology, for allowing me to access the I.P.R. Depository at the School of Legal Studies. I sincerely thank the librarians and all the other library staff of NALSAR University of Law, Hyderabad, National Law School of India University, Bangalore, School of Legal Studies, Cochin University of Science and Technology, and Hyderabad Central University, Hyderabad, for their support during my research work. I cheerfully acknowledge the discussions with and the help I received from Hardeep Singh Aujla, Roney

Jose Kurian, K. Parameshwar, Mayank Bharanwal, and Sophy Joseph at NALSAR.

I am also thankful to the two anonymous reviewers of the Oxford University Press (OUP), whose critical as well as complimentary comments helped immensely to refine the present work. It was a pleasant experience to work with the Commissioning Editor of OUP and she was cheerful and unfailing in her support throughout. She, along with the entire OUP team, deserves special appreciation for bringing the book out promptly and efficiently.

My special thanks to Anil K. Gupta and all the other members of my Honey Bee family, of which the National Innovation Foundation is an integral part, for the intellectual environment they gave me during the final stages of this work.

My parents, Scaria Zacharia and Marykutty Scaria, my sister Suma, and my wife Sandy, gladly and effusively shared the pangs and joys of the book's making right from the beginning. This work would not have been possible without the unfailing backing and trust I have always enjoyed from their side.

Hoping earnestly that the challenging field of ambush marketing will be as absorbing to many, as it has been fascinating to me, I submit this book to my readers.

ARUL GEORGE SCARIA

Introduction

When cricket fans across the world were passionately waiting for 13 March 2007, the day on which the ICC Cricket World Cup 2007 started in the Caribbean Islands, other groups were undergoing intense anxieties but not about cricket per se. The much awaited cricket carnival in actuality caters to varied constituencies, taking it beyond the pleasure-logics of the sport and the entertainment of genuine sports fan. Events of this kind, which have an obsessive transcontinental spectatorship, provide fabulous opportunities to the corporate world, as sponsorship of events is considered one of the best conduits for making an entry into the minds of prospective consumers. It is not surprising that among the contemporary techniques of marketing, sponsorship of mega sports events has acquired a talismanic standing whether for launching new brands or to bump up a product identity to the status of a consumer commonsense.

But the pro-active measure of winning new customers or consolidating the existing corpus tends to coincide in general with exclusionary strategies of marketing where the sponsors resort to actually preventing their competitors from using the event to promote the latter's goods. It was with this exclusionist rationality that Hutch telecom approached the International Cricket Council to disallow the celebrated Indian player Sachin Tendulkar from endorsing the competing Reliance Telecom advertisements during the Cricket World Cup, 2007.

The strategies and formulas of marketing have become enormously divergent and extremely innovative, warranting invariable exclusionary surveillance to guard the domain of marketing that one is legitimately entitled to. This is particularly important when contending groups, who are not lawfully part of the event in terms of sponsorship, resort to illegitimate and surprising modes of promotion. It is but natural that one of the most hated words as far as a sponsor of an event is concerned are 'ambush marketing'.

In most simple terms, ambush marketing is a type of marketing of goods or services wherein the companies endeavour to associate themselves with a sponsored event, without being formally part of it, or without meeting the financial liabilities of sponsorship. Through their unexpected interventions, these companies attempt to create an impression upon the spectators or consumers that they are very much associated with the event. This type of marketing that usually takes legitimate sponsors by surprise, could happen in any event having a significant marketing potentiality. However, the lofty endorsement value attached with sports events and the resultant investment of sponsorship on them on a massive scale makes sports a highly rewarding ground for ambush marketing. Some of the frequently employed tactics of ambush marketing include, dispatching hundreds of spectators wearing t-shirts and caps with the company logo or mark into the stadium, placing of billboards with ambush marketer's name and logo adjacent to the site of the event, supplying the crowd with paper flags imprinted with the company logo, organizing publicity contests offering tickets to the event or prizes, etc.

During the course of such exercises to get spuriously connected to the event, the ambush marketers transgress various intellectual property rights associated with the very event. Those who resort to ambush marketing are often seen referring to the events and their own products in an ingenious and subtle manner to circumvent the laws. These innovative as well as deceptive methods often place their actions beyond the reach of established legal mechanisms like trade mark infringement laws or copyright infringement rules, making the issue enormously complicated to tackle. The delicateness involved in this menacing issue led to serious deliberations about it in the legal, sports, and corporate circles. One of the outcomes of such wide-ranging discussions at various levels was the enactment of event-specific legislation to effectively weed out ambush marketing. The Sydney 2000 Games (Indicia and symbols) Protection Act 1996, London Olympic Games and Paralympic Games Act 2006, ICC Cricket World Cup West Indies 2007 Act, etc. are a few examples of such event-specific legislation. In jurisdictions which do not have specific legislation for combating ambush marketing, the event organizers still rely on conventional laws of trade mark, copyright, and passing off.

As it appears now, the situation is rather paradoxical or at least uncomplimentary. On the one side, we are witnessing a sharp increase in the cost of organizing bigger events with a satisfactory amount of pomp and splendour. In the absence or insufficiency of adequate sponsorships, events like the World Cup and Olympics would either vanish into history or become archaic festivities failing to meet the contemporary standards and expectations. But on the other side, we see a sharp multiplication in the number and devices of ambush marketing today, to the extent where the websites of advertising agencies are used to publicize their proficiency in ambush marketing.

This parasitic problem needs to be taken up with meticulous application of intellect to arrive at far reaching solutions for the good of all those who love such events. The contemporary scenario of escalating incidents of ambush marketing awaiting persuasive answers is the inspiration for the present study. The attempt here is to look at the issue of ambush marketing and the measures for averting it from the perspective of intellectual property rights. Though we are encountering the issue of ambush marketing for a significant time now, there seems to be a dearth of serious academic investigation into the subject. One would hardly come across a comprehensive study developed into a full-fledged monograph dealing with the question of ambush marketing. There are of course quite a few research articles, especially coming from the West which include 'Consumer Attitudes of Deception and the Legality of Ambush Marketing Practices' authored by Anita M. Moorman and T. Christopher Greenwell; 'Ambush Marketing: Robbery or Smart Advertising' written by Cristina Garrigues; 'Ambush Marketing: Not Just an Olympic-Sized Problem' by Jacqueline A. Leimer; 'Ambush Marketing: Sports Sponsorship Confusion and the Lanham Act' by Lori L. Bean; 'Reconciling Sports Sponsorship Exclusivity with Antitrust Law' by John A. Fortunato and 'Ambush Marketing: What it is, What it isn't?' by Jerry Welsh. There are also a few useful research articles by Steve McKelvey and Anne M. Wall. An interesting research article coming from India, worth mentioning here is 'Ambush Marketing—The Problem and the Projected Solutions vis-à-vis Intellectual Property Law—A Global Perspective' by Sudipta Bhattacharjee. However, though these articles are competent and methodical works, in the specific issues being taken up respectively for discussion, none of them have been taken as comprehensive. The analysis of scholarly articles on this issue leaves an impression that the established or traditional legal measures are ineffective to a great extent in fighting ambush marketing. Therefore, this study proceeds on a considered presumption that the best possible way of combating the menace of this deceitful marketing would be event-specific legislation.

The main objectives of this study are:

(1) To survey the varied ambush marketing practices found today;
(2) To examine the role played by the existing legal regimes in combating it;
(3) To discuss the possible solutions for this problem, especially the role event-specific legislation can play; and
(4) To analyse the incidental effects of such preventive measures against ambush marketing.

The present study is based on secondary sources. The major sources of information are statistics collected from the official websites of event organizers and various scholarly articles from academic journals discussing various ambush marketing techniques and the (in)effectiveness of the traditional legal measures. The Sydney 2000 Games (Indicia and symbols) Protection Act 1996, the London Olympic Games and Paralympic Games Act 2006 and the Chinese Regulation on the Protection of Olympic Symbols are collected from the Australian Government website, the UK Parliament website and the BOCOG website respectively.

Chapter 1 is an opening to the new world of ambush marketing and its intricacies. Any manoeuvre to comprehend ambush marketing without discerning the functions of a trade mark is akin to attempts at constructing walls without laying the foundation. The chapter therefore takes off with a general analysis on the significance of intellectual property rights in the new information era and then proceeds to elucidate the vitality of a key member of the intellectual property family—the trade mark. The advantages of a trade mark are explicated by disentangling the advertising functions and the license earning potential of it in detail. The second part of the chapter is preoccupied primarily with the question of how a trade mark becomes a brand in due course. It also looks into the manifold ways, often resorted to, for brand promotion where sponsorship of events is given a detailed consideration. It delves into various dimensions of rights often linked with sponsorships and thereby sets the background for a methodical discussion on ambush marketing.

Chapter 2 is an investigation into the real scope and extent of ambush marketing practices in the contemporary market. This begins with an attempt to offer a satisfactory definition to 'ambush marketing' and then moves on to different modes of marketing strategies that fit with the nuances of that definition. This is done by juxtaposing the marketing practices and procedures that have been seen in major sponsored events of recent times. This chapter will also examine some of the burgeoning issues arising from the misuse of the Internet as a medium and platform for ambush marketing. The last section of the chapter examines the impact of ambush marketing in a broad perspective, which includes a discussion about those companies that are engaged in ambush marketing from the angle of corporate social responsibility.

Chapter 3 scrutinizes the traditional legal measures used in combating ambush marketing. The efficacy of trade mark infringement action, copyright infringement action, and passing off action are discussed in detail. This is done by analysing the criteria for invoking these actions and by examining whether these criteria are fulfilled in those specific instances of ambush marketing. The examination of case law will bring to light the effectiveness of traditional legal measures along side the urgency to exceed the inadequacies of those conventional legal procedures.

Chapter 4 commences with an explication of the role played by the event-specific legislation against ambush marketing by delving into the Sydney 2000 Games (Indicia and symbols) Protection Act 1996 and the London Olympic Games and Paralympic Games Act 2006. Here, a detailed consideration is given to assessing the competence of the Sydney 2000 Games Act in preventing ambush marketing during the Olympics at 'the Harbour City'. The second part of this chapter is an investigation as to how the developing countries perceive and tackle the issues of ambush marketing. This discussion is carried with a detailed examination of the measures taken by China as the host of Beijing Olympics 2008 and the anti-ambush marketing approaches found in India, which is preparing to host the Common Wealth Games in 2010. The Chinese Regulation on the Protection of Olympic Symbols is analysed in contrast with the Sydney 2000 Games Act and the London Olympics Act in this part.

Chapter 5 pursues the arguments levelled in general against the efforts to curb ambush marketing. This is done particularly by pondering over the incidental effects of event-specific legislation on the freedom of speech and expression. This is done through a reflection on the question whether advertisements can be considered as 'commercial speech' and if so, would ambush marketing advertisements come within the purview of that protection. The second section of the chapter is devoted to the interface of anti-ambush marketing efforts with the fundamental assumptions of competition law. The discussion here focuses primarily on two issues. Firstly, whether the event-specific legislation and other measures against ambush marketing are essentially anti-competitive in nature and secondly, whether an abuse of a dominant position by the event organizers, within the meaning of competition law, happens when the event organizer imposes unjustifiable restrictions that harm competition.

The concluding chapter summarizes the findings of the work by pointing out some of the areas and issues that demand the prompt attention of the event organizers as well as the sponsors of events to effectively tackle the perilous issues of ambush marketing. These suggestions assume vital significance in the light of some of the recent controversies and public outcry concerning anti-ambush marketing efforts. Such contentions would be replicated with varying intensity if the event organizers tend to overlook public interests and if the public, in self-interest, eschew constraints of the event organizers. Striking a careful and informed line of balance between these apparently conflicting rationalities, rather than counter-posing them against one another is the only plausible way out.

1

The Long Road from Trade Marks to Sponsorship

Intellectual Property could be called the Cinderella of the new economy. A drab, but useful servant, consigned to the dusty and uneventful offices of corporate legal departments until the Princes of globalization and technological innovation—revealing her true value—swept her to prominence and gave her an enticing allure.[1]

The history of the human race is the history of application of imagination, innovation, and creativity.[2] The progress of arts and science rests on the power of imagination. When the power of imagination is used in solving a technical or artistic challenge, it becomes valuable intellectual property.[3] Intellectual Property, in other words, is the term that describes ideas, inventions, technologies, art works, music, and literature, which are intangible when first created, but become valuable in tangible form as products. The old brick and mortar economy is being fast replaced with an economy of ideas wherein the most valuable currency is intellectual property and this new economy banks on the power of technology and knowledge for its robust economic growth.[4] This makes even the shareholders of a company sensitive to the value of intellectual property assets, using them as an indicator for assessing the competitive edge of the company.[5]

The new management gurus are well aware of this strategic use of intellectual property and it has become a major element in the corporate business management. For example, Microsoft, which is considered to have a book value of US $90 billion, has a market capitalization value of around US $270 billion and a major part of this extra US $180 billion is said to come from its intellectual property assets in the form of trade marks, patents, trade secrets, and know-how.[6]

The importance of different forms of intellectual property to a business enterprise varies with the activities and the markets in which it operates.[7] But one thing is sure. Firms that fail to fully comprehend the value of their intellectual property run the risk of revenue loss, poor positioning in the market, diminishing market value, and even a possible collapse in this knowledge-driven economy.[8]

ROLE OF TRADE MARKS TODAY

Trade mark is a core member of the wider family of intellectual property and as such receives legal protection against unauthorized use by third parties.[9] A trade mark is a visual symbol in the form of a word, device, or label applied to articles of commerce with a view to indicate to the purchasing public that they are the goods manufactured or otherwise dealt in by a particular person, as distinguished from similar goods manufactured or dealt in by other persons.[10] It is a symbol of the product and is necessarily an element of a process of communication—a communication that originates with the owner or seller of a product and is received by a prospective buyer of that product.[11] Trade mark allows firms to create a robust brand which is essential to cultivate recognition and trust in the market. This increasing role played by trade marks in the promotion of a product through the creation of recognition and trust in the market makes them possess a strong influence on private investment and marketing decisions and also at the same time a potential point for conflicts.[12]

To qualify as a trade mark, a mark must be a sign which is capable of being represented graphically and it should also be able to distinguish the goods or services of one undertaking from those of other undertakings.[13] Economically, legally, and historically, the most important function of a trade mark is its role as an indication of origin.[14] All the other subsidiary functions that the trade mark fulfils during its economic life are evolved from this basic function.[15] The practice of marking goods for various purposes was known centuries before legal protection was even an issue. There are cited examples of cattle marking and pottery marking from as early as 5000 BC.[16] The marking of goods indicated the ownership of goods and functioned as proprietary marks.[17] The twelfth and thirteenth centuries witnessed the emergence of one more type of mark—regulation or production mark.[18]

Two trades that were instrumental in transforming the trade mark to its modern form were the cloth industry and the cutlery industry. The concept of collective goodwill originated from the cloth industry.[19] The products of a particular person or industry came to be identified for quality and could be purchased subsequently with the help of the attached symbol. The Courts also recognized such marks as being worthy of protection because of their functional use in pointing out whether the goods were of desirable quality or defective. Interestingly, in the cutlery trade, trade marks were treated as something similar to that of a tangible personality, which is a characteristic that exists even in the modern trade mark.[20] This was a clear shift of marks from the nature of a liability to that of an asset, with specific legal rights of ownership including the right to transfer.[21]

But it was the industrial revolution in the eighteenth and early nineteenth centuries that crystallized the evolution of trade marks to today's highly valuable assets. With the development of canals and railways, goods began to be manufactured on a large scale from a centralized location and were subsequently transported and marketed throughout the country. Along with this emerged a free market economy. Identification of a producer, who might have been at some distance from the consumers, and distinguishing the goods required from those manufactured and supplied by others, became a necessity in such a free market economy. Trade marks became the vital link between the consumer and the producer and also the valuable symbol of 'goodwill' which had previously been attached to a local or a known trader.[22] The courts also recognized this need for protection.[23]

Today a trade mark is seen as a badge of origin and as guarantee of consistency, carrying an implied assurance of quality, arising from personal experience of the product, word of mouth recommendation or the image projected through advertising.[24] Trade marks serve two macro-economic functions now: They facilitate the consumer's decision-making process in the market, and they provide incentives for an enterprise to invest in the development and delivery of goods and services with the qualities preferred by the consumer.[25]

Trade marks help in consumers' decision-making process by reducing the search costs incurred by them.[26] Consumers who have purchased a product with the same mark in the past can easily recall their experiences with the quality of a product the moment they see the trade mark and this in essence is a communication of information about the product.[27] On the other hand, they also play an instrumental role in encouraging investment in quality, as the brand value of a product rises only when a customer's post-purchase experiences are in tune with the message communicated by the trade mark and the claims made through the advertisements containing the trade mark.[28] Trade marks that have become popular in the past stand testimony to this fact. The concept of brand building is dealt with in detail in the next section of this chapter.

Studies have shown that trade marks play an instrumental role in increasing sales, cementing customer loyalty, responding to competition, increasing revenues and profit, expanding and maintaining market share, differentiating products, introducing new product lines, gaining royalties through licensing programmes, providing foundation for franchises, supporting strategic partnerships and marketing alliances, justifying corporate valuation in financial transactions, indicating compliance with safety and technical requirements, and ensuring interoperability of complex technical systems.[29]

Two aspects of trade marks, worth mentioning in detail in the broader context of our discussion on ambush marketing are the advertising function of a trade mark, and the license revenue earning potential of a trade mark.

Advertisements are used for persuading customers to purchase a product or a service.[30] They are used by the manufacturers to highlight their products and promote consumer recognition with the help of its trade marks. Trade marks play a pivotal role in advertisements by conveying information about the source or identity of the product in advertisement. This information can either be a prior experience with the product or any other information about the product from others. On the other hand, trade marks also help consumers in identifying a product seen in advertisements. This definitely plays a crucial role in improving the sales at retail outlets, especially the super markets and hypermarkets wherein a large number of products from different producers are placed side by side.

The growth of advertisements and promotions in modern commerce was instrumental in increasing the use of trade marks separately from the goods to which they are actually applied.[31] The increasing reach of visual media has resulted in many changes in advertising as well as in consumer behaviour. For example, today children play an instrumental role in the purchasing decisions in many families. They often demand products they are familiar with through advertisements. In such cases, it is the marks that play a crucial role in creating the demand for goods and services.[32]

But it needs to be specifically mentioned that two classes of thought exist with regard to advertisements. The pro-advertising view suggests that advertisements and trade marks reduce consumer search costs and foster quality management and quality improvement in goods and services, which results in a more orderly marketing of goods and services and less consumer deception.[33] On the other hand, there are some economists who view advertising as a medium that creates unnatural demand and therefore criticize it for perpetuating oligopoly through artificial product differentiation.[34] This group considers advertising as a form of psychological manipulation that could influence customers to differentiate mentally between products that are in reality similar or identical and to persuade them to accept the exaggerated or false quality claims.[35]

The other important aspect of a trade mark, in the context of our discussion on ambush marketing, is its royalty earning capacity through licensing contracts. Trade mark licensing is an agreement wherein one party consents to the use of its trade mark by another party on certain specified terms and conditions.[36] Today, trade mark licensing has become a multi-billion dollar activity that pervades the ways in which goods and services are distributed, marketed, and sold, both domestically and internationally.[37]

A trade mark attains licensing value when it becomes widely recognizable.[38] It has much less value when only one vertically-integrated company takes advantage of the trade mark and this is the main economic rationale behind the licensing of trade marks.[39] On the other hand, a trade mark license allows the licensee to take advantage of the goodwill that the mark enjoys or has the potential of acquiring, in the market.[40] This goodwill has the power to attract, convince, and sell the products of the licensee in the market.

During licensing negotiations, a trade mark owner can decide how the trade mark should be used, concentrate on those situations that will be positive for the company, and take steps to avoid situations that pose a risk to the reputation of the company.[41] Different types of trade mark licensing are found today. One of the common types is simple licensing of the trade mark, wherein the trade mark is licensed for use in a market segment other than the one used by the trade mark owner.[42] One of the examples for simple licensing is the use of the name of a cricket team on a T-Shirt. Character licensing is another kind of trade mark licensing wherein a popular character from a book or movie is licensed to licensees, who exploit the character in a different business segment.[43] For example, in the advertisements of Reid and Taylor suiting, one sees the use of the character 'James Bond', and the slogan 'Bond with the Best', for marketing clothes.

The increasing licensing potential of trade marks has turned them into a bundle of rights. One of the best examples in this regard is the licensing of world wide merchandising rights for the character 'Harry Potter' in the popular children's book series. Mrs J.K. Rowling assigned the rights to Warner Brothers. Warner Brothers has in turn divided the license rights among various other business partners.[44] Thus, for example, Hasbro will have the rights to develop and distribute trading cards and youth electronic games, Mattel will make toys, Electronic Arts will have the right to use it for making computer and video programmes, and Coca-Cola will have the rights relating to the marketing of the first Harry Potter film. This phenomenon is nothing but the evolution of trade marks to a bundle of rights. The revenue earned from this bundle of rights is often very high and unexpected.

In certain situations, the trade marks may be part of a larger licensing programme which includes rights to manufacture some product, assignment of patent rights, rights to technical documents, etc. In such comprehensive IP licenses, the trade marks play a very vital role, as the right to manufacture and sell a patented product turns out to be far more valuable when the right to use a recognized trade mark is incorporated in the deal. One of the case studies worth citing in this regard is that of Bayer Aspirin.[45] Even though Bayer did not have a patent protection in many countries for its pure Acetyl Salicylic Acid and its market rivals were successful in producing the same compound, Bayer was able to retain its dominant market share in the global analgesic market through the value attached to its trade mark 'Bayer Aspirin'. This shows the true power of a trade mark and its revenue earning potential. The licensing potential of a trade mark will become clearer if we try and think, for example, about the use of a license to manufacture and distribute Coca-Cola without the right to use the name 'Coca-Cola'.

But there is a substantial segment of the legal fraternity who argue against trade mark licensing. Their most important argument is that it destroys the very function of a trade mark, that is, to identify the source of goods. But those on the other side try to negate this argument by pointing out that the function of a trade mark has changed considerably with time, from an indicator of source of goods to an assurance of a consistent expectation of quality.[46] If one is willing to accept this changed definition, the trade mark licensing function can be considered as a truly legitimate one. Most jurisdictions appear to have accepted this reality since in most statues the right to license a trade mark is predicated on quality control.[47]

The Indian Trade Marks Act and the Indian courts have taken into consideration these changes happening across the world. The licensing of trade marks, both registered and unregistered, is permitted in India provided the licensing does not result in causing confusion or deception among the public, does not destroy the distinctiveness of the mark, and a connection in the course of trade consistent with the definition of trade mark continues to exist between the goods and the proprietor of the mark.[48]

But in recent times, the concept of trade mark has moved even further from the identification function, as it has been observed that certain marks now enjoy a drawing power, whereby the consumer wishes to be identified with the mark itself.[49] This makes the issue of licensing much more complicated.

WHEN A TRADE MARK BECOMES A BRAND

'Take water and sugar: They are *commodities.* Process them into cola drinks, and you have *products.* Market and promote them into Coca-Cola and Pepsi-Cola, you have *brands.*'[50]

Valuation of brands as assets is an important financial service today and these valuations play a major role in the take-over battles across the world.[51] An analysis done by the *Business Week* with the help of Interbrand, cites that the brand Coca-Cola was worth US $ 67 billion in the year 2006.[52] According to this study, the top three brands in the world are Coca-Cola, Microsoft, and IBM.[53]

It is a fact that there is no universally accepted definition for a brand. While some segments of the public including lawyers refer to brands in the same way as a trade mark, with source identification and differentiation as its key objectives, we need to realize that a brand is distinct from a trade mark in so far as it incorporates the total visual and emotional representation of the augmented product and its associated marketing, although through use a mark becomes a cue for the brand.[54] A brand is better defined as 'the product itself, the packaging, the brand name, the promotion, the advertising, and the over all presentation. The brand is therefore the synthesis of all these elements—physical, aesthetic, rational, and emotional.'[55] In other words a brand is a product plus the added values, or a blend of functional, economic, and psychological benefits for the end user. It is more about the way people perceive it and not about the product in isolation.[56] At the same time, we should not confuse branding with marketing. While branding consists of the development and maintenance of a set of product attributes and values which are appropriate, distinctive, protectable, and coherent, marketing is a broader function which includes branding and is concerned with the development and implementation of strategies for moving products from the producer to the consumer in a profitable fashion.[57]

Brands of the present world offer consumers an attitude or a philosophy of life, increasing the emphasis on the intangible nature of the brand concept.[58] The same also invites criticism from several quarters that trade marks and logos in particular, are part of a negative cultural phenomenon in which brands have become cultural icons or abstract expressions of emotions and psychological states, rather than beneficial tools for consumers.[59]

THE CONCEPT OF BRAND STRETCHING

A closely related subject, worth a brief discussion at this point, is brand stretching. Brand stretching is the use of a brand name established in one product or class on to another product or class.[60] It is the goodwill attached to an established brand name that prompts the business houses to extend the use of that brand name to another area.[61] A successful brand extension example in India can be ITC's extension of the brand name 'Wills' from tobacco products to apparels. In the past, Wills was a term synonymous with high quality cigarettes in India and today Wills Life Style holds a considerable market share in the high end casual apparels.

But extending the brand to an area inconsistent with the original brand has to be done very carefully and the past has witnessed many failures in this regard.[62] Studies have shown that consumer evaluations of brand extensions depend on the perceived fit of the new product with the existing brand and this fit generally depends on two factors namely, product feature similarity and brand concept consistency.[63] For example, if the Indian Cricket team is to permit the use of its name on products like cricket bats or other sports goods, it will be a perfect fit and will be good brand stretching. On the other hand, if the name of the team is used on some medicinal product, it might be a failure. This is because the particular product category of medicinal products does not fit with the original brand.

The main advantage of brand stretching is that it enables a new product to take advantage of the already established functional attributes and symbolic values associated with the original brand. It speeds up the process of establishing the product's awareness, helps in consumer recognition, reduces communication costs and the risk of purchase for a first time buyer, and makes it easy to obtain distribution and shelf space from a retailer.[64]

THE CONCEPT OF BRAND PROMOTION

Brand Stretching is made possible through an area of marketing referred to as 'brand promotion'. Brand promotion is a term used for the combination of three factors—advertising, promotion, and sponsorship. Brand promotion plays an indispensable part in building and maintaining a brand. It helps to inform consumers about a product and in the process helps them to reduce the time spent on making purchasing decisions.[65]

The most important component of brand promotion is advertising. There is a substantial section of economists who argue that advertisement is an investment in a brand and therefore the amount spent on advertisement must be entered on the balance sheet as an indicator of the value of a brand.[66] Advertisements act as a dialogue between the brand owner and the consumer, introducing the brand to the consumer and explaining to him or her the product benefits and attributes.[67] This dialogue gets completed when brand owners get feedback from the consumer with the help of market researches.[68] An advertisement for a brand can be considered as successful if that brand achieves significant market share, where the differences between competing brands are negligible and the product itself is of low risk.

According to Belinda Issac, the classical model of consumer decision making process involves six steps starting from brand awareness and moving through knowledge, liking, preference, conviction, and finally purchasing.[69] Depending on the nature of the brand in question and the time period from its introduction, the advertisements will focus on one or more facets of this decision making process.[70] The various forms of advertisements used are conventional advertising, comparative advertising, tandem advertising, shock tactics, product sponsorship, ambush marketing, product placement, and celebrity endorsement.[71]

THE ALLURING WORLD OF SPONSORSHIP

The other important component of brand promotion is sponsorship. Though sponsorship is purely a marketing concept, a detailed discussion on this concept is necessary at this stage as ambush marketing occurs in the context of sponsorship of events.

Sponsorship is a form of marketing whereby a sponsor contributes to, or underwrites, the cost of staging an event, or the cost of a participant in a prestigious event, or the cost of an individual competitor or a team under a periodic agreement in return for the grant of marketing and promotion rights by the sponsored party.[72] The sponsorship right provides an opportunity for the sponsor to promote the image of his products through an association with the event or individuals concerned. Though the prime purpose of sponsorship is to give financial assistance to a wide range of beneficiaries in the world of sports and entertainment, from a commercial angle it is for enabling the sponsor to benefit from the marketing opportunities associated with the event or the individuals which it sponsors.[73]

Even though the range of events, activities, individuals, and things that receive sponsorship today is very wide, arts and sports are usually the primary beneficiaries of sponsorship due to the higher popularity and public appeal in these two streams.[74] Between arts and sports, sports score a higher position in sponsorship as a result of the potential world wide audience for games. It was the increase in media coverage in the late 1980s and 1990s that converted sports into a real investment opportunity.[75]

Today, almost all the sporting events across the world depend on sponsorship.[76] It is generally seen that in sports events, sponsorship accounts for about 35 per cent of the revenues, while broadcasting provides for about half and the remaining comes from the sale of tickets and licensing.[77] But finding sponsorship and the required funding is a difficult task even for prestigious events and often the event organizers are seen struggling to make the promotional value of the event attractive to the type of sponsors being sought.[78]

The event organizers need a sponsor with the right image and status to project the event and they also have to ensure that the particular sponsor is compatible with the context of the event.[79] On the other hand, a sponsor has to use the event in such a way as to promote its corporate image in general terms, such as by having its logo identified with the relevant sector of the sponsored activity.[80] The long association with a good event can certainly add incalculable value for the sponsor.[81] A successful sponsor will become synonymous with the event they have sponsored and it is often seen that this new brand image is retained for a very long period.

There are different kinds of sponsorship and they may broadly be classified into sole sponsorship, primary sponsorship, and secondary sponsorship.[82] In the case of sole sponsorship, the sole sponsor is the exclusive source of funding for the event and receives the exclusive right to be publicly known as supporting the event. It exercises absolute control over the promotion rights granted under the sponsorship agreement and normally the name and logo of the sole sponsor is permitted to be used in conjunction with that of the sponsored party without any dilution of the promotional impact which may otherwise exist as a result of the presence of other sponsors. A primary sponsor, on the other hand, shares the overall sponsorship costs of the event with one or more subsidiary sponsors and they have different levels of marketing rights. The third category is secondary sponsorship and a secondary sponsor is a person who provides specialized goods or services as his sponsorship contribution and he can also be a lower level provider of a cash fee. But he plays an equally important role for the success of the event. The most common role played by the secondary sponsor is the 'official supplier' status. For a football match, it can be the supply of footballs. For an international company with a high level of sponsorship commitment as part of its world wide marketing strategy, the official supplier status at unique international events like the world cup football or world cup cricket will certainly be a boost to its image.[83] But it needs to be accepted that a sole sponsor is always in a better position during the sponsorship agreement negotiation. When there are multiple sponsors, each of them will negotiate hard to get the best deal and reaching the final agreement is a very difficult task.

Creating a sponsorship property is the most important and difficult task for the organizers of an event. A distinctive title, emblem, device, or logo is commonly devised as a means of giving an instant identity to a sponsored event, which when efficiently promoted, comes to be recognized as the event's visual-graphic representation.[84] Consistent and frequent use of the title and logo creates a permanent association with the event and it turns out to be a trade mark.[85]

One of the important rights granted to a sponsor is the right to use the sponsored party's trade mark for advertising the sponsor's association with the event and promoting the sponsor's brand.[86] A prudent sponsor will ensure from the sponsored party that the event's trade marks are protected across a wide range of goods and services so as to cover the sponsor's proposed activities. But most of the times events are found to have both registered and unregistered marks.

The event managers apply for the registration of trade marks in advance as the registration process of trade marks generally takes a minimum of twelve months time in most of the jurisdictions. An application for registration has to be made in all the classes for which the registration is relevant and this decision needs to be taken only after a due consideration of the potential areas. The sponsor has also to protect the use of logo in connection with its own business and goods and may seek authorization from the sponsored party to apply for such registration.[87] In cases of infringement where words ineligible for trade mark registration are used, the promoters may rely on the common law remedy of passing off.

The extent of rights available to a sponsor depends on the kind of event being sponsored. A sponsor is entitled to certain forms of exclusivity, depending on its role in sponsorship. The most prestigious form of exclusivity is to get associated with the title of the event.[88] Another right normally accrued to a sponsor is to use the event name and its association with it as sponsor to promote its own image and products.[89] A sponsor may use all kinds of media advertising for this purpose. Some products are also suitable for posters, billboards, and other forms of passive advertising.[90] A sponsor is also entitled to use its association with the event for sales promotion campaigns.[91] In certain situations the sponsors ask for the use of photographs of the event for their product promotion campaigns.

One of the most important concerns for event sponsors today is ensuring their presence in the broadcasting of the event. Otherwise there are chances that it may get ambushed by a competitor sponsoring the broadcasting of that event.[92] The past has witnessed this issue many a time. Some of these issues are discussed in the next chapter.

Another right that may be granted to a sponsor is merchandising right which is different from sponsorship. It is a commercial exercise of its own, whereby a company is granted the exclusive right to make and sell specified categories of products which display the title or logo of the event.[93] The categories of goods for which the merchandising license is issued may be limited to those approved by the sole or primary sponsor of the event. As the quality and presentation of the products will reflect the reputation of the event and the sponsored party, considerable care is usually given to these issues at the stage of drafting of merchandising agreements.

In return for these rights, a sponsor is also given an important duty—a duty to promote the event by all fair means.[94] With this clear understanding of rights and duties associated with sponsorship, we can move to our core theme, ambush marketing, which can be described as an uninvited guest intruding into an exclusive event.

NOTES

1. Kamil Idris, *Intellectual Property: A Power Tool for Economic Growth* (Geneva: World Intellectual Property Organization, 2003), 24.

2. Ibid., at 8.

3. In fact it is the challenges which unlock the true power of imagination in most situations. This is particularly true with respect to the innovations from the grassroot levels. During the author's experiences of interaction with innovators from the grassroot levels at the National Innovation Foundation, it is often found that it is the challenges which they face in the agricultural field or other fields of life that made them think about solutions for overcoming those challenges and bring out extremely useful innovations like modified tractors, cars for the physically challenged, amphibious bicycles, tree climbing machines, etc. The same holds true for artists also, who make classical works when they use their power of imagination to face intellectual and artistic challenges.

4. Classical economists like Joseph A. Schumpeter argue that a dynamic economy is not one in equilibrium, but one that is constantly disrupted by technological innovations. The neoclassical economists like Robert M. Solow also saw technological progress as an important variable in economic growth.

According to him, growth in labour and capital contributed only to half of the growth of total GDP and the remaining unexplained portion of growth came from technological progress. Later this finding was supported by a study conducted by Edward Denison, who revealed that between 1929 and 1957, 40 percent of the increase in per capita income of USA was due to advancement of knowledge. According to the model propounded by Solow, economic progress had little to do with internal economy, and progress in science and technology depended little on monetary or fiscal policy. Later in the 1980s we can see economists like Paul Romer supporting a model which suggested that the accumulation of knowledge was the driving force behind economic growth of countries. It is also interesting to note in this context the changes that have happened in the asset holding patterns of companies. While the 1982 figures show that around 62 percent of the Corporate assets in the US were physical assets, the 2000 figures show it nose diving to about 30 percent. For a detailed discussion on the relation of technological progress and economic growth, see Kamil Idris, 8–75. For another empirical discussion on the increasing share of knowledge intensive products in international trade, see generally, Carsten Fink and Carlos A. Primo Braga, 'How Stronger Protection of Intellectual Property Rights Affects International Trade Flows' in Carsten Fink and Keith E. Maskus (eds), *Intellectual Property and Development* (Washington DC: World Bank and Oxford University Press, 2005), 19–40.

5. For a discussion on some of the common strategies used for obtaining and maintaining competitive edge over competitors through intellectual property rights, see Taran Atwal, 'Canada: Keeping your Competitive Edge', *Mondaq Law Review*, May 30, 2006.

6. See Kamil Idris, 63.

7. For a detailed discussion, see Alan S. Gutterman and Bently J. Anderson, *Intellectual Property in Global Markets* (London: Kluwer Law International, 1997), 21.

8. Kamil Idris, 57.

9. Carsten Fink and Beata K. Smarzynska, 'Trade marks, Geographical Indications, and Developing Countries' in Bernard Hoekman, Aaditya Mattoo and Philip English (eds), *Development, Trade and the WTO*, (Washington DC: The World Bank, 2002), 403.

10. P. Narayanan, *Law of Trade Marks and Passing Off* (Kolkata: Eastern Law House, 2004), 1.

11. For further discussion on this point, see A. G. Papandreou, 'The Economic Effect of Trademarks' in Ruth Towse and Rudi Holzhauer (eds), *The Economics of Intellectual Property- Volume III* (Glos: Edward Elgar Publishing Ltd, 2002), 290.

12. One of the best examples in this regard is the ongoing conflict between the Indian group Wadia and the French group Danone over the trade mark 'Tiger' for biscuits. The trade mark 'Tiger' was registered in India and many other countries in the name of Britannia under Wadia group and is a popular brand in many markets in the biscuits segment. As stake holders in Britannia, Danone was granted the license to use this trade mark in some of the markets. Wadia now alleges that Danone has registered this trade mark in the name of Danone in 72 markets without their permission. The dispute has now gone up to the point of blocking the sale of Danone's stake in Britannia to other companies.

13. For a very detailed discussion on each of these requirements, see, David Kitchin, David Llewelyn, James Mellor, Richard Meade, and Thomas Moody Stuart (eds), *Kerly's Law of Trade Marks* (London: Sweet and Maxwell, 2001), 8–43.

14. The US Supreme Court upheld this view in its famous decision in *Hanover Star Milling Co* v. *Metcalf,* 240 US 403 (1916). Also see Peter J. Groves, *Source Book on Intellectual Property Law* (London: Cavendish Publishing Limited, 1997), 512.

15. See Bulletin of the European Communities, Supplement 8/76, adopted by the Commission on 6 July 1976, cited in Christopher Morcom, Ashley Roughton and James Graham, *The Modern Law of Trade Marks* (London: Butterworths, 1999), 7.

16. For a very detailed discussion on the history of trade marks, see C.D.G. Pickering, *Trade Marks in Theory and Practice* (Oxford: Hatt Publishing, 1998), 36–41.

17. For example in cases of ship wreck, piracy, etc. this marking helped in identifying the true owners. But the fall of Roman Empire in the 5th century led to the disappearance of the custom of marking goods. See, Lionel Bently and Brad Sherman, *Intellectual Property Law* (New Delhi: Oxford University Press, 2003), 655.

18. During the medieval period, along with the rise of towns as autonomous urban units, guilds came within towns. Each guild was a federation of master craftsmen, frequently established by some form of charter and had two main aims: to monopolize trade in a particular town or city and to promote the guild as a whole. Agreements were made between the members regarding standards of workmanship, amount to be charged for goods, prohibition of advertisement or competition between the members or with other guilds. Trade in goods by members of each craft took place locally with the result that consumer was always in close contact with producer. Each producer (guild member) was obliged to attach his mark to his goods, which had previously been recorded with the guild. Their main aim was to

identify the origin of goods so that any substandard produce could be traced easily. This was a medieval form of consumer protection. See C.D.G. Pickering, 37.

19. Ibid., at 38.

20. Ibid.

21. Ibid., at 39.

22. Ibid.

23. Under common law, the first reported decision in this regard was *Sykes* v. *Sykes,* (1824) 3 B and C 543 wherein an action for damages was allowed on the evidence of deliberate deceit. The mark in question was SYKES PATENT. See C.D.G. Pickering, 2.

24. See Amanda Michaels, *A Practical Guide to Trade Mark Law* (London: Sweet and Maxwell, 2002), 2.

25. For details, *see* Kamil Idris, 150.

26. For a critical analysis of the role of trade marks in reducing consumer search costs and consumer errors, see Robert Feinberg, 'Trademarks, Market Power, and Information' in Ruth Towse and Rudi Holzhauer (eds), *The Economics of Intellectual Property, Volume III* (Glos: Edward Elgar Publishing Ltd, 2002), 432–8. Also see William M. Landes and Richard A. Posner, 'The Economics of Trademark Law' in Ruth Towse and Rudi Holzhauer (eds), *The Economics of Intellectual Property, Volume III*, 318. According to the authors, the benefit of a trade mark is analogous to that of designating individuals by last name as well as first names.

27. See Kamil Idris, 151.

28. Ibid. These two functions are complementary and mutually reinforcing. When the consumers choose a product for the qualities suggested by the mark and when the businesses invest in quality, the result should be improved quality that yields customer loyalty to the brand.

29. A small example in this regard can be the Windows logo attached to computer CPUs and laptops which show that the system is compatible with Windows operating system. Without telling or writing anything in detail, such information is being able to be passed to the consumer through that small logo. For a detailed discussion on each of these functions, see Kamil Idris, 154–68.

30. See Joanna R. Jeremiah, *Merchandising Intellectual Property Rights* (Chichester: John Wiley and Sons, 1997), 121.

31. For a detailed discussion, see Neil. J. Wilkof and Daniel Burkitt, *Trademark Licensing* (London: Sweet and Maxwell, 2005), 36.

32. This view is supported by Schechter. According to him, 'today trademark is not merely the symbol of goodwill but often the most effective agent for the creation of goodwill, imprinting upon the public mind an

anonymous and impersonal guarantee of satisfaction, creating a desire for further satisfactions. The mark actually sells goods. And, self evidently, the more distinctive the mark, the more effective is its selling power.' Cited in Neil. J. Wilkof and Daniel Burkitt, 36.

33. Ibid., at 37.

34. For a detailed discussion, see Kamil Idris, 152.

35. See Neil. J. Wilkof and Daniel Burkitt, 36–7.

36. Special attention needs to be given in the drafting of the conditions relating to trade mark licensing. Any vagueness in the agreement can result in substantial harm to the parties. The conflicts between the Wadia group and Danone over the trade mark 'Tiger', mentioned in the earlier part of this chapter, is a classical example for the potential post licensing conflicts.

37. Some studies show that over $50 billion worth of licensed consumer goods are sold at the retail level in US in one year. See Neil. J. Wilkof and Daniel Burkitt, 1.

38. H. Jackson Knight, 'Intellectual Property '101' ' in Bruce Berman (ed.), *From Ideas to Assets—Investing Wisely in Intellectual Property* (New York: John Wiley & Sons, 2002), 12.

39. See *TMT North America Inc* v. *Magic Touch GmbH*, 43 USPQ 2d 1913. This case relates to a dispute between a German manufacturer and its American licensee. This case discusses licensing related issues in detail. In this case the Court is seen making an interesting observation that 'licensing allows more information to be conveyed to more consumers without the licensor having to risk losing title to its mark... indeed trade marks would be of much less value to society if only vertically-integrated firms could safely take advantage of trade mark law's protections.' 43 USPQ 2d 1913, 1916.

40. See Neil. J. Wilkof and Daniel Burkitt, 16.

41. See H. Jackson Knight, 12.

42. For a detailed discussion, see Kamil Idris, 162.

43. Ibid.

44. Ibid., at 163.

45. For a very detailed case study on the role played by the trade mark 'Bayer Aspirin' in maintaining the dominant share of Bayer in global analgesic market even after loss of its technological advantage, see Klaus Jennewein, *Intellectual Property Management* (Heidelberg: Physica-Verlag, 2005).

46. This argument stems out from the fact that where the licensor exercised satisfactory control over the use of a mark, it did not matter in principle whether the goods actually emanated from the proprietor of the mark or from someone under his control. See Neil. J. Wilkof and Daniel Burkitt, 21.

47. For a discussion on the quality control stipulations in statutes see Neil. J. Wilkof and Daniel Burkitt, 30–6.

48. See P. Narayanan, 432–433. In India, the Act permits the use of a registered trade mark by third persons under a scheme of registered users. The provisions relating to registration of a person as registered user are dealt in Secs 48 to 52 of the Act. The new Act also permits the use of a registered trade mark by a third party without that party being registered as a registered user. But there must be a written agreement regarding the consent of the registered proprietor. To find the approach taken by the Indian Judiciary towards licensing of trade marks, see *Gujarat Bottling Company Ltd.* v. *Coca-Cola Company,* AIR 1995 SC 2732 wherein Coca-Cola was the licensor and the appellant Gujarat company was the licensee. Due to breach of contract by the appellant, Coca-Cola company revoked that license. This case examined the issues involved in licensing in detail.

49. For a detailed discussion, see Neil. J. Wilkof and Daniel Burkitt, 21.

50. *The Economist*, 'The Year of the Brand', (24 December 1988).

51. For a detailed discussion on the concept of brand valuation see Gordon V. Smith, 'Brand Valuation: Too Long Neglected', *EIPR* 1990, 12(5), 159–64 (1990) and Tony Tollington, 'The Separable Nature of Brands as Assets: The United Kingdom Legal and Accounting Perspective', *EIPR* 2001, 23(1), 6–13 (2001).

52. See 'The 100 Top Brands 2006', http://bwnt.businessweek.com/brand/2006/, accessed on 22 March 2007.

53. Ibid. According to this report the top three brands are from US. While Coca-Cola is estimated at US $ 67 billion, Microsoft brand is worth US $ 56.9 billion and IBM brand is worth US $ 56.2 billion. This report shows the true power of brands.

54. For a detailed discussion on the differences, see Belinda Issac, *Brand Protection Matters* (London: Sweet and Maxwell, 2000), 26.

55. This definition was given by John Murphy, the founder of Interbrand, *cited* in Belinda Issac, 5.

56. A product can be defined as anything that is offered to a market for attention, acquisition, use or consumption that might satisfy a want or need and it includes physical objects, services, persons, places, organizations, ideas, and mixtures of these entities. A product usually comprise of three distinct levels. They are core product, actual product, and augmented product. At the most basic level is the 'core product' or the product concept, the basic idea behind the product which may have different ways of implementation. For example, the core product in relation to IFB Washing Machine is a washing machine incorporating a front door filling facility. From a consumer perspective the core benefit could be a clean and safe washing. The second

level is known as 'actual product' and it includes packaging, product name, logo, colour, quality level, features of the product, design of the product and shape as a specific manifestation of the core product. The third level is known as 'augmented product' where in addition to the actual product, the manufacturer may provide additional customer services such as after sales service, guarantee, insurance, helpline, etc. Quality, price, and image are essential factors in the evolution of a brand and consistency in all forms of packaging and promotion supports the process. See generally, Belinda Issac, 2–11.

57. Ibid., at 13. One of the good case studies where creation of product attributes and values is visible is that of Kingfisher Airlines in India. In the domestic aviation sector they introduced many new services like offering of a valet to take bags of passengers and cleaning of spectacles by airhostess in Business Class, etc. to induce a feeling that customer is the King. They also introduced a new system of referring to customers as 'guests' instead of 'passengers'. Some of the recent surveys says that it has become the most favoured brand in the domestic aviation sector. See Aarti Dua, 'Not a Flight of Fancy', *Businessworld* (April 2, 2007), 56.

58. Ibid., at 28. For example, see the 'Life is Good' caption on the products from LG. It is a good example for an attitude or philosophy of life propagated by a brand.

59. Kamil Idris, 152.

60. Brand Stretching is also known by the name brand extension. This should not be confused with 'line extensions' wherein a company introduces additional items like new flavours, package sizes, etc. in a given product category under the same brand name. One of the best examples will be Diet Cola from Coca-Cola. For details, see Belinda Issac, 131.

61. Belinda Issac, 131.

62. One of the classical examples for the failure in this regard was the extension of the brand name Levi to a new product area by Levi Strauss & Co in 1979. Levi, which is famous for men's casuals tried to introduce a brand 'David Hunter-Levi Tailored Classics' in men's tailored wool suits. But consumers of tailored wool suits felt the name 'Levi' as inconsistent with top quality men's suits and as a result, the new product failed and was withdrawn within a year. An example for successful brand stretching can be the extension of the brand name 'Marks & Spencer', which was originally associated with clothing, to even financial services. For a detailed discussion based on these case studies, see, Belinda Issac, 132–6.

63. Ibid., at 133–4. An analysis of the possibility of the extension of Coca-Cola brand to fruit juice segment will highlight this issue. Brand analysts have found out that extension of the brand Coca-Cola to orange juice will not

be successful. But Coca-Cola sweat shirts may be acceptable and successful. This was one reason for cola companies to roll out new brands like 'Tropicana' for their fruit juice segment and 'Kinley' for mineral water.

64. Ibid, at 134–5.

65. Ibid., at 172.

66. Ibid., at 174.

67. Through this dialogue, advertisements are intended to influence consumer behaviour. A successful advertisement saves considerable time and energy required for making the consumer aware of the development of new brands or improvements in existing brands.

68. See Belinda Issac, 173.

69. Ibid., at 176.

70. In the case of new products, the advertisements are seen focusing on the first two steps namely brand awareness and knowledge. They provide information with prominent and frequent references to the name with an emphasis on the novel aspects of the particular product.

71. The conventional advertising focuses on the brand and its characteristics. In comparative advertising one brand is directly or indirectly compared with the competitor. In tandem advertising one product is advertised on the back of another. In shock tactics particular settings that offend public morals are used as advertisements. In the case of product sponsorships, an event or programme is endorsed with the objective of creating awareness and brand associations. In product placement method, endorsement through contextual use in films or television programmes are used. In the case of celebrity endorsement, a particular celebrity is associated with a particular product. For a detailed discussion on form and content of advertisements, see Belinda Issac, 177–8.

72. For a detailed discussion on sponsorship and rights and duties associated therewith, see generally, Hayley Stallard (ed), *Bagehot on Sponsorship, Merchandising and Endorsement* (London: Sweet and Maxwell, 1998).

73. Ibid., at 1.

74. See Avril Martindale, 'Let the Sponsor Beware', *Ent. L.R.* 1993, 4(6), 165–8, 165 (1993).

75. See Anne M. Wall, 'Sports Marketing And The Law: Protecting Proprietary Interests In Sports Entertainment Events', 7 *Marq. Sports L.J.* 77, 84 (1996).

76. For example, during the years 2001 to 2004, the revenue of International Olympic Committee from sponsorship alone was $1459 million. It was about 34 percent of the total income of the organization. See http://www.olympic.org/uk/organisation/facts/introduction/index_uk.asp, accessed 5 April 2006. Another example pointing to this direction is that of Winter

Olympics in Turin. The budget for the Winter Olympics in Turin was $1.4 billion. Apart from that, around 2.5 billion Euros was to be spent on infrastructure by the host country. The corporate sponsors have put up more than $1 billion for this Winter Olympics. See *The Economist*, 'War Minus Shooting', (February 16, 2006).

77. *The Economist*, 'War Minus Shooting', (February 16, 2006).

78. See Hayley Stallard, 5.

79. For a detailed discussion, Ibid., at 6.

80. Ibid., at 7.

81. Most of the sponsors for the major events like Olympics and FIFA are long term partners with contracts of eight years and more. This long term association helps them build up a strong brand image in association with the event. The longer duration of the sports events is also a positive factor in this process of brand building.

82. See Hayley Stallard, 11–16.

83. Ibid., at 16.

84. Ibid., at 20. The best example in this regard would be the five Olympic rings. Even small children recognize it as the identity of Olympic event.

85. Ibid.

86. See Avril Martindale, 'Let the Sponsor Beware', 166.

87. See Hayley Stallard, 22.

88. One of the examples in this regard can be *Ponds Femina Miss India 2006*. Here Ponds and Femina was used in conjunction with the title and was visible through all media reports.

89. Hayley Stallard, 53.

90. Ibid.

91. Ibid.

92. To prevent such ambushing, the Institute of Sports Sponsorship Code of Conduct advises members to refrain from undertaking programme sponsorship unless it has first been offered to the event sponsor by the television contractor. For details, see Hayley Stallard, 59.

93. The common examples are T-Shirts, Caps, Mugs, etc. with the title or logo of the event. For more on merchandising rights, see ibid., 91–108.

94. For a detailed discussion on the duties of sponsors, see ibid., 66–78.

2

Definition, Extent, and Effects of Ambush Marketing

As discussed in the previous chapter, the major events provide golden opportunities not only for the participants, but also for the companies aiming to secure a mass audience through the sponsorship of such events. Whatever be the type of event, these global events give companies a platform to promote their brands to a potential worldwide audience and to benefit in image terms by associating themselves with the event and with the real heroes of the event.[1] The core theme of our discussion, ambush marketing, makes its appearance in various guises during such events of high value.

WHAT IS AMBUSH MARKETING?

Ambush Marketing can be defined as a marketing strategy wherein the advertisers associate themselves with, and therefore capitalize on, a particular event without paying any sponsorship fee.[2] The Macmillan English Dictionary defines ambush marketing as a marketing strategy in which a competing brand connects itself with a major sporting event without paying sponsorship fee.[3]

For example, in the case of the Olympic Games, the International Olympic Committee (IOC), a non-governmental, non-profit organization, is the supreme authority and it owns all rights relating to the Olympic symbol, the Olympic flag, the Olympic motto, the Olympic anthem, and the Olympic Games.[4] It is for the IOC to decide the sponsors of the Olympic Games and only those sponsors are entitled to use the Olympic related symbols.[5] All others who try to represent themselves as being associated with the Olympics, without the permission of the IOC, will be considered as ambush marketers.

Or take the example of FIFA World Cup 2006 held in Germany. The fifteen official partners of this event were Adidas, Anheuser-Busch, Avaya, Coca-Cola, Continental, Deutsche Telekom, Emirates, Fuji film, Gillette, Hyundai, MasterCard, McDonald's, Philips, Toshiba, and Yahoo!.[6] The six official suppliers were Energie Baden-Württemberg AG (EnBW), OBI, Hamburg-Mannheimer Versicherung, Postbank, ODDSET, and Deutsche Bahn AG.[7] If any company, other than those official partners, tried to associate their products with the FIFA World Cup 2006, it would have amounted to ambush marketing. These are just two examples. Ambush marketing can also happen in events like fashion shows, literary events, or art events.[8] It can even happen during a party hosted by someone.

According to McCarthy, ambush marketing is a type of marketing by a company that is not an official sponsor of an event, but which places advertisements using the event, to induce customers to pay attention to the advertisement.[9] In some cases, the advertisements may only be a reminder about the event. But in some others, it may go further to create a misleading impression that the company is an official sponsor regarding these goods or services or that it is affiliated with the event.[10] In other words, ambush marketing is an attempt to align a brand with an event for which it has not acquired any rights.[11] For example, if Coke was the successful candidate to the official sponsorship of Cricket World Cup, Pepsi may use the ambush marketing medium to create an impression among the spectators of that event that it is connected with the Cricket World Cup.

From a theoretical perspective, ambush marketing refers to a company's attempt to capitalize on the goodwill, reputation, and popularity of a particular event by creating an association with it, without the authorization or consent of the necessary parties.[12] In a narrow sense, it is the direct effort of one company to weaken or attack a competitor's official association with a sports organization acquired through the payment of sponsorship fee.[13] These ambush marketing objectives are achieved mainly with the help of advertisements and promotional campaigns. So if Nike has acquired the official sponsorship of World Cup Football, Reebok may use ambush marketing techniques for confusing the public as to who is the official sponsor of the game. Through its ambush marketing it will cast a shadow on the sponsorship made by Nike. There have been many instances in the past where ambush marketers have successfully overshadowed the official sponsors, through their ingenious ambush marketing strategies. Some of the best examples in this regard are the ambush marketing attacks made by Qantas Airways against the official sponsor Ansett Airways during the Sydney 2000 Olympic Games, Samsung efforts against JVC and Philips during the FIFA World Cup 2002 and the efforts made by Nike during the 1984 Los Angeles Olympic Games and 1996 Olympic Games. All of these issues will be discussed as the book progresses.

Ambush marketing is also known by the names 'parasitic marketing' and 'guerilla marketing'.[14] The word 'ambush' as used in the expression ambush marketing, means 'an attack from a hidden position' and is derived from the old French verb *embuschier*, having the meaning 'to place in a wood'.[15] The term 'ambush marketing' was coined by the famous marketing strategist Jerry Welsh, while he was working as the manager of global marketing efforts for the American Express Company in the 1980s.[16] Though today's world considers ambush marketing as something akin to commercial theft, Jerry Welsh disagrees with this view and explains that in the world of modern marketing, sponsor and ambusher are not moral labels to be assigned by the self-appointed arbiters of ethics, but merely the names to be given to two different and complementary, though competing roles played by competitors vying for consumer loyalty and recognition in the same thematic space.[17] According to him, the roots of ambush marketing can be found in the escalating prices and 'the distressed imagery of category-exclusive sponsorships'.

It is virtually impossible for a sponsor to buy rights to all avenues leading to the public's awareness of a given sponsorship property. In such situations, all except that which is specifically purchased is for grabs and this is what ambush marketers capitalize on.[18] Whatever be the definitions we accept, it is a fact that ambush marketing has become a major cause of concern for event organizers as well as sponsors across the globe and we can see its frequent appearance in different modes in all most all the major events.

DIFFERENT TYPES OF AMBUSH MARKETING PRACTICES

The ambush marketing practices are not a recent phenomenon and have been in existence for a long time. In the early days they appeared in simple methods like giving away promotional items in the form of ambusher's products or giving free trips to the event. But with time, ambush marketing tactics have become more sophisticated and today they cover a wider range of scenarios.[19] We can generally see two types of ambush marketing methods. In the first type, we see a direct reference to the event. In the second type, which is more common, ambush official sponsors and event organizers indirectly through their creative advertising. For the first type, remedies are comparatively easy. But the second type does not have a clear cut remedy and it makes the issue of ambush marketing a very serious one. This part of the chapter is an investigation into different ambushing practices that are witnessed in the modern marketing scenario.

While moving through the examples of ambush marketing cited in this chapter, a reader may question why the examples of ambush marketing cited here are limited to sports events. This was primarily the result of a conscious decision to cite only real life incidents, which happened in some of the major events of the past. Though sponsorship exists also in areas like arts and education, sponsorship is more common and more visible in sports. As sports events give a much wider audience, it is always a tempting option for sponsors, and today the global sports sponsorship is a multi billion dollar business.[20] It is also to be noted that sports sponsorship constitutes 63–65 percent of the total corporate sponsorship spending.[21] The potential worldwide audience and the loyalty of the followers of global sports events also make the sports events a thriving place for ambush marketers.[22] Hence, our examples are also forced to focus on such sports events.

One of the most common methods used by ambush marketers is buying commercial time over the broadcasting of events.[23] A big corporate famous (or infamous!) for this type of ambush marketing technique is the American Express company.[24] During the Norway Olympics, while it's rival Visa spent around $40 million to become a worldwide Olympics sponsor, which included the 1994 Winter Games in Norway, American Express baffled Visa and IOC through advertisements with the slogan 'If you're travelling to Norway, you'll need a passport, but you don't need a visa'. In fact, this was an improved version of their 1992 attack on Visa. Visa had invested over $20 million to become the official sponsor of the 1992 Olympic Winter and Summer Games and at that time also American Express purchased substantial advertising time on the major media networks and made advertisements that showed the French Alps with the caption 'Winter Fun and Games'. In the same year, during the Games at Barcelona in Spain, American Express ran another advertisement with the slogan 'And remember, to visit Spain, you don't need a visa'. It needs to be observed here that the word 'Olympics' was never used in any of these advertisements from American Express. As an event organizer who is really conscious of the sponsorship value, the IOC got disturbed by the frequent ambush marketing attempts from this company and threatened to sue it for 'repeatedly' trying to create an impression that it was an Olympic sponsor. But it was too late and those advertisements had really gained the attention of the world. Many people still consider American Express as an official sponsor of the game at that time. The novel approaches from American Express made its marketing story enter books and articles on marketing and is still considered as an inspirational theme for ambush marketers.

Another instance of this type of ambush marketing can be seen during the 1984 Olympics, wherein the exclusive sponsorship rights for the film category was for Fuji.[25] During this Olympics, Fuji made the fatal mistake of not locking up related broadcasting rights. As a result, their main rival, Kodak was able to sponsor the broadcasting of the Olympic Games on ABC television and it could also receive the attention of people without any breach of the agreement between the IOC and Fuji. A similar fate was met by McDonald's during the 1988 Winter Games in Calgary. Its main rival Wendy's responded to the official sponsorship of McDonald's by sponsoring the broadcast of the Games on ABC network. Wendy's also made ski-racing posters in front of its stores with the caption 'We'll Be There!' and they printed Olympic stories on its tray liners, and a drawing resembling Olympic rings was inscribed on its napkins.[26]

Another example worth citing in this regard happened during the 1984 Los Angeles Olympic Games where Converse was the official sponsor. Their main rival Nike used the advertisement with a theme, 'I Love LA' and made a good impact. A different approach was shown by Reebok during the 1988 Seoul Olympics. Reebok was not a sponsor of this game and it adopted a counter strategy to attack the official sponsor by using the advertisement with the theme '[A]ll the games aren't in Seoul'.[27]

One more example worth citing in this category is the one that happened during the 2004 Olympics. In May 2004, the Choice Hotels began airing advertisements with the slogan 'win a trip to the big events in Athens, Greece' to ambush USOC's official hotel lodging and timeshare services supplier, Marriott. Choice Hotels got the tickets from the Olympic Games broadcaster NBC, as part of its commercial time purchase agreement. But in this case, the USOC intervened quickly to make it clear to the Choice Hotels that its advertisements could not imply that Olympic Games tickets were the prize in the promotion. Subsequently Choice Hotels had to delete the reference to the 'big events' from its online, television, and radio advertisements.[28]

In all these situations, it is seen that the ambush marketers avoided the use of official trade marks or event symbols in advertising campaigns and they instead referred to the event site to associate themselves with the event. This was very much visible in the advertisements made by American Express. But in some instances, ambush marketers even avoid reference to place names and adopt other unique strategies. For example, during the 2002 Winter Olympic Games at Salt Lake City, Utah, Nabisco made advertisements for its Fig Newton cookies depicting an ancient Olympic athlete throwing a discus and it contained a text, 'The ancient Olympians worshipped the fig and used it for energy during training'. Viewed in isolation, it might appear as a factual statement. But this statement was used in the advertisements of Nabisco with the view to ambush its rival, PowerBar, who was an official sponsor. As a result, the USOC filed a suit against Nabisco alleging that it was attempting to create an association in the consumer's minds between the Fig Newton cookies and the Olympic Movement.[29]

In most of the ambush marketing instances in this method, the ambush marketers made a greater impact on the audience, when compared to that of the official sponsors. A good example in this regard is the ambush marketing that happened during the Canadian National Hockey League, wherein it was shown that the advertisements made by Pepsi during the television broadcast of the Canadian National Hockey League made a greater impact on the audience than that made by the official sponsor Coca-Cola.[30]

Another common type of ambush marketing is making independent contracts with athletes and teams.[31] One of the best examples for the use of athletes in ambush marketing can be found from the 1992 Olympics wherein Coca-Cola was an official sponsor. Pepsi cleverly ambushed Coca-Cola by airing a commercial, featuring Magic Johnson, a member of the United States Olympic basketball team.[32] A similar strategy was found during the 2002 Winter Olympic Games in Salt Lake City, Utah, wherein AT&T and Qwest were the official sponsors. Sprint PCS, in an attempt to promote their wireless services, made a tactical move by signing up high-profile Olympic athletes such as Jimmy Shea and Jonny Moseley one year in advance of the 2002 Games and featured them in Olympic-themed advertisements before and after the actual Games.[33]

This method is very much in demand even now and it was witnessed during the ICC Cricket World Cup 2007. Hutch Telecom was one of the official sponsors of this World Cup. Reliance Telecom, one of the main rivals to Hutch Telecom (now Vodafone) in India, tied up with Sachin Tendulkar, the high profile Indian cricket team player, and advertisements featuring him and score updates using his voice were telecast during the tournament. Hutch has approached the ICC seeking compensation for failing to stop Reliance Telecom from ambush marketing.

But the use of athletes in ambush marketing has moved further on, from mere presence in advertisements. During the 1992 Olympics, Reebok was an official sponsor. When the US basketball Dream Team went to the dais to receive their gold medal, two of its famous players, Michael Jordan and Charles Barkley who were having sponsorship contracts with Nike, covered the Reebok logo on their tracksuits with a US flag.[34] This was shocking to sponsors across the world and the conduct of those players and Nike was severely criticized. But a similar, if not more creative, method was witnessed in the 1996 Olympics. Here, Reebok was the official sponsor. They were clearly ambushed when the British 100 meters runner Linford Christie appeared at a press conference wearing blue contact lenses with a highly recognizable Puma logo in white at the centre of each lens.[35] The lenses with the Puma logo received world wide media coverage, as it reached the front page of almost all the international newspapers.

But with years, this method of using athletes has become much more sophisticated and today we can even see the use of an athlete's body as billboards. This latest trend is mainly in the form of tattoos on the body of athletes and this has become a major headache for the event organizers.[36] For example, in September 2001, boxer Bernard Hopkins was seen with the logo of an internet gambling casino named

GoldenPalace.com across his back. It is reported that the online casino paid him $100,000 for the advertisement and the casino was able to recoup the money easily with increased traffic on its website.[37] This was a shocking incident for both the advertising world and the event organizers.

Sponsoring a participating team for the purpose of ambush marketing was very much popular earlier and a good example in this regard is the ambush marketing by Fuji during the 1988 Olympics. During those Olympics, IOC had granted official film sponsor status to Kodak. But Fuji made its appearance in the event by sponsoring the US swimming team.[38] But now most of the event organizers incorporate specific stipulations regarding the sponsorship of teams as a condition for participation and as a result recent times have seen a sharp decline in the use of this method.

Another common technique of ambush marketing is distribution of tickets of the events as prizes in consumer giveaways, sweepstakes, etc.[39] This unauthorized use of tickets falls within the broader definition of ambushing, as these promotions use an event's popularity or goodwill, rather than directly ambushing a competitor's sponsorship.[40] Companies use different methods to protect themselves from legal battles that can arise by using this technique.[41] This type of ambush marketing in its classical form is observable in the facts of two cases from India. They are *ICC Development (International) Ltd.* v. *Arvee Enterprises*[42] and *ICC Development (International) Ltd.* v. *Ever Green Service Station.*[43] Both these cases came up during the ICC Cricket World Cup in 2003.

In the first case, the defendant Arvee enterprises who was one of the authorized dealers of Philips created advertisements before the World Cup Cricket 2003 using slogans 'Philips: Diwali Manao World Cup Jao' and 'Buy a Philips Audio System, win a ticket to the World Cup'. They also inserted a pictorial representation of a ticket with an imaginative seat and gate number saying 'Cricket World Cup 2003'. This advertisement was shown in all media, including newspapers, television, internet, and magazines. But as they were not the official sponsors and not entitled to distribute tickets, the plaintiff-ICC Development (International) Ltd., who was the owner of all the commercial rights relating to media, sponsorship, and other intellectual property rights relating to the ICC events, approached the Court for preventing the defendant from ambush marketing.[44]

The second case is similar and in this case the defendant Ever Green Service Station was a dealer of the Hindustan Petroleum Corporation

Limited. Although they were not the official sponsors, they advertised a contest with the title 'Race 4 the World Cup Offer', without any permission from the event organizers.[45]

Another example for this type of ambush marketing can be taken from the year 2001. The Brewing Company in Indiana offered NCAA game tickets as prizes in a sweepstakes promotion enabling the winners to attend the men's 'Final Four' basketball games.[46] It was actually a breach of the terms of the revocable ticket license that appeared on the back of NCAA tickets and ticket application forms. When the matter came before the Court, the Coors argued that the NCAA's remedy was to revoke the tickets of the sweepstakes winners. But NCAA knew that it was in effect a 'no-win remedy', as even if the NCAA could identify the winners among 45,000 ticket holders, it would suffer a really adverse publicity for throwing out the spectators. This shows the real issues involved in using this type of ambush marketing.

But this method of ambush marketing is still popular and was witnessed during the recent FIFA World Cup 2006. The famous fast food chain Burger King tried to run a contest that distributed tickets and travel packages to the FIFA World Cup in Germany as prizes, even though it was not an official sponsor. One of the official sponsors of this FIFA World Cup was McDonald's, their main rival. As a result, FIFA immediately sought an injunction against the ambush marketing attempt by Burger King and was successful in the attempt.[47]

Ambush marketers use prize contests in certain other forms also. The famous case *NHL* v. *Pepsi* is often considered as a good illustration of ambush marketing in this regard.[48] Coca-Cola was the official sponsor of the NHL. In the spring of 1990, during the NHL Stanley Cup Playoffs, its arch rival Pepsi launched an advertising campaign named the 'Diet Pepsi $4,000,000 Pro Hockey Playoff Pool'. In this widely publicized contest, fans were eligible for $10,000 prize, if they matched actual NHL Playoff results with information on Pepsi bottle cap liners, specially marked cups, or contest scratch cards. Pepsi was careful in referring to the event as 'Pro Playoff Hockey Pool' instead of the 'NHL Playoff Pool'. The promotional materials also displayed a disclaimer that disassociated the contest from NHL. The promotional materials used city names like 'Boston', instead of names like 'Boston Bruins' which was registered as a trade mark by NHL.

Pepsi used this contest in the advertisements during the television broadcast of the event. The advertisements also featured spokesperson Don Cherry, a former NHL coach, sitting in a locker room with several men dressed in generic hockey uniforms. NHL approached the Court claiming that Pepsi designed its advertising to take a free ride on the reputation of the NHL, thereby creating public confusion about the relationship between the NHL and Pepsi.[49]

Another common technique used for ambush marketing is the 'good luck' or 'congratulatory' advertisements, wherein the companies associate themselves with an event or achievement through some greeting messages.[50] During most of the major events, we can see such advertisements appearing in different kinds of media, wishing the teams or athletes 'good luck' or 'congratulations'. Many a times those companies who make such advertisements do not have any 'contractual' relationship with those teams. But these advertisements may cast an impression upon the viewers and the prospective consumers that the products are associated with or endorsed by those teams or athletes. One example worth citing in this regard is from the 1992 Olympics at Barcelona. Pepsi which was not a sponsor for the Olympics at Barcelona made commercials shortly before the summer games, featuring Pepsi endorser and Dream Team member Magic Johnson with the message 'From all of us at Pepsi to our friend and partner Earvin Johnson: Go get 'em, Magic'. Coke was the official sponsor of that game and this was a clever ambush marketing strategy against them.

Another ambush marketing practice commonly witnessed is throwing parties and arranging other events in host cities before, during, and after the main event.[51] The hosting of such events is mainly intended to convey their commercial messages to event attendees and to secure media coverage. For example, during the 1996 Atlanta Olympics, the official beer sponsor was Budweiser. But the thirsty sports fans moving to the Olympic stadium were greeted by a large tented beer garden hosted by the German brewer-Warsteiner Beer. At the same time, Miller Brewing also hosted a well-attended eighteen-day series of pop music concerts in Atlanta. The end result of all these parties was the considerable hampering of exclusivity of the official beer sponsor.

Buying advertisement spaces in and around the event place is another ambush marketing technique. It can include local bill boards, hanging of banners, signs on buildings, etc.[52] One of the often cited examples in this regard happened during the 1984 Los Angeles Olympic Games wherein Converse was an official sponsor. Their main rival Nike built huge murals near the Los Angeles stadium displaying the Nike logo and also the pictures of several athletes wearing Nike sporting clothes.[53] This was a shocking gift from Nike to the Olympics committee and its official sponsors.

In a similar manner, during the 2002 Winter Olympic Games at Salt Lake City, Utah, the Discount Tire Company used a billboard advertising campaign that depicted tires in the form of the Olympic Rings.[54] The billboard also welcomed the visitors to the Games in several languages. According to the USOC, it was using Olympic terminology and Olympic Games imagery to inaccurately suggest a commercial affiliation with the Olympic Games and the Olympic Movement and as a result a complaint was filed to remove the billboards.

But the world was shown better advertisement spaces by a local company during the Winter Games 2002 in Salt Lake City. Anheuser-Busch had paid more than US$ 50 million to become an official sponsor of the 2002 Winter Olympics. But a local company named Schirf Brewery came up with an ingenious, but legal idea of marking its delivery trucks painted with the slogan 'Wasutch Beers: The Unofficial Beer- 2002 Winter Games'.[55]

Making people wear apparels with ambusher's mark and making them carry products, signs, or accessories bearing the ambusher's marks are some of the common ambushing methods which have almost become synonymous with the term 'ambush marketing' through their frequent appearances in events across the world.[56] The ambush marketing during the 1996 Olympic Games at Atlanta is a classical example on this point. Reebok, who was the official sponsor, was terribly shocked when it saw the paper flags bearing the logo of Nike in the hands of a large number of spectators inside the stadium. These paper flags were handed out to the crowds by Nike marketers outside the venue. The TV cameras captured the images of the crowd waving the Nike flags, much to the despair of the official sponsor.[57]

A similar story was repeated at the FIFA World Cup 2002, hosted by Korea and Japan. Here the official sponsors were JVC and Philips. But Samsung distributed baseball caps with the logo of Samsung among the spectators and consequently gained a competitive edge over the official sponsors during the event as the Samsung mark was perfectly visible among the spectators during the broadcasting of this event.

But ambush marketing has become much more sophisticated these days and flying planes and helicopters towing banners have found favour with ambush marketers now.[58] For example during the 1994 Goodwill Games at St. Petersburg, Reebok was the official sponsor. Nike ambushed Reebok's sponsorship by flying a balloon over the Goodwill Games stadium and by supplying a truck to sell sneakers on the path of the Goodwill Games cycling race.[59]

Another area where ambush marketing happens on a wider scale is through merchandise sale. For example, during the Winter Olympic Games in Salt Lake City in Utah in 2002, Quick Silver Inc., without taking any permission, marketed Olympic themed T-shirts, sweatshirts, pins, and key chains through its Park City and Salt Lake City stores.[60] It used designs that included the company's logo, which depicted a wave and a mountain inside a circle, in five interlocking circles similar to those of the Olympic rings. The words, 'Salt Lake City-Winter 2002' were superimposed over the design and the word 'Olympian' was printed above it.

In another instance, Intelicense, a Swiss corporation, and its sub-licensee tried to market, and sublicense the official pictograms of the IOC within the United States, without taking consent from the USOC. They were graphic designs of athletes participating in various summer and winter Olympic sports, with a background that explicitly incorporated the Olympic symbol consisting of five interlocking rings. The USOC moved the Court and successfully prevented the attempt.[61]

Another interesting incident is an ambush marketing attempt from the side of a government agency—United States Postal Service.[62] In May, 1996, it released a series of stamps with Olympic themes and announced its plans to license such stamps to merchandisers selling T-shirts, mugs, and pins. But the Olympic committee immediately opposed this proposal as the plan would have considerably diminished the value of sponsorships and licenses. Though the postal service initially claimed that none of their merchandise contained any official Olympic phrases or marks, they later reached an agreement to grant the exclusive licensing rights to all art-works from its stamps.

Two other ambush marketing practices worth mentioning separately in this part are the background of the cases—*The New Zealand Olympic and Commonwealth Games Association Inc.* v. *Telecom New Zealand Limited*[63] and *Mastercard International Inc.* v. *Sprint Communications Co.*[64] In the first case, a few months before the 1996 Atlanta Olympic Games, the New Zealand Telecom company launched an advertisement that featured five repetitions of the word 'ring' using colors and disposition, identical to that of the rings of the Olympic symbol. It was accompanied by a slogan 'With Telecom mobile you can take your own phone to the Olympic'. The company was not an official sponsor, but because of the advertisement, the company was thought to be associated with the Olympic movement by the viewers.

The second case happened during the 1994 World Cup Soccer Tournament. The ISL was given the right to issue sponsorships for the 1994 World Cup Soccer Tournament by FIFA. ISL granted Mastercard International Inc. the right to be an official sponsor of the World Cup and this gave Mastercard the exclusive right to use 'World Cup '94' trade marks on all card-based payments and account access devices. It was written in the agreement that it included, without limitation, credit cards, charge cards, travel and entertainment cards, on-line and off-line point-of-sale debit cards, check guarantee cards, and cards that combined two or more of the foregoing functions. World Cup USA 1994 Inc. was the Local Organizing Committee ('LOC') for this World Cup and ISL had permitted LOC to contract with companies to become 'official partners' of the games and to authorize the use of the World Cup mark on their products. But the official partners were clearly told not to use the World Cup marks on any card-based payment or account-access devices as the LOC was not permitted to grant any rights that would infringe the rights of the official sponsors.

The LOC entered into an agreement with the telecom company Sprint, whereby it provided Sprint the exclusive long-distance telecommunication carrier rights for the World Cup Games and the right to use World Cup logos and marks in its advertising, marketing, and promotions. Subsequently, Sprint, based on its understanding of the agreement with the LOC on official partners' rights, issued over 100,000 telephone cards bearing the World Cup mark. Though the cards contained a number for each user, they neither had a magnetic strip for a card reader to scan nor did they allow users to make credit purchases with the cards. But Mastercard objected to these cards by arguing that the cards issued by Sprint were an activity within the domain of its exclusive rights conferred on it through official sponsor status and they approached the Court to prohibit Sprint's cards.[65] These two cases really show how complex the issue of ambush marketing can become.

Today ambush marketing is not limited to the real world. The recent events expose the entry of ambush marketers to the virtual world also. The ambush marketers are now using the internet as a medium of ambush marketing to reach the consumers. Considering the number of pages that go online everyday, it is a difficult task to trace the paths of ambush marketing in the virtual world. But it is interesting to note here that the Salt Lake Organizing Committee, the USOC, and the IOC brought an action for cyber squatting against the registered owners of over one thousand eight hundred domain names which contained registered Olympic marks, making it the single largest cyber squatting suit.[66] As a result, ownership of dozens of domain names with words like Salt Lake 2002, Olympic, Olympic Winter Games, and SLOC 2002 were transferred.[67] One of the examples is that of Brighton Ski Resort which created a logo with five linked snowflakes resembling the five Olympic rings and used them on their website www.brightonupthegames.com.[68] The USOC sought an injunction from the federal court to stop Brighton Ski Resort from using the word 'games' as part of its Internet domain name and also directed it to remove billboard advertising at the Salt Lake City airport that showed five overlapping snowflakes logo. Eventually, the ski resort agreed to comply with the directions.

The survey of different ambush marketing techniques that were witnessed during the major events of the past show the real gravity of the problem. The examples cited here are just a sample of the hundreds of ambush marketing practices found across the world. But they shows the real sophistication that has been achieved by ambush marketers across the world. Today we even find many websites of advertising agencies proclaiming their skills in ambush marketing.[69] But how the event organizers and the corporate world will tackle this problem is something to be watched with patience. But let us conclude by perceiving a very recent incident. During the opening ceremony of the Common Wealth Games in March 2006, the Gold Coast Mayor Ron Clarke, who was one of the four persons to run in the final stage of Queen's Baton Relay, wore a cap bearing the 'Very GC' logo.[70] The word 'GC' stands for Gold Coast. When we realize that it was an event watched by millions across the world and that no one else wore any caps, can we consider it as an ambush marketing strategy to promote his city? The answer is not easy. So also is the list of novel techniques of ambush marketing.

AMBUSH MARKETING THROUGH INTERNET—EMERGING ISSUES

We have made a detailed survey of the ambush marketing practices from past events. But as a work with an objective to discuss pragmatic solutions to the issue of ambush marketing, we also need to have an eye on some of the budding and possible spaces of ambush marketing. The new challenges are mainly from the medium of the internet. The increasing reach of the internet is creating the additional burden on event organizers and sponsors in ensuring protection of exclusivity.

As we saw in the study of ambush marketing practices in the previous section, one of the most common methods adopted by ambush marketers is registering domain names containing the event title or names having reference to the events. Even though we can see successful examples of tackling domain name related issues, the increasing number of websites and web pages makes the issue a really complicated one. An equally important issue is the unauthorized use of information available on the internet. Most of the event organizers produce publications for providing information to the public about the event and when someone reproduces it, it needs to be ensured that it is done only with the permission of the event organizer.[71] The ambush marketers can misuse such information in quite ingenious ways so that they can create an impression that they are associated with the event.

Another challenging issue is the attempts from ambush marketers to pass off web sites and its content as its own, through methods like 'framing' within the ambusher's site instead of linking the visitor to the official website of the event organizer, or designing the links to the official website in such a way as to make a browser believe that the website is endorsed by the official sponsors.[72] Linking raises serious issues when it explicitly or implicitly suggests an unwarranted association with linking and linked sites or where it creates a belief that an unassociated page is associated, affiliated, approved, or sponsored by the event organizer. For example, if an ambush marketer's website shows a link to the official website of the FIFA World Cup in a prominent manner, it will certainly create an impression that FIFA has authorized that person to provide a link to the official page of FIFA.

Similar are the issues like the use of event titles as meta tags, without the permission from event organizers. Meta tags are the key words embedded in a website's html code for enabling search engines like Google and Altavista to identify the contents of a website. When a person searches the term 'world cup' in a search engine like Google, the search engine will look for websites containing the meta tag 'world cup' for producing the search result. The greater the number of meta tags, the higher will be the order of ranking in the result page. When an ambush marketer creates a webpage having the meta tag 'world cup' repeated many times in its html code, it may be shown even above the official website of 'world cup' in the search result page. Since meta tags are not visible to the normal users, it is very difficult to detect. One of the unreported Indian cases which discussed the issues relating to unauthorized use of meta tags is the decision of the Delhi High Court is *Tata Sons Ltd.* v. *Bodacious Tatas* in the year 1999.

Another area of concern is the possible misuse of use of pop-up advertisements and banner advertisements by ambush marketers. A pop-up advertisement is an advertisement that displays itself in a new browser window.[73] The pop-up advertisements are usually triggered with the help of adware or spyware programmes like Gator, Savenow, etc., which often gets installed into a computer without the knowledge of the computer user. Once the software gets installed, it will track the user's online activity and will present the pop-up advertisements according to the user's area of activity.[74] So, in the case of a soccer fan who visits the FIFA website often, this software will trigger advertisements relating to soccer and the world cup. When a pop-up advertisement appears, the user may click on it and that will take the viewer to an outside website containing information from the advertiser. The user may never realize that such an advertisement was put up without the knowledge or permission from FIFA.

The banner advertisements also present a similar probability. Banner advertisements are rectangular blocks positioned above, below, or to the side of the content of a web page.[75] Most of the internet users who use mail services like that of Yahoo are familiar with these rectangle blocks of advertisements that often appear above their inbox. But in certain cases, the advertisers give a simple appearance for these boxes which makes them look more or less like an information source, rather than an advertisement. Just like in a pop-up advertisement, when a person clicks on a banner advertisement, he will reach an outside website, providing information from the advertiser. The use of pop-up advertisements and banner advertisements can help the ambush marketer achieve his or her objective at a much lesser expense and risk of legal action. This is mainly because the legislatures and the courts have so far not been able to find a concrete solution to this issue.[76]

One more issue worth mentioning in this context is the sale of key words. In key word advertising, the advertisers tie up with search engine providers like Google or MSN to make their advertisements appear on the search result page, whenever a particular word is searched. So if a person searches the word 'FIFA World Cup' in Google, a number of unofficial web links will appear on the right side of the search result page. These are provided by the advertisers and only a careful internet user will know that it is an advertisement link and not one related to FIFA in any manner. Through this route, the advertising companies can successfully associate a non-sponsor with an event. All these emerging issues create additional challenges upon the event organizers and sponsors over the protection of intellectual property rights associated with an event.

IMPACT OF AMBUSH MARKETING

The corporate sponsors of an event involve themselves in a sponsorship programme with the hope of exclusivity in the use of the official marks, logos, and other designations. They enter the sponsorship with the hope of capitalizing on exclusive advertising and promotional opportunities and the right to describe themselves as the official sponsors of such events, in their marketing and promotional campaigns.[77] But when that exclusivity is lost, the value of sponsorship is also lost.[78] When a company engages in ambush marketing the exclusivity intended to be conferred through sponsorship to a sponsor is lost. Hence, the value of sponsorship is also loss. As it is an undeniable fact that corporate sponsorship is one of the biggest money-spinning sources of revenue for the event organizers, the loss in sponsorship value will definitely affect the financial strength of an event organizer. Hence, the most important argument against ambush marketing is that it dilutes the value of corporate sponsorships and thereby jeopardizes the financial vitality of events.[79]

The increasing cost of sponsorships has also increased sponsor's emphasis on return-on-investment. If sponsored events do not give exclusivity, the sponsor's interest on sponsorship property will be lost and the damage will extend to the whole sponsorship market.[80] A recent survey among the decision makers in sports sponsorship underlines this issue and shows that a vast majority of them consider ambush marketing as a growing menace and that they would be less likely to recommend sponsoring events that are routinely ambushed.[81]

From the perspective of intellectual property rights, ambush marketing is a clear case of transgression on the intellectual property rights associated with an event. Even when the ambush marketers are not making any direct references to the protected intellectual property rights, they in effect transgress those intellectual property rights. Take for example, the goodwill attached with the Olympic Games. An ambush marketing attempt in the Olympic Games is definitely an attempt to capitalize on such hard earned goodwill, without taking the permission of the creator of such goodwill. Direct and indirect references to the Olympic symbol or the Olympic Games are just different means for achieving illegal transgression on the rights of event organizers. Hence, ambush marketing activities need to be viewed with the same seriousness we attach to other property infringements. The fact that they refer to the events and their own products in an ingenious and subtle manner should not permit them to circumvent the laws.

Ambush marketing also brings in some ethical questions.[82] These questions are predominantly based on the differentiation of ambush marketing practices from just imaginative marketing. But the answer to ethical questions regarding ambush marketing varies depending on whether the response is from a corporate sponsor, event organizer, or a marketer.[83] According to corporate sponsors and event organizers, the piggybacking of non-sponsoring companies is clearly unethical and they claim that it threatens the integrity and future of these events. The corporate sponsors strongly claim that the ambush marketing tactics will reduce the effectiveness of their promotional efforts and event organizers are concerned that these practices will diminish their ability to retain top paying sponsors, and thereby jeopardizing the whole funding mechanism of events.[84]

These ethical issues also bring in the question of Corporate Social Responsibility (CSR) of companies engaged in ambush marketing. CSR refers to the obligations arising from an implicit social contract between business firms and the society, which compels the firms to be responsive to society's needs and wants and business firms are required to tune its conduct in such a way as to maximize the positive and minimize the negative effects of its actions on the society.[85] In simple words, CSR is all about how a company behaves with various stakeholders including its employees, consumers, and the society at large.[86]

Corporate Social Responsibility generally includes economic, legal, ethical, and philanthropic responsibilities.[87] In our discussion on ambush marketing, it is the ethical responsibilities of a company that are being referred to. These responsibilities make a company morally responsible to the society if it inflicts actual or potential injury to any individual or groups in the society. Ambush marketing advertisements are those which create a misleading association with a sponsored event, and this 'misleading' aspect makes the ambush marketing company ethically responsible to the consumers and the society at large. Moreover, we find serious injury to the sponsorship value of an event that is being frequently ambushed. As found from the survey discussed earlier, frequent ambush marketing in an event will dissuade companies from investing money in sponsorship of that event and this in turn will even threaten the existence of such events. It also causes considerable economic injury to the official sponsor, who invests heavily on sponsorship. These multifold ethical issues involved in ambush marketing should dissuade companies from ambush marketing, in view of the Corporate Social Responsibility vested on them.[88] Even if a company is not engaged in promoting philanthropic responsibilities, it is expected to comply with at least its ethical responsibilities.[89]

On the other hand, ambush marketing companies and their supporters attempt to counter these arguments by arguing that ambush marketing is a fair game and as we live in an open market, it is for the official sponsors to promote their sponsorships and brands in a way they wish to project to the public.[90] Marketing guru Jerry Welsh, who coined the term 'ambush marketing', supports this view.[91] This group argues that many a times the price of sponsorships is exorbitant and ambush marketing is a form of creative advertising for those companies who cannot pay exorbitant prices for exclusive rights packages.[92] But when we analyse this argument in a comprehensive perspective, we see that it is an argument not only against the sports sponsorship packages, but also against the whole intellectual property rights system. It is an argument similar to that of the copyleft activists! Most of the music pirates and software pirates argue that they go for piracy because of the high price of original CDs and original software. But in today's world, where knowledge is the most powerful capital for any establishment, we see an obligation for its apposite protection. Hence, this argument based on the excessive prices for exclusive rights packages fails.

Those who favour ambush marketing also resort to an argument that ambush marketing acts as a positive force in a free market.[93] According to them, by exposing the true scope of exclusivity that any sponsor can reasonably expect to enjoy, ambush marketers are in effect helping to quantify the true market value of sponsorship, while participating in the marketing blitz in a manner they deem most cost effective for their company.[94]

Another interesting argument put forward by ambush marketers is that ambush marketing is an exercise of their right of free speech. This group argues that words like 'world cup', 'Olympics', 'games', 'fashion week', etc., are in public domain and every human being has a right to use these terms freely. We can see a strong group of academicians from European countries supporting this argument, in the wake of the strong action taken by FIFA against ambush marketing during FIFA World Cup 2006 in Germany. According to this group, they have a right to paste the advertisement of their choice on their cars and caps and take it near the event venues. They consider it unconstitutional to curtail their choice of drinks and snacks, merely on the ground that the product is a rival to the official sponsor.[95] In many instances we can see the defendants invoking constitutional protection, as commercial speech falls within its protective hands.[96] But whether such protection extends to an advertisement which creates an untrue impression of the association of the company with an event is questionable. This question of free speech and fundamental rights protection is dealt with in detail in chapter 5 where the implications of legislation against ambush marketing are discussed.

Whatever be the arguments for and against ambush marketing, it is worth listening to some interesting facts which were revealed in a recent study on consumer attitudes towards ambush marketing and the legal issues involved.[97] Though the data revealed that majority of the consumers (spectators of the event) were generally indifferent to ambush marketing practices, it was found that people's reaction differed considerably to the type of ambush marketing involved.[98] Though the consumers accepted ambush activities relating to team sponsorship, television advertising and promotions as suggesting an official sponsorship, they did not see it as dishonest, misleading, unethical, or illegal. But at the same time the study also revealed that there was high awareness about the exclusivity of Olympic rings and as a result the consumers were seen as sensitive to activities involving Olympic related logos.

This study also showed that consumer attitudes differed with gender and age.[99] According to the findings, ambush marketing activities produced different results depending on the number of women in the audience, as women were seen as more sensitive to the dishonest aspects of ambush marketing activities.[100] Similarly, age differences also produced different opinions. Younger consumers in the age group of 18 to 39 viewed ambush marketing activities as dishonest, misleading, and unethical, whereas older consumers who were above the age of 40 did not have such an attitude.[101] This study is a clear pointer towards the need for creating greater awareness about the real effects of ambush marketing.

However, this is a never ending debate. The only argument that emerges from our survey of different types of ambush marketing practices the world has experienced is that ambush marketing has become, and will continue to be, an irritating fact of life for sports organizers and sponsors across the globe, in new and different forms, at least for some time more.

NOTES

1. For a detailed discussion, see Cristina Garrigues, 'Ambush Marketing: Robbery or Smart Advertising', *EIPR* 2002, 24(11), 505–7, 505 (2002).

2. Jacqueline A. Leimer, 'Ambush Marketing: Not Just an Olympic-Sized Problem', 2(4) *Intell. Prop. Strategist* 1, 3 (1996).

3. See http://www.macmillandictionary.com/New-Words/050815-ambush-marketing.htm, accessed 5 March 2006.

4. For details, see the official website of International Olympic Committee, http://www.olympic.org/uk/organisation/index_uk.asp, accessed 21 February 2006.

5. The corporate sponsor has to pay around $ 40 million to get the highest level corporate sponsorship in Olympics. See Steve McKelvey and John Grady, 'An Analysis of the Ongoing Global Efforts to Combat Ambush Marketing: Will Corporate Marketers "Take" the Gold in Greece?', 14 *J. Legal Aspects Sport* 191, 191 and Abram Sauer, 'Ambush Marketing: Steals the Show' available online at http://www.brandchannel.com/features_effect.asp?pf_id=98, accessed 21 January 2006.

6. See http://fifaworldcup.yahoo.com/06/en/partners.html, accessed 2 April 2006. It is interesting to observe that twelve of the fifteen official

partners are continuing the sponsorship with FIFA from the 2002 World cup and each of them paid around thirty to fourty million pounds for the four-year extension. See *http://www.tmcnet.com/usubmit/2006/03/31/1524884.htm*, accessed 2 April 2006.

7. Ibid.

8. Among all, it is found that sports events have higher brand awareness. For example studies show that the five interlocked rings which forms the Olympic symbol has a brand awareness of 93 percent. See Jason K. Schmitz, 'Ambush Marketing: The Off-Field Competition at the Olympic Games', 3 *Nw. J. Tech. & Intell. Prop.* 203, 4. (2005). Such a higher brand awareness is one reason for sports events turning to be the favourite hunting place for ambush marketers.

9. J. Thomas McCarthy, *McCarthy on Trademarks and Unfair Competition*, Fourth Edition, 4 McCarthy on Trademarks and Unfair Competition Â§ 27:66 (4th edn).

10. Ibid.

11. See Jamie Carr, 'Get real: Sport Costs', http://www.adfocus.co.za/adfocus2003/b8.htm, accessed 5 February 2006.

12. See Jason K. Schmitz, 'Ambush Marketing: The Off-Field Competition at the Olympic Games', 5.

13. See Lori L. Bean, 'Ambush Marketing: Sports Sponsorship Confusion and the Lanham Act', 75 *BUL Rev.* 1099, 1100 (1995).

14. Carolina Pina and Ana Gil-Roble, 'Sponsorship of Sports Events and Ambush Marketing', *EIPR* 2005, 27(3), 93–6, 93 (2005).

15. http://www.macmillandictionary.com/New-Words/050815-ambush-marketing.htm, accessed 5 March 2006.

16. To know more about Jerry Welsh, see http://www.poolonline.com/bios/biojwelsh.html, accessed 6 March 2006.

17. To find more about Jerry Welsh's views on Ambush Marketing, see Jerry Welsh, 'Ambush Marketing: What it is, What it isn't', http://www.poolonline.com/archive/issue19/iss19fea5.html, accessed 6 March 2006.

18. For a detailed discussion, see Michael A. Lisi, 'Ambush Marketing: Here to Stay?', 12(1) *Intell. Prop. Strategist* 3 (2005).

19. For further discussion on this practical aspect, see Cristina garrigues, 'Ambush Marketing: Robbery or Smart Advertising', 505.

20. For example, the 2004 Olympic Games at Athens was seen live by about 4 billion people from 220 countries. See Andrew Moss, 'The Olympics: A Celebration of Sport and the Role of Law', *Ent. LR* 2004, 15(8), 237–42, 237 (2004). Though every author agrees that global sports sponsorship is a multi billion dollar business, it is very difficult to find the exact amount spent in sponsorship. The data is scattered. According to Anne M. Wall, the

global expenditure on sports sponsorship in the year 1995 was $10 billion. See Anne M. Wall, 'Sports Marketing and the Law: Protecting Proprietary Interests in Sports Entertainment Events', 86. This amount is expected to rise to $26.5 billion in 2005. See Anita M. Moorman and T. Christopher Greenwell, 'Consumer Attitudes of Deception and the Legality of Ambush Marketing Practices', 15 *J. Legal Aspects Sport* 183, (2005). According to the data available on the official website of International Olympic Committee, between 2001 and 2004, its revenue from sponsorship alone was $1459 million. This was about 34 percent of the total income of the organization.

See http://www.olympic.org/uk/organisation/facts/introduction/index_uk.asp, accessed 5 April 2006.

According to the *Economist*, the total sponsorship for FIFA World Cup 2006 was around $700 million. See *The Economist*, 'War Minus Shooting' (February 16, 2006).

21. See Anita M. Moorman and T. Christopher Greenwell, 'Consumer Attitudes of Deception and the Legality of Ambush Marketing Practices', 183. But some other authors consider sports sponsorship as even going up to 85 per cent of the total sponsorship expenditure. For example, see http://www.tmcnet.com/usubmit/2006/03/31/1524884.htm, accessed 15 April 2006.

22. Cristina Garrigues, 'Ambush Marketing: Robbery or Smart Advertising', 505.

23. See Stephen M. Mckelvey, 'Atlanta '96: Olympic Countdown To Ambush Armageddon?', 4 *Seton Hall J. Sport L.* 397, 403–4 (1994).

24. It is worth remembering here that Jerry Welsh who coined the term 'ambush marketing' was working as the manager of global marketing efforts for the American Express Company.

25. See Michael A. Lisi, 'Ambush Marketing: Here to Stay?', 3.

26. See Lori L. Bean, 'Ambush Marketing: Sports Sponsorship Confusion and the Lanham Act', 1104.

27. Ibid.

28. See Steve McKelvey and John Grady, 'An Analysis of the Ongoing Global Efforts to Combat Ambush Marketing: Will Corporate Marketers "Take" The Gold In Greece?', 192–3.

29. Nabisco settled the case for a confidential amount and ceased its advertising campaign later. See, Ibid., 206–7.

30. Coca-Cola had paid $ 2.6 million to achieve official sponsorship in this game. See Carolina Pina and Ana Gil-Roble, 'Sponsorship of Sports Events and Ambush Marketing', 94.

31. See Jacqueline A. Leimer, 'Ambush Marketing: Not Just an Olympic-Sized Problem', 3.

32. This has to be read in the light of the fact that Coca-Cola had paid $33 million to become an official sponsor of the 1992 Olympics. See Lori L. Bean, 'Ambush Marketing: Sports Sponsorship Confusion and the Lanham Act', 1105.

33. See Steve McKelvey and John Grady, 'An Analysis of the Ongoing Global Efforts to Combat Ambush Marketing: Will Corporate Marketers "Take" the Gold in Greece?', 207.

34. See Cristina Garrigues, 'Ambush Marketing: Robbery or Smart Advertising', 505.

35. Ibid., at 506.

36. For a very detailed discussion on the legal aspects of this new trend, especially the first amendment rights related issues, see generally, Stephen M. McKelvey, 'Commercial "Branding": The Final Frontier or False Start for Athletes' Use of Temporary Tattoos as Body Billboards', 13 *J. Legal Aspects Sport* 1 (2003) and John Vukelj, 'Post No Bills: Can the NBA Prohibit its Players from Wearing Tattoo Advertisements?', 15 *Fordham Intell. Prop. Media and Ent. LJ* 507, 507–46 (2005).

The problem is much more complicated as there are many players who are addicted to tattoo fixing. For example, it is widely reported that the famous soccer star David Beckham is addicted to the pain of fixing tattoos. He already has 12 tattoos on his body. See *The Deccan Chronicle*, 'Beckham Addicted to the Pain of Tattoos' (Hyderabad: 4 April 2006), 20.

37. For details, see Stephen M. McKelvey, 'Commercial "Branding": The Final Frontier or False Start for Athletes' Use of Temporary Tattoos as Body Billboards', 4.

38. See Michael A. Lisi, 'Ambush Marketing: Here to Stay?', 3.

39. See Jacqueline A. Leimer, 'Ambush Marketing: Not Just an Olympic-Sized Problem', 3.

40. For a detailed discussion, see Lori L. Bean, 'Ambush Marketing: Sports Sponsorship Confusion and the Lanham Act', 1105.

41. While adopting this method the companies are seen referring to the event generically and usually avoid using the event's registered name in the contest headlines. In many situations, the companies are also seen using disclaimers 'Not Endorsed or Sponsored By ——' to protect themselves from lawsuits. The Courts are generally seen favoring the use of disclaimers and one of the best examples in this regard will be *National Football League* v. *Governor of Delaware* 435 F. Supp 1372 (1977). In this case, the Delaware State Lottery had started a state football lottery game wherein the participants could buy a lottery ticket on which they guessed the winning team for the weekly professional football games. At the back of each ticket it was written that 'The "Scoreboard Lottery" is sponsored solely by the Delaware State

Lottery'. When the matter was taken to the court alleging it as an attempt of ambush marketing, the court took the view that the lottery used the National Football League service mark not to identify the service it offered, but to describe its game. A more detailed discussion of this case and the implication of using disclaimers are dealt in detail in the next chapter.

42. *ICC Development (International) Ltd.* v. *Arvee Enterprises and Anr.* 2003 (26) PTC 245 (Del).

43. *ICC Development (International) Ltd.* v. *Ever Green Service Station and Anr.* 2003 (26) PTC 228 (Del).

44. In this case the plaintiff was not successful. The reasons found by the Court in arriving at this decision is analysed in detail in the next chapter.

45. Interestingly in this case also the plaintiff was not successful on the claim of ambush marketing. The decision in this case is also analysed in detail in the next chapter.

46. See Steve McKelvey and John Grady, 'Ambush Marketing: The Legal Battleground for Sport Marketers', 21-WTR *Ent. and Sports Law* 8 (2004).

47. It is interesting to note here that FIFA has already filed about 1200 infringement cases in 65 countries in relation to World Cup 2006. See *The Economist*, 'War Minus Shooting', (16 February 2006).

48. See, *NHL* v. *Pepsi Cola Canada Ltd.* 1995 CarswellBC 15.

49. Ibid. This case is analysed in detail in the next chapter.

50. See Stephen M. Mckelvey, 'Atlanta '96: Olympic Countdown to Ambush Armageddon?', 408.

51. See Michael A. Lisi, 'Ambush Marketing: Here to Stay?', 3.

52. Ibid.

53. See Cristina Garrigues, 'Ambush Marketing: Robbery or Smart Advertising', 505.

54. For details, *see* Steve McKelvey and John Grady, 'An Analysis of the Ongoing Global Efforts to Combat Ambush Marketing: Will Corporate Marketers "Take" the Gold in Greece?', 205–6.

55. See Abram Sauer, 'Ambush Marketing: Steals the Show'.

56. See Michael A. Lisi, 'Ambush Marketing: Here to Stay?', 3.

57. For a detailed analysis of this incident, see Christina Garrigues, 'Ambush Marketing: Robbery or Smart Advertising', 506.

58. See, Michael A. Lisi, 'Ambush Marketing: Here to Stay?', 3.

59. For more details on this incident, see Lori L. Bean, 'Ambush Marketing: Sports Sponsorship Confusion and the Lanham Act', 1104–5.

60. The USOC approached the Court arguing that the references to the upcoming Games were meant to mislead and deceive consumers. See Steve McKelvey and John Grady, 'An Analysis of the Ongoing Global Efforts to

Combat Ambush Marketing: Will Corporate Marketers "Take" The Gold In Greece?', 207.

61. See *United States Olympic Committee* v. *Intelicense Corporation and others*, 737 F.2d 263 (1984).

62. For more details, *see* Erinn M. Batcha, 'Who are the Real Competitors in the Olympic Games? Dual Olympic Battles: Trademark Infringement and Ambush Marketing Harm Corporate Sponsors—Violations Against The USOC and its Corporate Sponsors', 8 *Seton Hall J. Sport L.* 229, 254 (1998).

63. *The New Zealand Olympic and Commonwealth Games Association Inc.* v. *Telecom New Zealand Limited* [1996] FSR 757 (New Zealand HC).

64. *Mastercard International Inc.* v. *Sprint Communications Co.* 1994 WL 97097 (SDNY).

65. Ibid. In this case, the main issue to be decided by the Court was whether Mastercard was granted an exclusive license for the World Cup marks which can preclude Sprint from using those marks on the payment cards which it has issued and plans to issue in connection with its World Cup promotion. In this case the Court noted that the use of the World Cup mark by Sprint on telephone cards will convey to the world a false impression that its use of the marks on calling cards is officially sanctioned by the World Cup organization. Since Mastercard was having the exclusive right to use the mark with respect to payment services, the Court enjoined Sprint from using the World Cup mark on any card issued in connection with the payment for its services or in any other manner that conflicts with the exclusive rights granted to Mastercard.

66. Steve McKelvey and John Grady, 'An Analysis of the Ongoing Global Efforts to Combat Ambush Marketing: Will Corporate Marketers "Take" the gold in Greece?', 205.

67. Ibid.

68. Ibid., at 206.

69. For example, see http://www.onpoint-marketing.com/beverage-marketing.htm, accessed 13 March 2006. There are several other advertising agencies like this which offer ambush marketing services.

70. See, http://www.abc.net.au/goldcoast/stories/s1593547.htm, accessed 20 March 2006.

71. Take the example of the contents of www.ioc.org, through which the Olympic committee tries to educate public and provides information to the public. Ensuing dissemination of information without violating the copyright of the International Olympic Committee is a really challenging issue in this digital world. For a detailed discussion on this issue, see Scott A. Bearby, 'Marketing, Protection and Enforcement of NCAA Marks', 12 *Marq. Sports*

L. Rev. 543, 554–5. In this article, the author discusses the issue in the context of NCAA marks.

72. Ibid., at 554.

73. See Geoffrey D. Wilson, 'Internet Pop-Up Ads: Your Days Are Numbered! The Supreme Court of California Announces a Workable Standard for Trespass to Chattels in Electronic Communications', 24 *Loy. LA Ent. L. Rev.* 567, 569 (2004).

74. See Kristen M. Beystehner, 'See Ya Later, Gator: Assessing Whether Placing Pop-Up Advertisements on Another Company's Website Violates Trademark Law', 11 *J. Intell. Prop. L.* 87, 87 (2003).

75. Ibid.

76. In most of the jurisdictions, online advertising is not governed by any specific legislation devoted solely to regulate advertising practices in cyberspace. Such situation often leads to diverse judicial opinions. In the case of *Washingtonpost.Newsweek Interactive Company* v. *Gator Corporation* 2002 WL 31356645, some publishers approached the Court contending that the defendant Gator Corporation's pop-up advertising scheme was inherently deceptive and mislead users into falsely believing that the pop-up advertisements supplied by Gator were advertisements authorized by and originating with the underlying websites. In July 2002, the United States District Court for the Eastern District of Virginia granted the Publishers' motion for a preliminary injunction, enjoining Gator from several acts relating to its pop-up advertising scheme, based on likely violations of the Publishers' intellectual property rights. But when the trial was about to begin in early 2003, the parties reached a settlement. But in a more recent case *1–800 Contacts Inc.* v. *Whenu.Com Inc.* 414 F.3d 400 (2005), we can see the Court of Appeals taking an approach in favour of pop-up advertisers.

77. For a detailed discussion on this aspect, *see* Cristina Garrigues, 'Ambush Marketing: Robbery or Smart Advertising', 505.

78. Ibid.

79. See Lori L. Bean, 'Ambush Marketing: Sports Sponsorship Confusion and the Lanham Act', 1100–1.

80. Ibid., at 1101.

81. For details, see, Steve McKelvey and John Grady, 'Ambush Marketing: The Legal Battleground For Sport Marketers', 13.

82. For a detailed discussion on these ethical issues, see Christina Garrigues, 'Ambush Marketing: Robbery or Smart Advertising', 507.

83. Ibid.

84. Ibid.

85. The term 'social contract' is used here with a meaning similar to that

of the social contract between citizens and government discussed by philosophers like Locke. For a very detailed discussion on the relevance of CSR, especially from its historical context, see generally, Geoffrey P. Lantos, 'The Boundaries of Strategic Corporate Social Responsibility', available online at http://faculty.stonehill.edu/glantos/Lantos1/PDF_Folder/Pub_arts_pdf/Strategic%20CSR.pdf, accessed 15 July 2007.

86. For a critical review of this general definition, see *The Economist*, 'The Good Company', 20 January 2005.

87. The term economic responsibility includes delivering good quality products at a fair price to customers. Legal responsibilities includes complying all the laws regulating business conduct. Ethical responsibilities includes doing what is right, just, and fair; respecting peoples' moral rights; and avoiding harm or social injury as well as preventing harm caused by others. Philanthropic responsibilities include giving time and money in the form of voluntary service, voluntary association, and donations. For a detailed discussion on these responsibilities, see Geoffrey P. Lantos, 'The Boundaries of Strategic Corporate Social Responsibility', 3–5.

88. It is a sad reality that for many companies, CSR is something that remains with colour and splendor in their Annual Reports, which do not get implemented in their day to day activities.

89. Philanthropic responsibilities may even include donations for the organizing of a public event. But among the four general areas of CSR, it was the philanthropic responsibilities which were most controversial. There is a substantial group of authors who says that philanthropic activities shall not be done with the money of share holders and the duty of those who manage companies is only to promote the interests of share holders and not to give money from some one else's pocket. They try to establish this point by arguing that companies cannot and should not take up the responsibilities of a Government, as their functions and objectives are different. For a series of articles which focuses on this issue, see *The Economist* 20 January 2005.

90. Christina Garrigues, 'Ambush Marketing: Robbery or Smart Advertising', 507.

91. See Jerry Welsh, 'Ambush Marketing: What it is, What it isn't'.

92. For further discussion on this argument, see Robert N. Davis, 'Ambushing the Olympic Games', 3 *Vill. Sports and Ent. L.J.* 423–5 (1996).

93. For a detailed discussion on this point, see Jason K. Schmitz, 'Ambush Marketing: The Off-Field Competition at the Olympic Games', 14.

94. Ibid.

95. In most of the recent events we see the event organizers not permitting

the products of rivals of official sponsors inside the stadium. For example, where Coca-Cola is the official sponsor of the event, those persons coming with Pepsi bottles will have to drop them at the entrance of the stadium.

96. See Lori L. Bean, 'Ambush Marketing: Sports Sponsorship Confusion and the Lanham Act', 1120.

97. This study was based on questionnaires distributed to spectators attending two events involving US Olympic teams. For more details about this study and the methodology used in the study, see Anita M. Moorman and T. Christopher Greenwell, 'Consumer Attitudes of Deception and the Legality of Ambush Marketing Practices', 196–207.

98. Ibid., at 203.

99. Ibid., at 204.

100. Ibid.

101. Ibid.

3

Ambush Marketing and the Traditional Legal Measures

Though the world has been witnessing ambush marketing practices on an escalating scale in recent years, only few of them who have been victims to this practice have reached the Courts. One of the main reasons behind this trend was the absence of specific regulations against ambush marketing in most of the legal regimes.[1] Because of this absence of specific regulations, the event organizers are often forced to resort to traditional legal weapons like action for trade mark infringement, copyright infringement, and passing off. But how far these weapons are effective against the sophisticated methods of ambush marketing is doubtful. This chapter tries to examine the effectiveness of each of these weapons in the context of ambush marketing.

TRADE MARK INFRINGEMENT ACTION

Most of the time, the event organizers register the event related logos and marks at the national trade mark registries in different classes, covering a wide range of goods and services. This is mainly to facilitate the licensing of these marks. For example, before the FIFA World Cup in 2010, FIFA will try to register marks like 'FIFA World Cup 2010', '2010 Games', etc. in trade mark registries across the world. Granting of registration for such applications is a matter entirely within the discretion of the national trade mark registries. If an ambush marketer uses any such registered marks without permission of the event organizers, the organizers can take the path of trade mark infringement action to prevent the ambusher.

Basic Ingredients of a Trade Mark Infringement Action

A trade mark is infringed when a person, other than the registered proprietor or a permitted user, uses a mark which is identical with or deceptively similar to that of a registered trade mark in the course of trade.[2] When we analyse this condition in detail, we see that the mark used should be either identical or deceptively similar to the registered mark; the goods or services in respect of which it is used must be specifically covered by registration; the use must be in the course of trade in areas covered by registration; the use must be in such a manner as to reflect its use as a trade mark; and the defendant must not be a permitted user.[3]

A person is considered to have used a registered mark when he affixes it to goods or the packaging thereof; offers the goods for sale, market, or stock or supply services under the registered mark; imports or exports goods under the mark; or uses the registered trade mark on business papers or in advertising.[4]

In situations wherein an identical mark is used in relation to similar goods or services, or where a similar mark is used in relation to identical or similar goods or services, there will be infringement if such use is likely to cause confusion among the public or is likely to create an association with the registered mark.[5] In the case of identical marks on identical goods or services, there is no need to prove confusion as there will be a presumption that it is likely to cause confusion in the minds of the public.[6]

Two cases that provide useful guidelines in determining infringement in such situations are the *Pianotist's Application*[7] and *British Sugar Plc* v. *James Robertson*[8] . According to the decision in the *Pianotist's Application*, look and sound of words, goods to which the mark is applied, nature of customers, surrounding circumstances and result of the simultaneous use of both the marks are the main determining factors.[9]

The *British Sugar case* explains in further detail and says that the most relevant factors in finding out whether goods are similar or not are the respective uses of the goods; physical nature of goods; respective channels of trade; in case of consumer items found in super market shelves, whether they are placed on same shelves or not; and whether the marketing companies classify the goods as belonging to same or different sectors.[10]

Indian Courts are generally of the view that the resemblance may be visual or phonetic or even in the basic idea represented by the plaintiff's mark.[11]

An analysis of provisions relating to infringement of trade marks and the relevant case law show that these provisions can be used successfully against ambush marketing, in certain situations. For example, if ICC is successful in registering 'Cricket World Cup' as a trade mark in respect of certain goods and services and if someone uses that mark on a class of products or services for which ICC has obtained registration, ICC can approach the Court on grounds of trade mark infringement. But in such an imaginative situation, the success of the infringement action depends on the registration of the mark by ICC; the use of an identical or a similar mark by the defendant; and the use of such identical or similar marks by the defendant in respect of the same class of goods and services for which ICC had obtained registration.

A very good case law that can tell us more about the effectiveness of trade mark infringement action in ambush marketing related issues is *Boston Athletic Association* v. *Mark Sullivan*.[12] In this case the organizers of the Boston Marathon, an annual event, approached the Court to enjoin the defendant from manufacture and sale of T-shirts and other wearing apparel with marks infringing BAA's 'Boston Marathon', 'BAA Marathon' and its unicorn logo. Like most other ambush marketing related cases, the main argument of the defendant case was that 'Boston Marathon' had become a generic term. But we can see the Court rejecting that argument in this case. Based on the eight factors to be weighed in assessing likelihood of confusion, laid down by the Courts in *Pignons S.A. de Mecanique de Precision* v. *Polaroid Corp.* [657 F.2d 487 (1981)] and *Astra Pharmaceutical Products Inc.* v. *Beckman Instruments Inc.* [718 F.2d 1201 (1983)], the Court ruled in favour of the plaintiff and enjoined the defendant from infringing the service marks of the plaintiff.[13] This case stands as a good example for the situations wherein trade mark infringement actions can be used successfully against ambush marketers.

Trade Mark Infringement Action with Respect to Dissimilar Goods or Services

The use of identical or similar marks on dissimilar goods or services shall constitute infringement, if the registered trade mark has reputation in India and the use of the mark by the defendant was without due cause and takes an unfair advantage of, or is detrimental to the distinctive character or reputation of the registered trade mark.[14] Marks having reputation are also referred by the name 'well known marks' by most of the legal scholars. One of the useful case law in this regard is *Pfizer Ltd. v Eurofood Link (UK) Ltd*[15]. In this case, the Court pointed out that the assessment of confusion was a matter of global appreciation and references were to be made to the distinctiveness of the mark in question and greater the distinctiveness, the greater was the likelihood of confusion.[16] According to the Court, the mere association between two marks as a result of their analogous semantic context was not sufficient and a confusion which included the likelihood of association with the earlier trade mark was a necessary ingredient.[17] In such circumstances, the dissimilarity in the products in some respects was no bar to finding infringement.[18]

When we apply these principles in the context of ambush marketing, with the help of the same imaginative example of ICC, we find its relevance. If 'ICC Cricket World Cup' can be proved as a mark with reputation in India, ICC will be able to prevent the use of its mark on any goods or services, irrespective of the classes in which ICC has registration. But ICC will be successful in an infringement action only if it can prove that its registered trade mark has reputation in India and the use of the mark by the defendant was without due cause and takes an unfair advantage of, or is detrimental to the distinctive character or repute of the registered trade mark of ICC. In such situations it is advisable for the event organizers to emphasize on the detrimental effects of the infringement on the distinctive character and reputation achieved by the registered trade mark of ICC.

Ambush Marketing Advertisements and Trade Mark Infringement Action

The most important type of infringement, in the context of our discussion on ambush marketing is infringement by way of advertisements. A registered trade mark is infringed by an advertisement containing that trade mark, if such advertising takes unfair advantage of and is contrary to honest practices in industrial or commercial matters; or is detrimental to the distinctive character or reputation of the trade mark.[19]

For example, if 'world cup' is *registered* as a mark in India and if Philips uses the mark 'world cup' in its advertisement by way of a slogan, 'Philips: Diwali Manao World Cup Jao' and 'Buy a Philips Audio System, win a ticket to the World Cup', without permission from the registered owner of the mark 'world cup', Philips shall be liable for trade mark infringement.[20] In fact if the marks relating to the event are registered ones, this provision can play a very good role in the prevention of ambush marketing in the form of contests.

Additional Protection Given to Olympic Symbols in India

We can see an additional layer of protection given to Olympic related symbols in most of the trade mark statutes. The Olympic marks and symbols are protected as official marks falling under the 'prohibited marks' section in most of the national trade mark statutes.[21] For example, the Indian Trade Marks Act provides that a mark shall not be registered as a trade mark if its use is prohibited under the Emblems and Names (Prevention of Improper Use) Act, 1950.[22] When we look at the Emblems and Names (Prevention of Improper Use) Act, we see the specific inclusion of the name and emblem of the International Olympic Committee.[23] This 'official mark status' gives it far greater protection compared to ordinary trade marks.[24]

Where Trade Mark Infringement Action Fails

One of the main limitations of trade mark law in fighting ambush marketing is the fact that ambush marketers often do not use or display registered marks of the event.[25] They instead create a false association with the marks through their ingenious methods. The best example in this regard will be the famous American Express Advertisement cited in the previous chapter. When they used the slogan 'And remember, to visit Spain, you don't need a visa' during the Barcelona Olympics, they did not use any of the marks associated with the event. But at the same time they ambushed the event organizer and the sponsor in a clear way.

Moreover, the trade mark law will be of little or no help in most of the common ambush marketing practices like buying commercial time during the telecast of events; making independent contracts with the athletes and teams; throwing parties and other events in the host cities before, during, and after the main event; buying advertisement spaces in and around the event place; and making people wear apparels with ambusher's mark and carry products, signs, or accessories bearing the ambusher's marks to the event place. The same difficulties may also be found in the case of complex ambush marketing methods like tattoo advertisements, which was discussed in the previous chapter.[26] Ineffectiveness against these major forms of ambush marketing makes trade mark infringement action futile to a great extent.

Another area of difficulty is proving the 'likelihood of confusion', a necessary ingredient in an infringement action, as it often does not apply to the facts of ambush marketing cases.[27] This is because the consumers in most situations do not care about sponsorship and hence, in general, they do not get confused as to who sponsors the main event.[28] This view is further supported by the findings in the study on consumer attitudes towards ambush marketing, which was discussed in the previous chapter.[29] Moreover, the applicability of fair use doctrine which permits a party to use a word or phrase to describe its goods or services, even if that word or phrase is another person's trade mark, goes in favour of the ambush marketers.[30]

A noteworthy case in this regard is *WCVB-TV* v. *Boston Athletic Association* wherein the Court pointed out that a television station's use of the words 'Boston Marathon' during its unauthorized television broadcasting of that event was fair and there was no infringement of the mark 'Boston Marathon', as the viewers thought that the channel showed the marathon and not that channel had some special approval from the trade mark owner to do so.[31]

The application of nominative fair use theory also saves the non-trade mark use of a mark.[32] This theory was used by the Court in *New Kids on the Block* v. *News America Publishing Inc.*[33] According to this theory, where a defendant uses a trade mark to describe the plaintiff's product, rather than its own, the commercial user is entitled to nominative fair use defense, provided that the product or service in question is one not really identifiable without use of that trade mark, that only so much of the mark or marks may be used as is reasonably necessary to identify the product or service and the user does nothing that would come in conjunction with mark to suggest sponsorship or endorsement by the trade mark holder.[34] The ambush marketers across the world can use these defenses in their own ingenious ways to shield their ambush marketing activities.

Another major issue is that in most countries like India, the title of events like 'World Cup' would be considered as generic words and hence not capable of registration. For example in *ICC Development (International) Ltd.* v. *Arvee Enterprises and Anr.*, the Court was seen expressing the view that 'World Cup' was a dictionary word having the meaning 'a tournament or event, where several nations participate' and in consequence the Court considered it as a generic term, not capable of conferring any exclusive rights for event organizers.[35] All these factors narrow down the scope of trade mark law in preventing ambush marketing.

COPYRIGHT INFRINGEMENT ACTION

Another weapon used by organizers of events in fighting ambush marketing is copyright infringement action. Copyright protection exists in different areas relating to an event. It may be in the form of an artistic work in the logo created by the organizers of the event. It can also exist in various literatures relating to the event, like the official document that provides details about time, venue, etc. provided it satisfies the minimum requirements for achieving the status of a literary work.

One of the main features of copyright that distinguishes it from other forms of intellectual property rights is that it springs into life immediately on creation of the work.[36] There is no requirement for registration of the work to achieve protection. Registration is an optional affair with regard to copyright protection. The result of this distinguishing feature is that the work is protected as soon as it is recorded in writing or otherwise on paper, canvas, tape, disc, film, or any other recording medium from which it is capable of being reproduced.[37] When a person, other than the organizer reproduces or imitates any of those copyrighted materials relating to the event, he shall be liable for copyright infringement.

The Essential Elements in a Copyright Infringement Action

Copyright is infringed by a person, who, without the license of the author, does, or authorizes another to do, any of the acts restricted by copyright.[38] In India, Sec.51 of the Copyright Act, 1957 deals with infringement of copyright.

Infringement of copyright can broadly be classified into primary infringement and secondary infringement. Transgression of any of the rights provided under copyright is known as primary infringement and when any person aids or abets the primary infringement, s/he becomes liable for secondary infringement.[39] Primary infringement is concerned with people who are directly involved in the reproduction, performance, etc. of the copyrighted work whereas secondary infringement is concerned with people in a commercial context who either deal with infringing copies or facilitate such copying or facilitate public performance.[40] In the case of secondary infringement the state of mind of the defendant has a significant importance, as the liability depends on whether the defendant knows or has reason to believe that the activities in question are wrongful.[41] For our discussion on ambush marketing, both types of infringement are important. This is mainly because, many a times, the ambusher may not be indulging in the ambush marketing directly, but through a third person or a different medium.

The most important factors to be taken into consideration while determining a question of infringement are whether the plaintiff is the owner of the work, whether the defendant has carried out any activities falling within the domain of the copyright owner's rights, whether the defendant's work was derived from the copyrighted work and whether the defendant has copied whole or substantial portion of the copyrighted work.

For example, in a typical situation of ambush marketers using the logo of an event, the event organizers will first have to prove that they have copyright of that particular logo of the event. Once the ownership of copyright is proved, then the question of misappropriation is looked into. Here the plaintiff will have to prove that the defendant's alleged infringing work was taken directly or indirectly from the plaintiff's work.[42] Here the plaintiff has to prove that this casual connection is the reason for the similarity between the work and the infringement.[43] This requirement makes copyright differ substantially from strong monopolies like that conferred by a patent.[44] It is also to be noted that infringement can happen also through subconscious copying and indirect copying.[45]

In the next step, the question whether the defendant copied whole or substantial portion of the copyrighted work comes into play. The underlying rationale of this requirement is to protect and adequately reward the interests of authors and copyright owners and to prevent others from unfairly appropriating the benefit of effort, skill, and labour which the copyright owner has invested during the creation of a work.[46] This question of substantial portion is a mixture of law and facts and it has to be considered according to the facts of each case.[47] Generally, it is seen that the overriding question in this regard is whether substantial use has been made of the features which had made the plaintiff's work an original one.[48] It is also to be borne in mind that in assessing whether a substantial portion has been taken or not, it is the quality of the portion which matters and not the quantity.[49] The extent to which the defendant's work is different from the plaintiff's is irrelevant and in the context of artistic works it is wrong to enquire whether the defendant's work looks like that of claimant's.[50] One of the questions to be asked in determining this is whether both the works are in competition.[51]

Accumulation of insubstantial taking, over a period of time, can also be an infringement. A useful case law in this regard is *Football League Ltd* v. *Littlewoods Pools Ltd*[52]. It is also to be remembered that to constitute copying, it is not essential that the same words from the claimant's work need to be used.[53] This concept of non-literal and non-textual copying extends to all cases where there has been a substantial taking of the original skill and labour of the author in expressing his ideas, thoughts, etc. When an ambush marketer makes use of a poster relating to Olympics, even if s/he has not copied the whole poster, s/he may be liable for copyright infringement, if it can be proved that the copied part was a substantial part of the original skill and labour of the copyright owner of that poster. A good case law that illustrates this view is *Designers Guild Ltd* v. *Russell Williams (Textiles) Ltd.*[54] According to the House of Lords, the fact that the overall appearance of the defendant's work might be very different from the copyrighted work did not make the defendant's work a non-infringing one.[55] The Court pointed out that in cases of altered copying, a useful test to determine whether such an altered copy constituted an infringement is to see whether the infringer incorporated a substantial part of independent skill, labour, etc. contributed by the original author for creating the copyrighted work.[56]

These principles are of great importance to ambush marketing related cases, as they show that in cases where the ambush marketer copies the logos associated with an event, an action for copyright infringement is likely, even if the reproduced logos are not exactly similar. The logos relating to events are protected as artistic works and the reproduction of such logos in any medium results in its infringement. In the case of artistic works, infringement includes making a copy of the two dimensional work in three dimensions and also making a copy of three dimensional works in two dimensional forms.[57] The famous case of *British Leyland Motor Corp Ltd.* v. *Armstrong Patents* is a very good illustration of this point.[58]

The Indian judiciary also follows a similar approach towards copyright infringement and points out that one of the surest and the safest tests to determine whether or not there has been a violation of copyright is to see if the reader, spectator or the viewer, after having read or seen both the works, is clearly of the opinion and gets an unmistakable impression that the subsequent work appears to be a copy of the original.[59]

Successful Copyright Infringement Action against Ambush Marketing

One of the best methods to analyse the effectiveness of copyright infringement action against ambush marketing is to analyse ambush marketing related cases involving copyright infringement claims. One of the examples of a successful copyright infringement action in the context of ambush marketing, worth citing here, happened in the year 2002. The SLOC was successful in preventing a music store in Salt Lake City which was conducting a print campaign that made direct reference to 'The 2002 Olympic Mascots' and the '2002 Winter Olympics'.[60] The advertisement contained pictures similar to the official Olympic mascots—'Powder', 'Copper' and 'Coal' and had a slogan 'Proud not to be sponsors of the 2002 Winter Olympics'.[61] Citing copyright infringement, the organization sent a cease and desist letter and subsequently the advertiser had to pull out the advertisement.[62]

Another example of a successful copyright infringement action can be seen in *ICC Development (International) Ltd.* v. *Ever Green Service Station and Anr.*[63] In this case the defendant used the logo of the plaintiff during its promotion campaign. The Delhi High Court took the view that the logo denoting black and white stripes of Zebra was an artistic work within the meaning of copyright law and hence subject to copyright protection.[64] As a result the defendant was restrained from using the logo of the plaintiff in its advertisements.

These cases definitely show the effectiveness of copyright infringement action in certain types of ambush marketing. But one thing to be remembered in the context of both the cases discussed here is that they were instances of direct copying, wherein copyright infringement claims are easy to establish.

Where Copyright Infringement Action Fails

All the provisions and case laws discussed in this section show the strength of a copyright infringement action. But when it comes to ambush marketing, the reasons that fail a trade mark infringement action are mostly likely to fail copyright infringements actions also. A copyright infringement action will be successful where the ambush marketer uses the logo or name of the events. But ambush marketers often do not use or display marks of the event and they normally create a false association with the marks through ingenious methods. In such circumstances, it is very difficult to bring them within the parameters of copyright infringement action.

When an ambush marketer copies the logo of Olympics, it is easy to book him/her under copyright infringement action. But when s/he uses a slogan like 'And remember, to visit Spain, you don't need a visa' s/he is not infringing any copyright. But at the same time the event organizer and the sponsor are ambushed.

Moreover, like the trade mark infringement action, copyright infringement action will also be of little or no help in most of the common ambush marketing practices like buying commercial time during the telecast of events; making independent contracts with the athletes and teams; throwing parties and other events in the host cities before, during, and after the main event; buying advertisement spaces in and around the event place; making people wear apparels with the ambusher's mark; making arrangements to give the spectators products, signs, or accessories bearing the ambusher's marks; making tattoo advertisements, etc.

ACTION FOR PASSING OFF

Action for Passing off is a common law remedy widely used in the fight against ambush marketing. It is the oldest action of the modern legal regimes for the protection of trade symbols.[65] Though passing off and trade mark law overlap in certain factual situations, they are different and deal with the issues in different ways and from different standpoints.[66] Passing off action is a remedy that can be applied to a wide range of situations, including some of the ambush marketing instances.

In simple words, an action for passing off is allowing trader A to prevent a competitor B from passing his goods off as if they were A's. Though it was earlier considered that this action was based on property right in the name or symbol, later it began to be viewed as based on the property right in 'goodwill'.[67]

A passing off action depends mainly on its facts.[68] There are three basic elements in every passing off action. These essential elements are reputation or goodwill acquired by the plaintiff in his goods, name, mark, etc. a misrepresentation by the defendant leading to confusion or deception; and damage as a result of such misrepresentation. These three elements are commonly referred to as the 'classical trinity'.[69] All three of these elements are inter-related.

In *Erven Warnink B.V.* v. *J. Townend and Sons (Hull) Ltd.*, the House of Lords went a little further and explained the characteristics required in an expanded manner.[70] According to this case, the five characteristics which must be present to create a valid cause of action for passing off are

(1) a misrepresentation;
(2) made by a trader in the course of trade;
(3) to prospective customers or ultimate consumers of goods or services supplied by him;
(4) which is calculated to injure the business or goodwill of another trader; and
(5) which causes actual damage to the business or goodwill of the trader by whom the action is brought.

To know the real effectiveness of passing off action, we need to analyse in detail the essential ingredients of a passing off action. The first requirement, goodwill, is a legal right of property associated with every business and is often considered as the attractive force which brings in customers.[71] It is a form of intangible property that is easy to describe, but difficult to define.[72] Goodwill is said to exist when the customers buy the goods or services just because of the reputation that it has developed.[73] Goodwill arises in relation to the name, symbol, or logo that has been employed by a trader and thus has come to be associated with the business.[74] It may also get associated with the packaging, get-up, trade dress of products and advertising style.[75] But in cases where descriptive words are used for selling goods or services, it will be very difficult to establish the existence of goodwill attached to those words.[76] In such cases, the trader will have to show that such a word has attained a 'secondary meaning' over the goods or services, of which they are the source.[77] It has to be noted that goodwill can be owned by a single trader or business house or by a group of traders as in the case of champagne.[78]

This requirement of proving goodwill needs to be fulfilled in ambush marketing related passing off action cases also. For example, if ambush marketing happens during the FIFA World Cup, the first thing that FIFA will have to prove is the goodwill attached to the term 'FIFA World Cup'. FIFA may meet this criterion by proving that FIFA World Cup has become the world's most favourite soccer tournament.

The second element in a passing off action, namely misrepresentation, happens when a representation is calculated to deceive in fact, even if it is literally true in some sense.[79] In most of the situations, a misrepresentation happens where the defendant through his act suggests that the defendant's goods or services derive from or are otherwise economically connected with the claimant.[80] But this has been expanded to misrepresentations as to quality and nature also.[81]

There can also be misrepresentations that the claimant has control or responsibility over the goods and services.[82] One of the useful cases in this regard is *British Legion* v. *British Legion Club (Street)* wherein it was held that an organization formed to assist first world war veterans named 'British Legion' could use passing off action to prevent the defendant from using the words 'British Legion Club (Street) to describe their local social club.[83] According to the Court, the rationale behind the decision was that the public would have thought that the social club was either a branch of the plaintiff's association or a club some way amalgamated with or under the supervision of the plaintiff's association. If we follow this point of law, we realize that where a person suggests in an ingenious manner that s/he is somehow associated with the event, s/he is making a misrepresentation and hence fulfills the second element in an action for passing off.

But this point of law, which is of enormous potential in the fight against ambush marketing is limited to a great extent by the fact that mere suggestion of being somehow connected to the claimant will not necessarily amount to passing off.[84] Misrepresentations have to be through words or actions.[85] In most cases, misrepresentation happens when a defendant adopts some materials like name, mark, get up, or other signs which are deceptively similar to materials that are distinctive to that of the claimant.[86] For example, when a person uses a logo similar to the Olympic rings, misrepresentation arises. Same will be the case where he uses advertisements similar to that of an event. For example, if the organizers of Femina Miss India Contest are using one unique advertisement and if a particular company uses a similar advertisement to promote its product, it would amount to misrepresentation.

In some instances misrepresentation occurs when the defendant makes a statement that links him either explicitly or implicitly to the claimant.[87] When a company make a statement that '[W]ith Telecom mobile you can take your own mobile phone to the Olympics', it is trying to link itself with the Olympic Games and thereby creates a misrepresentation.

One of the best examples for misrepresentation by action is when the defendant manufactures his/her goods having an identical or similar look to that of the plaintiff's. It also occurs in situations where the defendant supplies his own goods when he is asked to supply some other goods, or when he places his product in close proximity to the claimant's, or through registration of famous trade marks as domain names, or when he provides services under a famous name.[88] The list of misrepresentation is inexhaustive and the list will keep on increasing as long as the human ingenuity exists.

Misrepresentations can happen in the form of false endorsements also.[89] The case of *Irvine* v. *Talksport* is a good example.[90] One of the notable features of the decision in this case was the rejection of the argument that passing off action cannot exist in the absence of 'common field of activity' by both the plaintiff and the defendant. In this case the Court was of the view that it was not necessary to show that the claimant and the defendant shared a common field of activity or that sale of products or services would diminish.[91] This point is of much relevance to our discussion on ambush marketing as it removes the requirement of showing a common field of activity between the event organizer and the ambush marketer, while pursuing a passing off action.

To fulfill the requirement of misrepresentation, a claimant has to show that the defendant's actions have either confused or are likely to confuse the public or a substantial part thereof. In other words, the defendant's misrepresentation must be deceptive.[92] The question of whether a misrepresentation operated to deceive the public is generally seen by the Courts through the eyes of the *relevant public* and the *relevant public* varies in accordance with the type of misrepresentation being alleged.[93]

But the question as to the point at which the public had been misled depends mainly on the facts of the case.[94] The authors differ in their views with regard to this point. According to one group, misrepresentation is deemed to happen as soon as the goods are released into circulation, even if the immediate recipients are traders who themselves are not deceived.[95] But we can also see another group arguing that the relevant time is the time when the product is consumed or used, rather than the time at which it is purchased.[96]

The third requirement to sustain an action for passing off is the proof that the claimant has suffered, or is likely to suffer damage as a result of the defendant's misrepresentation. A real, tangible probability of damage is sufficient to fulfill this requirement.[97] The four types of damage that have been recognized by the Courts are loss of existing trade and profits, loss of potential trade and profits, damage to reputation, and dilution.[98]

Loss of existing trade and profits is comparatively easy to prove in cases of ambush marketing as the event organizers can easily prove the loss of sponsorship revenue as a result of ambushing activity. In many instances the event organizers are even forced to return money to the sponsors, if the sponsors have been ambushed.[99] The loss of potential trade and profit is also comparatively easy to prove in ambush marketing instances in terms of the reluctance of sponsors to sponsor an event which is being constantly ambushed. It can also illustrate situations where a defendant trades in a field or geographical area into which the claimant intends to expand in future.[100] In the case of sports organizers, this future expansion can be to areas like apparels, sports goods, etc. Similar is the case of other events like fashion shows, where the organizers can prove their future plans to expand to different areas like the cosmetics business or retailing of apparels. It can also include situations wherein the defendant's conduct undermines the claimant's ability to license its own mark.[101]

Damage to reputation is another area recognized by the Courts under the third element of damage. This may be in the form of inferior goods and services marketed by the defendant. Damage to reputation arises where the defendant's misrepresentation leads the public to believe that the goods or services of the claimant and the defendant are somehow related.[102] For example, if a company advertises a contest using an event name and if they market an inferior quality product causing health problems to those who consumed the product, it can damage the reputation of the event organizer also. Similar is the situation when one company provides a much unorganized trip to the event-hosting country and the winners of that contest suffer difficulties during their journey and stay in that country. This can cause irretrievable damage to the reputation of the event organizers. This is one of the major reasons that compel event organizers to prevent unauthorized contests that give tickets to the event as prizes.

Another form of damage recognized by the Courts is dilution. It occurs where the defendant's misrepresentation undermines the ability of the claimant's sign to summon up particular goods or values.[103] In other words it is the dilution of the pulling power or goodwill of the claimant's sign.[104] This approach was re-emphasized in the decision of *Tattinger* v. *Allbev*, wherein producers of champagne, who had a very high reputation in their field, were able to prevent the defendant from marketing a non-alcoholic beverage with the name 'Elderflower Champagne'.[105] In this case, the Court of Appeal was of the view that the requisite damage to sustain an action for passing off arose from the fact that there would have been blurring or erosion of the uniqueness associated with the name 'Champagne'. This principle is equally applicable in ambush marketing instances. If a person is allowed to freely use the word Olympics, gradually people will start using it for all kinds of products and it will lose its identity. For example, a condom manufacturer can then manufacture condoms under the name Olympic condoms or a tea stall can come under the name Olympic Tea Stall. All such actions can erode the distinctiveness of 'Olympics' and hence cause its dilution.

Passing Off Action against Ambush Marketing—How it Works

Most of the cases that have come up before the courts against ambush marketing are in the form of passing off action. There is no better method than to analyse some of these cases, to find out the real effectiveness of an action for passing off in preventing ambush marketing.

One of the landmark cases which relate to ambush marketing is *National Hockey League* v. *Pepsi-Cola Canada Ltd*, the facts of which were discussed in detail as an example of ambush marketing practices in chapter 2.[106] In this case, even though the court recognized the expanded role played by the tort of passing off, taking into account the changing commercial realities, the Court ultimately dismissed the action. The court noted that the plaintiffs' sole product was hockey games while that of the defendant was soft drinks. According to the Court, there was no possibility of the contest to mislead the public into believing the defendant's product as being that of the plaintiff's.[107] The Court held that neither the television commercials nor the printed material relating to the contest suggested that the plaintiff had approved, authorized, or endorsed the contest in any way or that there was some form of business connection between the parties. According to the Court, the disclaimer under the promotion material was effective to dispel any misleading impression that might have been created.[108] As a result, the action was dismissed with costs to the defendants.

Another case worth mentioning here is *The New Zealand Olympic and Commonwealth Games Association Inc.* v. *Telecom New Zealand Limited.*[109]

According to the plaintiff in this case, the advertisement in question passed off Telecom mobile phone services as associated with the Olympic movement, the Olympic Association, and the New Zealand Olympic team. But the defendants rebutted this argument by pointing that the mere conjunction of the word 'ring' as set out and Telecom's name was not sufficient to make the readers assume a sponsorship relationship between the plaintiff and defendant. This case also showed a reluctance on the part of the judiciary to accept passing off claims, in ambush marketing related incidents. The Court was of the view that those who read such newspaper advertisements would notice the five coloured 'ring' words, then drop their gaze to the next line picking up the reference to Olympics, and then refer back to the five 'ring' words, and then make an association with the five circle Olympic symbol, and would be mildly amused. According to the Court, it would then appear like a cartoon or a clever device where one pauses for a moment to laugh and acknowledge the lateral thinking involved. According to the Court there was a long way from this brief mental process to an assumption that this play on the Olympic five circles must have been with the authority of the Olympic organization or through sponsorship of the Olympics.[110] It is interesting to see that the Court was of the view that the outcome of this case illustrated the need for additional protection by way of legislation.[111]

Arsenal Football Club v. *Reed* is another case worth discussing here.[112] In this case, the defendant was operating a stall outside the Arsenal Football Ground wherein he sold unauthorized souvenirs or memorabilia bearing the names 'Arsenal' and 'The Gunners' and also used the badges of the club. Two cases of passing off existed in this case. The first one was a broad allegation that the unauthorized sales by the defendant would mislead members of the public into believing that those goods were the products of AFC or were goods associated or connected with or licensed by AFC as they bore one or more of the names 'Arsenal', 'The Gunners', the Crest Device, or the Cannon Device. The second was an allegation that a particular employee working for the defendant deliberately attempted to deceive customers by falsely representing that their unlicensed products were 'official' products.

In this case the Court pointed out that there would be a group of potential customers who would purchase memorabilia bearing the words 'Arsenal', 'Gunners' or devices *only* because those words or signs are of interest as signs of allegiance. They will have no interest in knowing who makes or markets these goods. In determining confusion and deception what was counted was whether there would be confusion amongst that part of the public who cares about the origin of such products.[113] It was pointed out that the use of the Arsenal signs on Mr. Reed's products carried no message of trade origin.[114] Though the Court accepted that there would be some fans who would want to purchase official Arsenal memorabilia to support the club, it was a *non-sequitur* to say that it meant that all the Arsenal memorabilia or memorabilia displaying one or more of the Arsenal Signs was believed by them to have come from or licensed by AFC.[115] According to the Court, what was necessary was some additional sign or circumstance of trading which said to the customer that the goods in question came from or were commercially connected with the source were and not some other source.[116] As AFC failed to prove relevant confusion, the Court was of the view that it also failed to show that it had suffered relevant damage as a result of the defendant's activities.[117] Thus the broad claim of passing off failed. The second claim of passing off also failed due to lack of evidence and a number of factors which suggested the possibility of a misunderstanding that could have taken place.[118]

Another case worth analysing in detail here is *ICC Development (International) Ltd.* v. *Arvee Enterprises and Anr.*[119] In this case, the main argument of the plaintiff was that the defendant's intentional use of the slogans in question and the insertion of the pictorial representation of the ticket with an imaginative seat and gate number saying 'Cricket World Cup 2003' during the advertising campaign amounted to passing off and ambush marketing, as it was to create an identification with the event and to sell its goods through that misrepresentation. The plaintiff focused its arguments on the real likelihood of confusion and unmistakable aura of deception.

Even though the court accepted that the law relating to passing off had been developing and expanding, it pointed out that this was a type of passing off claim wherein it was alleged that the defendant had promoted his product or business in such a way as to create a false impression that his product or business, was in some way approved, authorized, or endorsed by the plaintiff or that there was some business connection between them. According to the Court, the main question that was required to be answered in such a situation was whether a sufficient number of purchasers of the defendant's goods were likely to be unmistakably confused about the source of the defendant's goods or assume that the defendants had some connection with the official sponsors of the event.[120]

The Court observed that the defendants had not used the plaintiff's 'logo' or mascot 'Dazzler' on any of their advertisements or promotional campaigns. It also noted that the defendants had inserted only a pictorial representation of a ticket with an imaginative seat and gate number saying 'Cricket World Cup 2003', so as to draw the attention of the purchasing public to the event. The Court was of the view that this did not show any likelihood of confusion in the public mind that the defendants were sponsors or licensees of the event.[121] According to the Court the slogans merely showed that the purchasers of the defendant's goods may win a ticket and travel package to see the world cup and nothing more. Therefore, the Court came to the conclusion that the basic ingredients of passing off action were not present in this case.[122]

Regarding the specific plea of ambush marketing, the Court took a perilous view that the phrase 'ambush marketing' was a term used by marketing executives only and it was different from an action for passing off.[123] The real ambit of this dangerous dictum will be visible when we read it along with the explanation of the Court itself in the next sentence that in a passing off action there is an element of overt or covert deceit, whereas ambush marketing is opportunistic commercial exploitation of an event. The Court was of the view that the ambush marketer did not seek to suggest any connection with the event, but gave his own brand or other insignia, a larger exposure to the people attracted to the event, without any authorization from the event organizer. It is really threatening to see the observation of the Court that in such cases there was no deception and the conduct of the defendant was neither wrongful nor against public interest.[124] On the strength of these arguments, the Court ultimately reached the disappointing conclusion that an advertising campaign offering tickets to an event as prizes, without using the logo or the mark of the plaintiff could not be held as unlawful and as a result, the passing off action was held not applicable in such cases.[125] But the same Court can be seen passing the issue to the legislature by pointing out that it was for the legislators to find a proper solution to ambush marketing issues.[126] A similar fate for passing off action can be seen in another Indian ambush marketing case *ICC Development (International) Ltd. v. Ever Green Service Station* also.[127]

Among the traditional legal measures, passing off action is the most powerful and most frequently used weapon in fighting ambush marketing. But the case laws discussed here point out the real drawbacks of a passing off action in fighting ambush marketing. Even though we can see the Courts sympathizing with the larger issues involved, we see that passing off action cannot be of help in most of the situations. When we realize the limitations of passing off action along with the limitations found during the analysis of the scope and extent of other traditional legal measures like trade mark infringement action and copyright infringement action, we reach a disappointing observation, that that traditional legal measures have very limited scope in fighting the sophisticated ambush marketing methods. This forces us to search for a better solution to this parasitic problem.

NOTES

1. For a detailed discussion on this issue, see Carolina Pina and Ana Gil-Roble, 'Sponsorship of Sports Events and Ambush Marketing', 94. The other reasons often cited are high cost of litigation and long time period taken for settlement of disputes through Courts.

2. See, Sec. 29 (1) of the Trade Marks Act, 1999 of India Sec. 29(1). A registered trade mark is infringed by a person who, not being a registered proprietor or a person using by way of permitted use, uses in the course of trade, a mark which is identical with, or deceptively similar to, the trade mark in relation to goods or services in respect of which the trade mark is registered and in such manner as to render the use of the mark likely to be taken as being used as a trade mark.

3. See P. Narayanan, 531.

4. See Sec. 29 (6) of the Trade Marks Act 1999.

5. See Sec. 29 (2) of the Trade Marks Act, 1999. Also see *Durga Dutt Sharma* v. *Navaratna Pharmaceutical Laboratories* AIR 1965 SC 980. In this case, the Court pointed out that once the use of the mark which is claimed to infringe the plaintiff's mark is shown to be 'in the course of trade', the question of infringement has to be decided by comparison of the two marks. In this case the marks in question were 'Navaratna Pharmaceutical Laboratories' and 'Navaratna Pharmacy'. The Court was of the view that when two marks are not identical, the plaintiff would have to establish that the mark used by the defendant resembles the plaintiff's registered trade mark so nearly as is likely to deceive or cause confusion with goods in respect of which the mark is registered. See AIR 1965 SC 980, Para 29.

6. See Sec. 29(3) of the Trade Marks Act, 1999.

7. *Pianotist's Application* (1906) 23 RPC 774.

8. *British Sugar* v. *James Robertson* [1996] RPC 281.

9. See, *Pianotist's Application* (1906) 23 RPC 774, 777.

10. See, *British Sugar* v. *James Robertson* [1996] RPC 281, 296–7.

11. See, *Durga Dutt Sharma v Navaratna Pharmaceutical Laboratories* AIR 1965 SC 980, para 29.

12. See, *Boston Athletic Association* v. *Mark Sullivan* 867 F.2d 22 (1989).

13. The eight factors to be weighed in assessing likelihood of confusion according to *Pignons S.A. de Mecanique de Precision* v. *Polaroid Corp.* and *Astra Pharmaceutical Products, Inc.* v. *Beckman Instruments, Inc.* were (1) the similarity of the marks; (2) the similarity of the goods; (3) the relationship between the parties' channels of trade; (4) the relationship between the parties' advertising; (5) the classes of prospective purchasers; (6) evidence of actual confusion; (7) the defendant's intent in adopting its mark; and (8) the strength of the plaintiff's mark.

14. See Sec. 29 (4) of the Trade Marks Act 1999.

15. *Pfizer Ltd.* v. *Eurofood Link (UK) Ltd* [2001] FSR 3. In this case the main issue was whether the use of the word 'Viagrene' in respect of a beverage which was claimed to be capable of stimulating the libido of men and women was an infringement of 'Viagara' registered by the plaintiff, in respect of pharmaceutical and veterinary preparations.

16. Ibid. at para 19.

17. According to the Court, the relevant likelihood of confusion was a question of fact and if the court was satisfied as to the proof of confusion, relief should be granted, notwithstanding substantial dissimilarity between the goods. The nature of the confusion to be proved was confusion as to origin. Ibid., at para 29.

18. Ibid., at para 28.

19. See Sec. 29 (8) of the Trade Marks Act 1999.

20. In *ICC Development (International) Ltd.* v. *Arvee Enterprises and Anr.* [2003(26)PTC245(Del)] we can see a similar situation. But 'world cup' was not a registered mark in India. ICC had filed an application for registration of the mark 'ICC Cricket World Cup South Africa 2003' and logo and the dazzler when the matter was before the Court. In this case the plaintiff relied on passing off action and not trade mark infringement.

21. *See*, Juda Strawczynski, 'Is Canada Ready for the Vancouver Winter Games? An Examination of Canada's Olympic Intellectual Property Protection', 62 *U. Toronto Fac. L. Rev.* 213, 215 (2004).

22. See Sec. 9 (2) (d) of the Trade Marks Act, 1999.

23. See the schedule to the Emblems and Names (Prevention of Improper Use) Act, 1950.

24. For a detailed discussion, see Juda Strawczynski, 'Is Canada Ready for the Vancouver Winter Games? An Examination of Canada's Olympic Intellectual Property Protection', 216. Here the author points out that this additional protection prohibits all others from adopting a mark that resembles an official mark. It prevents the registration of similar marks and the owner of an official mark can approach the Courts to stop infringements, without the burden to prove injury or damage. Unlike regular trade marks which are confined to specific goods and services for which registration is sought, an official mark gets protection across classes. The author also points out that once public notice has been given for the adoption and use of an official mark, it is virtually inexpugnable.

25. For example see the decision in *National Hockey League* v. *Pepsi-Cola Canada Ltd.* 1992 CarswellBC 215. Dismissing the trade mark infringement claim, the Court was seen pointing that the defendant did not 'use' any of the plaintiffs' registered marks in conjunction with the contest or any of its products. See 1992 CarswellBC 215, para 61.

26. But some scholars have made their attempts in arguing that traditional legal measures can be stretched to fight even complex ambush marketing methods like tattoo advertisements. For example, see John Vukelj, 'Post No Bills: Can the NBA Prohibit its Players from Wearing Tattoo Advertisements?', 519–26.

27. For a detailed discussion, see Jason K. Schmitz, 'Ambush Marketing: The Off-Field Competition at the Olympic Games', 11.

28. See Lori L. Bean, 'Ambush Marketing: Sports Sponsorship Confusion and the Lanham Act', 1128.

29. See Anita M. Moorman and T. Christopher Greenwell, 'Consumer Attitudes Of Deception And The Legality Of Ambush Marketing Practices', 196–207.

30. For a detailed discussion on the applicability of fair use doctrine as a defense, see Jacqueline A. Leimer, 'Ambush Marketing: Not Just an Olympic-Sized Problem', 4.

31. *WCVB-TV* v. *Boston Athletic Association* , 926 F.2d 42 (1991). The Court was of the view that use of the mark by the channel was to describe the event that Channel was telecasting. According to the Court the use of words for descriptive purposes is a fair use and the law usually permits it even if the words themselves constitute a trade mark. See 926 F.2d 42, 46.

32. For details, see, Jacqueline A. Leimer, 'Ambush Marketing: Not Just an Olympic-Sized Problem', 4.

33. *New Kids on the Block* v. *News America Publishing Inc.* 971 F.2d 302 (1992).

34. Ibid., at 308. In this case the main issue was whether a newspaper's use of the trade mark of a musical group for the purpose of polls on group's popularity would amount to infringement of trade mark. The court ruled in favour of the newspaper by adopting the nominative fair use doctrine. The Court was of the view that a trade mark is a limited property right in a particular word, phrase, or symbol.

35. *ICC Development (International) Ltd.* v. *Arvee Enterprises and Anr.* 2003 (26) PTC 245 (Del), para. 18. According to the Court, the genericness of the words 'world cup' was also clear from the fact that these words have been used to refer to several other international sporting events, like Football-FIFA World Cup, Hockey-FIH World Cup, etc.

36. See Kevin Garnett, Gillian Davies and Gwilym Harbottle, *Copinger and Skone James on Copyright* (London: Sweet and Maxwell, 2005), 23.

37. Ibid.

38. Ibid., at 368.

39. For a detailed discussion on this classification, see Lionel Bently and Brad Sherman, 155.

40. Ibid.

41. Ibid.

42. See *Copinger and Skone James on Copyright*, 373.

43. See W.R. Cornish, *Intellectual Property: Patents, Copyright, Trademarks and Allied Rights* (Delhi: Universal Law Publishing Co. Pvt. Ltd., 2003) 360.

44. See *Copinger and Skone James on Copyright*, 373.

45. In the case of subconscious copying, a person reads, sees, or hears a work, forgets about it, but later reproduces it believing it to be his own. In the case of indirect copying, a work is being copied by imitating a copy of it. For example, in the case of a drawing, if someone makes a three dimensional article from that drawing and if it is copied in three dimensions by the defendant, there will be a casual connection for the indirect copying of the drawing. See W.R. Cornish, 361.

46. See *Copinger and Skone James on Copyright*, 381.

47. Ibid., at 384.

48. Ibid., at 384–5.

49. Ibid.

50. Ibid., at 386

51. This test has to be used with caution. A case in which the court considered this as useful, although not determinative, is *Cambridge University Press* v. *University Tutorial Press* (1928) 75 RPC 335 cited in *Copinger and Skone James on Copyright*, 388.

52. See *Football League Ltd* v. *Littlewoods Pools Ltd.* [1959] ch. 637. In this case the plaintiff was producing a chronological list of about 2000 weekly Football league championship fixtures to be played in the season. Every fortnight the defendant copied list of fixtures for that fortnight, for the purpose of preparing its pool coupons. Finding it as a case of systematic piracy, the court upheld the argument of infringement. See [1959] ch. 637, 658.

53. *Copinger and Skone James on Copyright*, 394.

54. *Designers Guild Ltd* v. *Russell Williams (Textiles) Ltd* [2001] FSR 11. In this case the main question was whether the defendant's fabric design 'Marguerite' infringed the copyright of the claimant's artistic work, from which its fabric 'Ixia' was made. So one of the answers to be found was whether the portion that had been copied amounted to 'whole or a substantial part' of 'Ixia'.

55. Ibid., at para 38.

56. Ibid., at para 64.

57. Ibid.

58. *British Leyland Motor Corp Ltd.* v. *Armstrong Patents* (1986) 2 WLR 400. In this case the plaintiffs were designers and manufacturers of motor cars and they also produced some of the spare parts for their cars. The defendants produced replacement exhaust pipes for the plaintiffs' cars by copying the shape and dimensions of the original part. The plaintiffs commenced a copyright infringement action by pointing out that the indirect copying of the defendants infringed copyright in plaintiffs' original drawings of the exhaust system. The Court held that the manufacture of exhaust pipes, although achieved by indirect copying, amounted to an infringement of the plaintiffs' copyright in the drawings.

59. See *R.G. Anand* v. *Delux Films,* AIR 1978 SC 1613, para 46. In this case the main issue was whether the film produced by the defendant titled 'New Delhi' was an infringement of the copyright of plaintiff in a drama called 'Hum Hindustani'. Both the film and the play were based on the subject of provincialism.

60. For details, see, Anne M. Wall, 'The Game Behind The Games', 12 Marq. Sports L. Rev. 557, 575–6 (2002).

61. Ibid.

62. Ibid.

63. *ICC Development (International) Ltd.* v. *Ever Green Service Station* 2003 (26) PTC 228 (Del). The facts of this case was discussed in detail in the earlier chapter.

64. Ibid., at para 20. But it needs to be noted here specifically that even though the Court upheld the argument of copyright infringement, the larger

question of violation of rights of plaintiff through ambush marketing was rejected by the Court. The only restraint imposed by the Court was the use of logo of plaintiff.

65. See Lionel Bently, 671.

66. For a detailed discussion, see Christopher Wadlow, *The Law of Passing Off* (London: Sweet and Maxwell, 2004), 6–7.

67. See Lionel Bently, 672.

68. See *Kerly's Law of Trade Marks,* 416.

69. For a detailed discussion on the 'classical trinity', see, Christopher Wadlow, 6.

70. *Erven Warnink B.V.* v. *J. Townend & Sons (Hull) Ltd.* [1979] A.C. 731.

71. See, Christopher Wadlow, 7.

72. See, Lionel Bently, 674.

73. Ibid.

74. Ibid.

75. One of the best examples in this regard will be the bottles of 'Coca-Cola'. Another example worth citing here can be seen in the facts of the famous case, *Reckitt & Colman* v. *Borden Inc* [1990] RPC 341, wherein the plaintiff was selling lemon juice in plastic container that resembled a lemon in size, shape, and color. When the defendant used plastic lemons that were very similar to the plaintiff's, the Court considered it as amounting to passing off. This was on the basis of the goodwill attached with the plaintiff's product.

76. See, Lionel Bently, 675.

77. Ibid., at 676.

78. Ibid., at 690.

79. See Christopher Wadlow, 6.

80. Lionel Bently, 692.

81. Ibid., at 672. More specifically, it was an extension in multifold manners. It was from sale of goods to services, from origin of goods or services to its quality, from simple pretences that the goods are those of another trader to cover pretences that the goods have been licensed by another trader. See *Spalding* v. *Gamage* [1915] 32 RPC 273, wherein the plaintiff who was the manufacturer of football brought a passing off action against the defendants who obtained some of the claimant's old stock and sold them as if they were new and improved footballs. This was held to be a misrepresentation. Another case useful to substantiate this point is *Taittinger SA* v. *Allbev* [1993] FSR 641, wherein the defendants were prevented from using the name Elderflower Champagne.

82. See Lionel Bently, 698.

83. *British Legion* v. *British Legion Club (Street)* (1931) 63 RPC 555.

84. See, Lionel Bently, 699.

85. Ibid., at 694.

86. See, Christopher Wadlow, 6.

87. See, Lionel Bently, 694.

88. Ibid. Also see, *Associated Press* v. *Insert Media* [1991] FSR 380 and *British Telecommunications* v. *One in A Million* [1998] 4 All.E.R. 476. The first case is an example for the situation where the defendant places their product in close proximity to the claimant's product. In this case the defendants inserted advertisement inside the plaintiff's newspapers after the delivery of newspaper to newsagents. The second case is an example for registering domain names containing the name of organizations having goodwill. In the instant case the defendant had secured domain names like virgin.com. The Court of Appeal considered this as an actionable misrepresentation.

89. In false endorsement related cases, it is generally seen that the unauthorized use of the name or picture of a real person is more likely to succeed than that of fictious characters. See Christopher Wadlow, 494.

90. *Irvine* v. *Talksport* [2002] FSR 60. In this case, the plaintiff Irvine was a well-known racing driver. The defendant, Talk Sports Limited (TSL) was a radio station and they had acquired rights to cover a number of prominent sporting events, including the FIA Formula One Grand Prix World Championship. In 1999 TSL embarked a promotional campaign and during the campaign they used a photographic image of Irvine, dressed in the racing gear of the Ferrari team and apparently holding up to his left ear a small radio on which the station's logo appeared clearly. Another photographic image of Irvine, standing on the winner's podium at the Monte Carlo F1 Grand Prix, was also used. As these photos were used without permission from Irvine, he approached the Court by saying that the distribution of the defendant's brochure bearing a manipulated picture of him was an actionable passing off. In this case, the Court granted a sum of £25,000 as damages to Irvine.

91. Ibid., at para 38.

92. See, Lionel Bently, 705. In deciding whether a defendant's misrepresentation is deceptive, the Courts take into consideration a number of factors and these includes strength of the public's association with the claimant's sign, similarity of the defendant's sign, proximity of the claimant's and defendant's field of business, characteristics of the market, intention of the defendant, existence of a disclaimer and finally, whether the defendant was attempting a parody or satire through its action.

93. Ibid.

94. Ibid., at 707.

95. See Christopher Wadlow, 6.

96. See Lionel Bently, 707.

97. See Christopher Wadlow, 7.

98. See Lionel Bently, 718.

99. For example, it is reported that ICC had to give back 20 per cent of the 30 million dollars that LG had paid as sponsorship fee for the world cup. See http://www.businessworldindia.com/innerSections.aspx?SectionId=382, accessed 2 April 2006.

100. See, Lionel Bently, 719.

101. Ibid.

102. Ibid.,at 720.

103. Ibid.,at 722.

104. Ibid.

105. See *Tattinger* v. *Allbev,* [1993] FSR 641.

106. *National Hockey League* v. *Pepsi-Cola Canada Ltd,* 1992 CarswellBC 215.

107. Ibid., at Para 28.

108. Ibid., at Para 55.

109. *The New Zealand Olympic and Commonwealth Games Association Inc.* v. *Telecom New Zealand Limited* [1996] FSR 757 (New Zealand HC). The facts of this case are discussed in detail in chapter 2.

110. In arriving at this decision, the Court also observed that there was no use of the five circles as such and there was not a circle in sight. The Court was of the view that there was no significant likelihood of assumption by readers that Telecom was a sponsor or was connected with Olympics. Ibid., at 763.

111. Ibid., at 765.

112. *Arsenal Football Club* v. *Reed* [2001] RPC 46.

113. Ibid., at para 25.

114. Ibid., at para 42.

115. Ibid.

116. Ibid.

117. Ibid., at para 43.

118. Ibid., at para 47.

119. *ICC Development (International) Ltd.* v. *Arvee Enterprises and Anr.* 2003 (26) PTC 245 (Del). The facts of this case is discussed in detail in chapter 2.

120. Ibid., at para 9.

121. Ibid.

122. Ibid.

123. Ibid., at para 10.

124. Ibid.

125. Ibid., at para 21.

126. Ibid., at para 10.

127. *ICC Development (International) Ltd.* v. *Ever Green Service Station* 2003 (26) PTC 228 (Del). The facts of this case were discussed in detail in chapter 2. But in this case, as seen from our previous discussion on copyright infringement action, the Court upheld a claim of copyright infringement as there was a direct copying of the logo of the event organizer.

4

Changing Times and Changing Resolutions

The analysis of the effectiveness of traditional legal measures in fighting ambush marketing is an eye opener to the fact that, though they were useful in some instances, they were helpless to a great extent in most types of sophisticated ambush marketing. The main reason for this is the fact that the purpose of traditional legal measures is not prevention of ambush marketing. They were just being used to prevent ambush marketing, as there was no other weapon in the armoury. The increasing instances of ambush marketing coupled with the lack of effectiveness of traditional legal measures, compelled event organizers and sponsors across the globe to think of new solutions. The result was event-specific legislation aimed at preventing this parasitic problem. Many a times, the courts had also pointed to this solution.

Today we see almost all the major event organizers requesting the host countries to enact new legislation for securing proper protection of properties associated with their events.[1] For example, in the case of the Olympics, a host country will have to ensure that the intellectual property associated with the organization and the Olympic Games get protected at all levels. Thus the world saw Australia enacting a new statute entitled 'Sydney 2000 Games (Indicia and Images) Protection Act 1996' for equipping itself against ambush marketing during the 2000 Sydney Olympics. Though the London Olympics is years away, the UK has already drafted 'London

Olympic Games and Paralympic Games Act 2006' which aims at protecting the valuable properties associated with the Olympic games, to be held in London in 2012. This Act received the Royal Assent on March 30, 2006. Meanwhile, China also contributed to this field, as early as in April 2002, through the legislation of Regulations on the Protection of Olympic Symbols, in view of the Olympics games to be held in Beijing in 2008.

Due to multifold reasons, these three statutes are taken up for analysis. Analysis of a statute like Sydney 2000 Games (Indicia and Images) Protection Act 1996 can give a clear idea as to how the event-specific legislation worked in the past. On the other hand, analysis of a statute like the London Olympic Games and Paralympic Games Act 2006 will provide the readers a brief idea about the process of evolution of event-specific legislation. The analysis of the Chinese law in the backdrop of these two statutes in turn will help us find the differences, if any, in the perspectives of developing countries and developed countries on the issue.

So the first part of this chapter will focus on the Sydney 2000 Games (Indicia and Images) Protection Act 1996 and the London Olympic Games and Paralympic Games Act 2006 in detail and will also analyse how far the Sydney 2000 Games (Indicia and Images) Protection Act 1996 was successful in preventing ambush marketing during Sydney 2000 Olympics. The second part of this chapter focuses on the question as to how the developing countries perceive and tackle issues of ambush marketing. Two major developing countries, China and India, are chosen for this purpose. The Chinese Regulation on the Protection of Olympic symbols 2002 is analysed in contrast with the other two statutes in that part. Anti-Ambush marketing approaches in India are also discussed in the context of its hosting of Common Wealth Games in 2010 and ICC Cricket World Cup in 2011.

FEATURES OF SYDNEY 2000 GAMES (INDICIA AND IMAGES) PROTECTION ACT 1996

The main aim of Sydney 2000 Games (Indicia and Images) Protection Act 1996 (herein after referred to as 'Sydney 2000 Games Act') was the regulation of the use of indicia and images associated with the Sydney 2000 Olympic Games and the Paralympic Games, for commercial purposes. The main feature of this statute is that it supplants and augments the existing intellectual property laws to protect a peculiar set of indicia.[2] The legislative history of this Act shows that it has its genesis in a parliamentary report entitled 'Cashing in on the Sydney Olympics: Protecting the Sydney Olympic Games from Ambush Marketing'.[3] The objective of this Act was to be achieved by facilitating the raising of licensing revenue with the help of a proper regulation regarding the use of distinctive marks and images associated with the Games.[4]

It is interesting to see that the applicability of this Act was specifically extended to the waters above the continental shelf of Australia and also the airspace above Australia and the continental shelf of Australia.[5] This extended applicability has to be read in the light of the ambush marketing instances with the help of air balloons and helicopters, as seen in chapter 2. The seriousness attached to countering this form of ambush marketing will be clearer, when we find that Australia has recently brought another comprehensive statute, the Major Events (Aerial Advertising) Act 2007, with the sole objective of regulating, managing, and controlling aerial advertising during major events in Australia.[6]

The Sydney 2000 Games Act defined Sydney 2000 Games indicia in a very broad manner to protect phrases like 'Games City', 'Millennium Games', 'Sydney Games', 'Sydney 2000' and the combination of the words 'Games' and the number '2000' or the words 'Two Thousand'.[7] Apart from this, the Act also protected the words 'Olympiad', 'Olympic' and the phrases like 'Share the Spirit', 'Summer Games', 'Team Millennium' and also the combination of '24th', 'Twenty-Fourth' or 'XXIVth' and the word 'Olympics' or 'Games'.[8]

The Act also made two lists wherein List A contained the words 'Olympian' and 'Olympics' and list B contained the words 'Bronze', 'Games', 'Gold', 'Green and Gold', 'Medals', 'Millennium', Silver', 'Spirit', 'Sponsor', 'Summer', 'Sydney', 'Two Thousand', and '2000'. Any combination of the words in List A with any word in List B was brought within the ambit of the meaning of Sydney 2000 Olympic Games indicia.[9] This broad strategy was aimed at preventing the common ambush marketing practice of referring to events in indirect ways. The Sydney 2000 Paralympic Games indicia was also defined in a similar way.

The same strategy was adopted in the Act with respect to the images associated with the Games. The Act defined the Sydney 2000 Olympic Games images in a broad manner to include all visual or aural representations that, to a reasonable person, in the circumstances of the presentation, *suggested a connection* with the Sydney 2000 Olympic Games.[10] Thus, if a person associated a product with the Olympic Games, by seeing an advertisement, the advertisement was liable to be brought within the purview of the Act. This makes certain authors view that, the Act tightly controlled a limited language and symbolic domain.[11]

It is also interesting to note the circumstances where the Sydney 2000 Games Indicia and Images were considered to as being applied. The Act specifically noted down certain situations, but at the same time explained that it should not be considered as limited to those circumstances. According to the Act, Sydney 2000 Games indicia and images was considered to have been applied to goods, if the indicia or images (1) were woven in, impressed on, worked into, or affixed to or annexed to, any goods; or (2) were applied to any covering, document, label, reel, or thing in or with which the goods were, or were intended to be, dealt with or provided in the course of trade.[12]

In the case of both goods and services, Sydney 2000 Games indicia and images was considered to have been applied, if they were (1) used on a signboard or in an advertisement (including a television or radio advertisement) that promoted the goods or services or (2) used in an invoice, price list, catalogue, brochure, business letter, business paper, or other commercial document that related it to those goods or services.[13] The Act also addressed the issues of importation of goods by specifically pointing out that Sydney 2000 Games indicia and images shall be considered to have been applied, if a person imports goods into Australia for the purpose of sale or distribution and when imported, the goods have already had applied to them the Sydney 2000 Games indicia or images.

Thus, by first defining what all things can constitute the Sydney 2000 Games Indicia and Images and then proceeding by defining the circumstances that will be considered as the application of Sydney 2000 Games Indicia and Images, the Act made the Sydney 2000 Olympics, a really challenging game for the ambush marketers.

The Act interdicted all other than SOCOG, or SPOC or a licensed user, from using Sydney 2000 Games indicia and images for commercial purposes.[14] The Act specifically pointed out that the use of an indicia closely resembling Sydney 2000 Games indicia, as to be likely to be mistaken by a reasonable person, would also amount to use of Sydney 2000 Games indicia.[15] So in situations wherein a person represented the word 'Olympics' in his own creative manner, but at the same time created a misrepresentation in the minds of reasonable persons, he was to be held liable under the provisions of this Act.

To ensure clarity and consistency in interpretation, the Act also defined 'use for commercial purposes' by pointing out that a person uses Sydney 2000 Games indicia and images for commercial purposes, if that person applies the indicia or images to goods or services of the person; the application is for advertising or promotional purposes, or is likely to enhance the demand for the goods or services; and the application, to a reasonable person would suggest that the first-mentioned person is or was a sponsor of, or is or was the provider of other support for the Sydney Games or any event arranged by Sydney Organizing Committee for the 2000 Olympic Games, the Australian Olympic Committee Inc., or the International Olympic Committee.[16]

The Act empowered the Sydney Organizing Committee for the 2000 Olympic Games (SOCOG) and the Sydney Paralympic Organizing Committee (SPOC) to license a person to use all or any of the Sydney 2000 Games indicia and images for commercial purposes and specifically required them to make an entry of such licenses in the register of licensed users.[17]

The use of Sydney 2000 Games indicia and images for the purpose of conveying information or for the purposes of criticism or review was specifically exempted from liability under this Act.[18] This included reporting of news or the presentation of current affairs and criticism or review in a newspaper, magazine, or similar periodical, or in a broadcast, or in a cinematograph film.[19]

Remedies Provided under the Act

The pragmatic approach of the Australian Legislature and the Olympics Committee is quite evident in the drafting of the remedies under this Act. Under it when a person other than the SOCOG, SPOC, or a licensed user uses the Sydney 2000 Games indicia and images for commercial purposes, a prescribed court will have the power to grant an injunction to restrain the person from such conduct.[20] It is worth noting here that the use of an indicia closely resembling the Sydney 2000 Games indicia was also subject to this provision for injunction, provided it could be proved that it is likely to be mistaken by a reasonable person as the Sydney 2000 Games indicia.[21] This application for injunction was to be made by

SOCOG, SPOC, or a licensed user.[22] During the pending of an application for injunction, they were permitted to seek an interim injunction also.[23]

This Act also provided specific measures to mitigate the possible economic losses that the SOCOG, SPOC, or a licensed user might undergo by specifically providing that the loss or damage they suffered as a result of any act done by any person in contravention of the provisions of the Act could be recovered through an action.[24] For example, if American Express tried to ambush Visa during the Sydney Olympics and if Visa could prove that it suffered loss of money due to ambush marketing of American Express, the Court was empowered to direct American Express to reimburse Visa. This provision should have made the ambush marketers think twice before making an attempt.

This legislation also empowered the SOCOG, SPOC, and licensed users to give the Chief Executive Officer of Customs (CEO) a written notice objecting to the importation of goods having Sydney 2000 Games indicia or images for using, for commercial purposes without proper authorization or license under the Act and the CEO was empowered to seize such goods.[25] In cases where the court ordered such goods to be forfeited to the Commonwealth, the goods were to be disposed off according to the directions of CEO.[26]

But the most interesting remedy that was introduced under this legislation was the provision for 'corrective advertisements'.[27] On an application from the SOCOG or SPOC, the prescribed court was empowered to make an order under its discretion requiring a person to publish advertisements by such means as the court thought fit (it included a broadcast), at the person's own expense and intervals specified in the order, if the Court was satisfied that s/he has used the Sydney 2000 Games indicia and images for commercial purpose without the required authorization. This provision was certainly an open threat to the ambush marketing experts across the world. No company would want to go for such a kind of corrective advertisements, as a series of corrective advertisements through different media could cause irreparable damage to their reputation and brand value.

As the operation of the Act was meant to supplement the already available remedies and not to supplant the application of remedies provided under various laws like the Trade Marks Act or the Designs Act, all the rights conferred or liabilities imposed by other laws also remained available for the event organizers and sponsors.[28] This implies that a person who engages in ambush marketing with the help of a registered trade mark of the event was to be held liable under this legislation as well as the Trade Marks Act.

Even while providing such strong remedies against ambush marketing, the legislation tried to ensure a balance to the whole system by providing remedies to persons aggrieved by groundless threats of legal proceedings. It entitled such persons to bring an action against SOCOG, SPOC, or the licensed user in cases wherein they faced a groundless threat.[29]

HOW THE LEGISLATION WORKED AT SYDNEY OLYMPICS

The enactment of a good law as such is never a solution to any problem and only a proper enforcement of its provisions can address the mischief against which it was drafted. When the Sydney 2000 Games Act was enforced along with the Olympic Arrangements Act 2000, which focused mainly on the administrative and practical aspects of the Games, the result was a very effective prevention of ambush marketing. This was mainly because they complemented each other, covering a very wide range of rights and scenarios.[30] As a result, most of the academicians consider the anti-ambush marketing strategy at the Sydney Olympics a big success.[31] They also consider this success as a proof of the potential commercial uses of intellectual properties associated with an event.[32]

But all these good words do not mean that there was no instance of ambush marketing at the Sydney Olympics. One group of authors thinks that the Sydney 2000 Act did not achieve its aim of preventing ambush marketing in a comprehensive manner.[33] They cite the example of ambush marketing done by Qantas Airlines and Reebok to substantiate this argument.

It is interesting to see that most of the consumer surveys during the Sydney Olympics showed that the public was more aware of Qantas Airways as an Olympic sponsor than Ansett Airways, which was the real official sponsor.[34] This ambushing was done mainly with help of advertising campaigns made by Qantas featuring a series of athletes. Qantas also ran a full-page advertisement titled 'Australia Wide Olympic* Sale' wherein through the asterisk it made a disclaimer in a small size font that 'Qantas is not an Olympic Sponsor'. Ansett brought proceedings in Federal Court for an injunction to prevent Qantas from engaging in ambush marketing activities. But this case was settled after a few hearings without a decision from the court. It is generally viewed that Qantas won this case as there was neither a declaration of infringing conduct nor any direction for corrective advertising.[35]

Another victim of ambush marketing during Sydney games was Nike. Nike was an official clothing supplier for the Australian Olympic team. One of the team members, Ian Thorpe, was sponsored by its rival Adidas. When he was called to the dais during a medal presentation ceremony, the swimmer had his towel draped over the Nike logo on his official team tracksuit and as a result his photo appeared throughout Australia without the logo of the official sponsor. It is interesting to note here that it was Nike itself which showed the scope of this ambush marketing method to the sponsorship world during the 1992 Barcelona Olympics and the same boomeranged on them at Sydney.[36] Though Thorpe and Adidas escaped liability by saying that it was not a deliberate act, this revealed loopholes in the new law also.

Even though such small instances of ambush marketing can be cited from the Sydney Olympics, for ambush marketers we can still consider them as the worst ever games.[37]

FEATURES OF LONDON OLYMPIC GAMES AND PARALYMPIC GAMES ACT 2006

The London Olympic Games and Paralympic Games Act 2006 (herein after referred to as 'London Olympics Act'), which received the Royal Assent on 30 March 2006, is another statute that needs to be considered in detail in this part. Like the Sydney 2000 Games Act, the principal aim of this Act is also the smooth conduct of the Olympic Games and it deals with the issue of ambush marketing in detail. The fact that it is aimed at preventing ambush marketing connected to an event due to be held after a long period of six years shows the seriousness with which the world views ambush marketing.

This Act creates a body corporate known as the Olympic Delivery Authority (ODA) for the purpose of the London Olympics.[38] The legislation explores in detail the issue of regulations relating to advertising and imposes a duty on the Secretary of State to make regulations regarding the advertisements in the vicinity of Olympic venues.[39] These regulations will specify the nature and extent of the restrictions including the place, time period, and type of advertisements which are to be restricted.[40]

According to this Act, any person who violates the advertising restrictions under Section 19 shall be committing a criminal offence punishable by a fine that can go up to £20,000.[41] ODA has been conferred the power to institute criminal proceedings.[42] The only defense available to a person to escape from the criminal liability is to show that the contravention of the regulations occurred without his knowledge or that they happened despite his having taken all reasonable steps to prevent it.[43] This is a feature which distinguishes it from the previous law regarding ambush marketing and this has come in for severe criticism from many quarters, especially from the academicians. According to them, criminal liability cannot be justified in cases of *'creative'* marketing techniques like ambush marketing.

This Act empowers a Constable or an Enforcement Officer designated by the ODA to enter any land or premises to prevent any unauthorized advertising that comes within the purview of the regulations. Interestingly, if a person is convicted as a result of such proceedings, s/he may also have to pay the expenses incurred by the ODA or Police Authority in undertaking such enforcement action.[44] But when we analyse this section from a wider perspective, we find that it is a section which gives really broad powers, as it permits entry even to land outside the area to which the advertising restrictions apply, provided such land is being used to project images into an area where advertising restrictions apply.[45] Here is an example of a law drafted with the foresight to include even the latest multi media projection techniques. Officers are empowered to seize the equipments used in the breach of the regulations, so as to prevent violations of the regulations and also to use them for evidential purposes.[46]

Another interesting feature of this Act is its attempt to cast a duty upon the ODA to educate people who are likely to be affected by the regulations and also to provide assistance to the public for complying with the regulations.[47] The local planning authorities are also given a duty under this Act to inform those whom they grant consent for advertisements about these advertisement regulations.[48] This kind of awareness creation is the most important step in tackling ambush marketing practices in an effective and democratic manner.

The statute casts a specific duty on the Secretary of State to make regulations, to control street trading, in the vicinity of Games venues and these regulations are to be applicable to trading on highways, public place, and even on private lands.[49] But trading within buildings, with the exception of car parks, is permitted under the legislation. The punishments and enforcement power seen in relation to advertising regulations have been made applicable also in the case of street trading.[50]

Another notable restriction is in the area of sale of tickets. The Act has made it an offence to sell a ticket or anything that purports to be a ticket, for an event held as part of the London Olympics or Paralympics in a public place or in the course of a business without written authorization from London Organizing Committee for the Olympic Games (LOCOG).[51] The person convicted for such an offence shall end up paying a fine of up to level 5 on the standard scale, which is presently £5,000.[52] The legislation gives a very broad definition for 'sale of tickets' by including within its ambit a wide range of activities like offering to sell a ticket, exposing a ticket for sale, advertising that a ticket is available for purchase and giving or offering to give a ticket to someone who is paying for other goods and services.[53] Under the Act, a person shall be considered as acting in the course of a business if he does anything as a result of which he makes a profit or aims to make a profit.[54] This section was included specifically to prevent ambush marketing situations wherein a ticket is offered as part of a package with other goods and we have seen such examples of ambush marketing in chapter 2.[55] A provision like this, which has been specifically crafted to prevent such activities, may effectively prevent ambush marketing practices in this line.

The pragmatic approach of this statute is once again visible when it says that the internet and other electronic communication service providers must withdraw services that are being misused for touting tickets, within the shortest time period from which they become aware of such misuses.[56] This provision can be applied successfully in the case of ambush marketing through the medium of the internet. Provisions like this assume significance in the light of the increasing possibilities of misuse of internet as a platform for ambush marketing, as we found in chapter 2.

This statute introduces a right, named the London Olympics Association Right, which is the right to be associated with the London Olympics.[57] Like the Sydney Act, this Act specifically sets out certain words and phrases, the combination of which may be taken into account by a court while considering whether the London Olympics association right has been contravened.[58] This can be a combination of the words 'games', 'Two Thousand and Twelve', '2012', or 'twenty twelve' with the words 'gold', 'silver', 'bronze', 'London', 'medals', 'sponsor', or 'summer'.[59] Without stopping there, the Secretary of State is given an additional power to add, remove, or vary an entry in either group of expressions to meet the challenging ambush marketing practices at that time.[60] It extends to the infringement of the Olympic association right to words that are similar to the protected words and which creates an association with the Olympic Games or the Olympic movement in the public's mind.[61] But like the Sydney 2000 Games Act, this Act also has provided certain exceptions and limitations like publishing or broadcasting of a report of the sporting or other event related to Olympics, publishing and broadcasting information about Olympic games, incidental inclusion in a literary work, dramatic work, artistic work, sound recording, film or broadcast within the meaning of Part I of the Copyright, Designs and Patents Act 1988, etc.[62]

Like the Sydney 2000 Games Act, the British Act also allows LOCOG to grant authorizations to individuals, who are mainly the sponsors, to associate themselves with the London Olympic Games.[63] The Act also imposes a duty on the LOCOG to maintain a public register of those individuals who have been granted the right to associate with the London Olympic Games.[64]

We also see an increased protection for the Olympic words, symbols and motto through this Act.[65] The offences under Olympic Symbol (Protection) Act 1995 (OSPA) has been made an arrestable offence through this Act.[66] The Act gives Her Majesty's Revenue and Customs (HMRC) officers the power to prevent the entry of OSPA infringing goods into the territory of UK and specifically empowers the officers to detain such goods when they have a notice in writing from LOCOG or the British Olympic Association, or the British Paralympics Association or when they find them during their normal duty.[67]

All these measures show a very comprehensive statute aimed at countering different types of ambush marketing. This Act can very well be considered as a further step from the Sydney 2000 Games Act. By making ambush marketing activities a criminally liable one, it has shocked the ambush marketers across the world. But we may have to wait for some more time to see how far this legislation will prevent ambush marketing during the 2012 Olympic Games.

DEVELOPING COUNTRIES AND ANTI-AMBUSH MARKETING EFFORTS

The two anti-ambush marketing statutes discussed in detail in the first part of this chapter may be viewed by some segment of academia as a developed country's capitalist perspective of protecting business interests. In this context it is certainly interesting to see how developing countries perceive and tackle the issues of ambush marketing.

For this let us analyse the issue from the perspective of two major developing countries—China and India. China is undoubtedly one of the leading developing countries. China invited opprobrium for its reluctance in giving due recognition and protection for valuable intellectual property rights during its initial pace in promoting domestic industries. However, in recent times a clearly different trend has emerged and it is now trying its best to project itself as a strong advocate of intellectual property protection.[68] As China will host the Olympics in 2008, it is a good choice for our analysis of developing countries perspective on the issue of ambush marketing. India is also going to host a major sports event in the year 2010—the Common Wealth Games. Hence we may choose these two countries for a comparative assessment of anti-ambush marketing efforts in the developing countries.

China is taking lot of measures to deal with the issues of ambush marketing as the host of 2008 Olympics. If we take into consideration the words of those who sit at the helm of organizing the Beijing Olympics, we sense a very similar perspective to that of developed countries. The official position as reflected from the words of senior officials is that only those who financially sponsor the Games have the right to market their products and maximize their commercial interests.[69]

China came out with a detailed law as early as April 2002, for the protection of intellectual property rights associated with the Olympic Games.[70] Like the two statutes we discussed in the previous section of this chapter, this one also approaches the issue of ambush marketing in a comprehensive manner. However, the number of provisions in it are fewer and the language used is jargon-free and very simple, which at times can make the reader confused as to whether it is a mere guideline or a regulation.

Strengthening of protection of Olympic symbols, safeguarding the lawful rights and interests of the right holders of Olympic symbols and maintaining the dignity of Olympic movement are considered as the three basic objectives of this Act.[71] Like the Sydney 2000 Games Act and London Olympics Act, this regulation also specifically says that it aims only to supplement or act as an additional remedy to the existing remedies and does not intend to substitute the already available remedies for the event organizers.[72]

But a major difference between the Chinese statute and law from other countries discussed in the previous section is their approach in defining 'Olympic symbols'. While the Sydney 2000 Games Act defined the Olympic indicia in the most comprehensive way by putting forward a list of words like 'Games City', 'Millennium Games', 'Sydney Games' or 'Sydney 2000', 'Games' and '2000' or 'Two Thousand' from a long list of words and the London Olympics Act placed restriction on combination of words like 'games', 'Two Thousand and Twelve', '2012' or 'twenty twelve' with the words 'gold', 'silver', 'bronze', 'London', 'medals', 'sponsor', or 'summer' and had empowered the Secretary of State to add entries to that list, the Chinese regulation takes a moderate approach by restricting itself to limited items while defining 'Olympic symbols'.[73]

According to the Chinese regulation, 'Olympic symbols' refer to (1) the five Olympic rings, Olympic flag, Olympic motto, Olympic emblem, and Olympic anthem of the International Olympic Committee (IOC); (2) expressions such as Olympic, Olympiad, Olympic Games, and their abbreviations; (3) name, emblem, and symbols of the Chinese Olympic Committee; (4) name, emblem, and symbols of Beijing 2008 Olympic Games Bid Committee;(5) symbols such as the name and emblem of Beijing Organizing Committee for the Games of the XXIX Olympiad, the mascots, anthem, and slogan of the 29th Olympic Games, 'Beijing2008', the 29th Olympic Games, and its abbreviations; and (6) other symbols related to the 29 Olympic Games laid down in the Olympic Charter and the Host City Contract for the Games of the XXIX Olympiad in the Year 2008.[74]

But this narrowed down approach can be seen compensated in another part of the regulation in quite an ingenious way. The Chinese regulation says that the Olympic symbols shall not be used for 'commercial purposes' without authorization of the right holders and in defining 'commercial purposes', it has included a specific provision whereby all acts that might mislead people into thinking that a sponsorship or any other supporting relationship exists between the doers and the rights holders of Olympic symbols are brought within the purview of 'commercial purpose'.[75]

The responsibility for protecting the Olympic symbols is vested upon the administrative authorities for industry and commerce under the State Council.[76] The regulation empowers them to inquire, investigate, conduct on the spot inspections, and also seal and seize infringing goods.[77] The regulation specifically talks about the need for concluding a license contract for all those who wish to use the Olympic related symbols.[78] A positive sign that needs special appreciation is the different steps taken from the side of the authorities in speeding up this process of licensing.[79]

With regard to infringements, the Chinese regulation takes a slightly different approach from that of the two statutes discussed in the previous section, in that it favours the settlement of disputes through a process of consultation between the parties concerned.[80] But in cases wherein the parties concerned are unwilling to consult or in situations wherein the consultation fails, the rights holders are given the right to institute legal proceedings in a people's court or to request the administrative department for industry and commerce to make a disposition.[81]

In cases wherein the administrative department for industry and commerce finds evidence of infringement, it will be the duty of the department to order an immediate cessation of the infringement or to confiscate or destroy the infringing goods and the special tools used for manufacturing those infringing goods.[82] In cases where it finds the generation of illegal income from such infringing activities, the department has the right and duty to confiscate such illegal income and may also impose a fine which can go up to five times the illegal income earned.[83] In cases where no evidence of illegal income is available, a fine of up to 50,000 Yuan may be imposed on the infringer.[84] In the year 2006 alone, the Chinese authorities have dealt with around 428 Olympic symbol related infringements.[85] Between the years 2004 and 2006, SAIC has dealt with a total of 1128 infringement cases, involving 1.95 million US dollars.[86] Fine of 1.16 million US dollars was imposed during this period.[87]

In cases where the party concerned refuses to accept the disposition, the administrative department for industry and commerce may apply to the People's Court for compulsory execution.[88] If the parties concerned request, the administrative department for industry and commerce may mediate on the amount of compensation for the loss caused by infringement of exclusive rights of Olympic symbols and if the mediation fails, the parties concerned can institute legal proceedings in a people's court in accordance with the Civil Procedure Law of the People's Republic of China.[89] All this does not mean that the infringers can escape from criminal liability as the Regulation specifically says that those who use Olympic symbols to conduct fraudulent or other illegal activities shall be held criminally liable.[90]

Like the other two statutes, the Chinese regulation also takes into consideration the possibility of infringements through the import or export channels and empowers the Customs authorities to investigate into such matters.[91] Another interesting feature of this regulation is the provision for determining the amount of compensation. According to the Regulation, the amount of compensation for the loss caused by infringement of the exclusive rights over Olympic symbols shall be determined on the basis of the loss that the rights holder has suffered through the infringement or on the basis of the profit that the infringer has earned through the infringement.[92] According to the Regulations, the compensation amount shall also include the reasonable expenses incurred for finding the infringement.[93] In cases where the loss suffered or the profit obtained by the infringer are difficult to determine, the compensation is to be determined with reference to the licensing fees for using the Olympic symbol.[94] But at the same time, under the regulation those who unknowingly sell infringing goods and those who can prove that the goods were acquired lawfully are not liable to pay compensation, provided they are willing to point out the real supplier.[95]

A very positive approach taken by the Chinese authorities is that they have begun to sensitize the public about the need for buying souvenirs from the genuine souvenir outlets.[96] This educational measure is certainly an important ingredient for a successful anti-ambush marketing campaign and the Chinese regulation needs to be appreciated in this attempt.

ANTI-AMBUSH MARKETING EFFORTS—THE INDIAN PERSPECTIVE

With a vibrant knowledge driven economy, India too is conscious of the real value of intellectual property rights and is now considered by many as a champion of protection of intellectual property rights. The Indian judiciary has also supported such a positive approach. But whether this interest in protecting intellectual property also extends to the intellectual property rights associated with events is some thing that needs to be explored from the practical realities.

India is soon going to be hosting two major sports events—the Common Wealth Games in 2010 and the ICC Cricket World Cup in 2011. Common Wealth Games is to be hosted alone and ICC Cricket Word Cup along with its neighbours. How India approaches the issue of ambush marketing in the context of these two mega events is something really worth exploring.

Experience from the past shows a clear lack of interest from the side of the legislature in dealing with issues relating to ambush marketing. Even though India has hosted many major events in the past, the Indian Parliament has not passed any legislation so far on the issue of ambush marketing. This legislative approach needs to be examined in contrast with the efforts taken by countries like the UK in protecting the rights relating to events coming as late as in 2012. The Indian judicial approach on the issue of ambush marketing also narrates a story of helplessness. In the absence of specific laws, the Indian courts have so far tried to tackle the issue with the help of traditional legal measures like passing off action, trade mark infringement action, and copyright infringement action. In the process they have indicated their limitations in addressing the issue of ambush marketing.[97] The three ambush marketing related Indian cases which have been discussed in detail in the previous chapter showed the Courts rejecting most of the arguments on the ground that the existing IP laws were not meant for preventing ambush marketing.[98] The real danger was visible when the Court made the observation that a passing off action contains an element of overt or covert deceit, while ambush marketing is an opportunistic commercial exploitation of an event.[99]

But even the Judiciary recognizes the larger issues involved in ambush marketing and has taken the view that it is for the legislators to find a proper solution to the problem.[100] As seen from our discussion in the previous chapter as well as the examination of event-specific legislation in this chapter, the proper solution would be event-specific legislation. So far no law has been drawn up for hosting the Common Wealth Games. With regard to the ICC Cricket World Cup in 2011, it is almost sure that ICC will be insisting on the drafting of specific legislation before the event. But whether India should wait till that time is debatable. The only positive trend seen in recent times is the significant amount of attention given by the print and electronic media to ambush marketing issues.[101]

It is high time that the Indian parliament came up with detailed event-specific legislation that can be amended according to the events that India hosts. This is necessary for attracting the major events of the world to Indian soil. By giving an assurance that it will protect the genuine interests of those who invest money in the organizing of such mega events, India can become a major host of spectacular global events. Let India learn useful lessons from the Australian, UK, and Chinese legislation and move in the right direction of democratic event-specific legislation that protects real Indian interests

NOTES

1. For example, London Olympic Games and Paralympic Games Act 2006 was drafted for the London Olympics to be held in 2012. This Act is discussed in detail in this chapter. Another example can be the legislation drafted for ICC Cricket World Cup 2007 in Caribbean Countries. A new legislation, officially known as the ICC Cricket World Cup West Indies 2007 Act, was drafted for the specific purpose of prevention of ambush marketing and successful conduct of the world cup. This legislation is often referred to as sunset legislation as it was added to the statute books only for a fixed period of time. For more details about this legislation, see http://www.icc-cricket.com/icc-cwc/content/story/243734.html, accessed 10 April 2006. Also see http://barbados.gov.bb/Docs/Act-World%20Cup.pdf, accessed 22 February 2007.
2. See Graeme Orr, 'Marketing Games: The Regulation of Olympic Indicia and Images in Australia', *EIPR* 1997, 19(9), 504–8, 504 (1997).
3. Ibid., at 505.
4. See Sec.3 of the Sydney 2000 Games Act 1996.
5. See Sec.5 of the Sydney 2000 Games Act 1996.
6. This legislation is available online at http://www.austlii.edu.au/au/legis/vic/consol_act/meaa2007309/, accessed 30 July 2007.
7. See Sec.8 of the Sydney 2000 Games Act.
8. These words were included specifically under the definition of 'Sydney 2000 Olympic Games indicia' in Sec. 8 of the Act.
9. Ibid.
10. See Sec. 9 of the Sydney 2000 Games Act.
11. For a detailed discussion on this point, see Graeme Orr, 'Marketing Games: The Regulation of Olympic Indicia and Images in Australia', 504.
12. See Sec. 10 (1) (a) of the Sydney 2000 Games Act.
13. See Sec. 10 (1) (b) of the Sydney 2000 Games Act.
14. See Sec. 12 of the Sydney 2000 Games Act.
15. See Sec. 12 (5) of the Sydney 2000 Games Act.
16. See Sec. 11 of the Sydney 2000 Games Act.

17. See Secs 14 and 15 of the Sydney 2000 Games Act.

18. See Sec. 25 of the Sydney 2000 Games Act.

19. See Sec. 25 (2) of the Sydney 2000 Games Act.

20. See Sec. 43 of the Sydney 2000 Games Act.

21. Sec. 43 (9) of the Sydney 2000 Games Act.

22. Sec. 43 (3) of the Sydney 2000 Games Act.

23. See Sec. 44 of the Sydney 2000 Games Act.

24. See Sec. 46 of the Act. The time limit prescribed for this action was specified as 3 years from the day on which the contravention occurred. It is also to be noted that the grant of an injunction was not a bar to request for award of damages. The prescribed courts for the purposes of this Act were the Federal Court, the Supreme Court of a State, the Supreme Court of the Australian Capital Territory, the Supreme Court of the Northern Territory, and the Supreme Court of Norfolk Island. See Sec. 50 of the Act.

25. To know more about the requirements of such notice, see Sec. 32 of the Act. Also see Sec. 33 of the Act.

26. See Sec. 38 of the Sydney 2000 Games Act.

27. See Sec. 45 of the Sydney 2000 Games Act.

28. See Sec. 24 of the Sydney 2000 Games Act.

29. See Sec. 48 of the Sydney 2000 Games Act.

30. For a detailed discussion, see Cristina Garrigues, 'Ambush Marketing: Robbery or Smart Advertising', 506.

31. For example, see Mark Roper-Drimie, 'Sydney 2000 Olympic Games—"The Worst Games Ever" for Ambush Marketers', Ent. L.R. 2001, 12(5), 150–3 (2001).

32. The Sydney licensing program generated nearly US $500 million in revenues. See Laura Misener, 'Safeguarding the Olympic Insignia: Protecting the Commercial Integrity of the Canadian Olympic Association', 13 *J. Legal Aspects Sport* 79, 89 (2003).

33. For example see Jeremy Curthoys and Christopher N. Kendall, 'Ambush Marketing and the Sydney 2000 Games (Indicia and Images) Protection Act: A Retrospective', *Murdoch University Electronic Journal of Law*, available online at http://www.murdoch.edu.au/elaw/issues/v8n2/kendall82.html, accessed 5 April 2006.

34. Ibid.

35. Ibid.

36. This ambush marketing method taken by Nike during 1992 Barcelona Olympics was discussed in chapter 2 that surveyed different kinds of ambush marketing practices.

37. For a detailed analysis of the effectiveness of Sydney 2000 Games Act

during the Sydney Olympics, see generally, Mark Roper-Drimie, 'Sydney 2000 Olympic Games—"The Worst Games Ever" for Ambush Marketers'.

38. See Sec. 3 of the London Olympic Games and Paralympic Games Act 2006.

39. See Sec. 19 of the Act. These regulations are required to fulfill the obligations imposed by the IOC. The Host City Contract specifically requires that no advertising must be placed around Olympic venues so as to be within the view of television cameras covering the events or spectators watching Olympic events. See explanatory notes to the London Olympic Games And Paralympic Games Act 2006 available online at http://www.opsi.gov.uk/acts/en2006/06en12-a.htm, accessed 19 April 2006.

40. The framing of regulations was left to secondary legislation with a view to drafting them with a consideration of the requirements in 2012. As ambush marketing practices are getting more and more sophisticated every year, a secondary legislation may give a better fight against ambush marketing in so far as it can meet the changing requirements.

41. See Sec. 21 of the London Olympics Act.

42. See Sec. 23 (4) of the London Olympics Act.

43. See Sec. 21 (2) of the London Olympics Act.

44. See Secs 21 (4) and 22 of London Olympics Act.

45. See the explanatory Notes to London Olympic Games and Paralympic Games Act 2006 available online at http://www.opsi.gov.uk/acts/en2006/06en12-a.htm, accessed 19 April 2006.

46. See Sec. 22 (5) of the London Olympics Act.

47. See Sec. 23 (3) of the London Olympics Act, which deals with the duties of the ODA.

48. See Sec. 24 of the London Olympics Act.

49. See Sec. 25 of the London Olympics Act.

50. See Sec. 27 –The contravention of the regulations against street trading is also made a criminal offence punishable by a fine upto £20,000.

51. See Sec. 31 of the London Olympics Act.

52. Ibid.

53. Sec. 31 (2)(b) of the London Olympics Act.

54. See Sec. 31 (2)(c).

55. The best examples in this regard are the facts of the cases *ICC Development (International) Ltd.* v. *Arvee Enterprises* and *ICC Development (International) Ltd.* v. *Ever Green Service Station,* which was discussed in detail in chapters 2 and 3.

56. See Sec. 31 (5) of the London Olympics Act.

57. See Sec. 33 along with Schedule 4 of the London Olympics Act.

58. See Para 3 of Schedule 4 of the London Olympics Act.

59. Ibid.

60. See Para. 3(6) of Schedule 4 of the London Olympics Act.

61. See Para. 3 of Schedule 3 of the London Olympics Act.

62. See Para. 4 of Schedule 3 of the London Olympics Act.

63. See Para. 4 of Schedule 4 of the London Olympics Act.

64. See Para. 5 of Schedule 4 of the London Olympics Act.

65. See Sec. 32 along with Schedule 3 of the London Olympics Act.

66. See Para. 13 of the Schedule 3 of the London Olympics Act.

67. See Para 14 of the Schedule 3 of the London Olympics Act.

68. For example, recent statistics shows that State Administration for Industry and Commerce (SAIC) has dealt with 1,93,332 cases of trade mark infringement since 2001. See http://news.xinhuanet.com/english/2007-06/14/content_6242374.htm, accessed 22 June 2007.

69. Chen Feng, Marketing Director of BOCOG, as quoted in *China Daily*. See www.chinadaily.com.cn/2008/2007-06/13/content_893703.htm, accessed 20 June 2007.

70. This regulation was adopted at the 54 executive meeting of the State Council held in January 30,2002 and was promulgated by Decree No.345 of the State Council of the People's Republic of China on February 4,2002. This legislation came into effect on April 1,2002. Copy of this regulation is available online at http://en.beijing2008.cn/98/69/article211986998.shtml, accessed 21 June 2007.

71. See Art. 1 of the Regulation.

72. See Art. 14 of the Regulation which says that in addition to the present regulation, Olympic symbols are also protected according to provisions of other laws and administrative regulations such as the Copyright Law of the People's Republic of China, Trade mark Law of the People's Republic of China, the Patent Law of the People's Republic of China, and the Regulations on Administration of Special Symbols.

73. A comparative analysis of Sec.8 of the Sydney 2000 Games Act, Para 3 of Schedule 4 of the London Olympics Act and Art. 2 of the Chinese Regulation will highlight this issue.

74. See Art. 2 of the Chinese Regulation.

75. See Art. 4 of the Regulation along with Art. 5(6).

Art. 4—The right holders of the Olympic symbols enjoy the exclusive rights of Olympic symbols in accordance with these Regulations.No one may use Olympic symbols for commercial purposes (including potential commercial purposes, and the same below) without the authorization of the right holders.

Art. 5—For the purpose of these Regulations, 'use for commercial purposes' means the use of Olympic symbols for profit-making purposes in the following ways:

(1) The use of Olympic symbols in goods, packages or containers of goods or trade documents of good;

(2) The use of Olympic symbols in services;

(3) The use of Olympic symbols in advertising, commercial exhibition, profit-making performance and other commercial activities;

(4) Selling, importing or exporting goods bearing Olympic symbols;

(5) Manufacturing or selling Olympic symbols;

(6) Other acts that might mislead people to think there are sponsorship or other supporting relations between the doers and the right holders of Olympic symbols

76. See Art. 6 of the Regulation.

77. See Art. 11 of the Regulation. For the real picture of powers vested in the authorities, Art. 6 has to be read with Art. 11 of the Regulation.

78. Unlike the other anti-ambush marketing laws, this regulation goes in very detail at this point. To make things easy for the public, this regulation talks in detail about whom to have the contract with for the use of different symbols associated with the games. According to the regulations, anyone who wants to use the five Olympic rings, Olympic flag, Olympic motto, Olympic emblem, and Olympic anthem of the IOC and expressions such as Olympic, Olympiad, Olympic Games, and their abbreviations shall conclude a contract with the International Olympic Committee and institutions authorized or approved by it. Anyone who wishes to use the name, emblem, and symbols of the Chinese Olympic Committee is required to conclude a contract with the Chinese Olympic Committee. Anyone who wants to use the name, emblem, and symbols of Beijing 2008 Olympic Games Bid Committee, symbols such as the name and emblem of Beijing Organizing Committee for the Games of the XXIX Olympiad, the mascots, anthem, and slogan of the 29th Olympic Games, 'Beijing 2008', the 29 Olympic Games and its abbreviations and other symbols related to the 29th Olympic Games laid down in the Olympic Charter and the Host City Contract is required to conclude a contract with Beijing Organizing Committee before December 31, 2008. The license contracts are also required to specifically mention about the geographical area and duration of permitted use of symbols. See generally, Art. 8.

79. For example the Organizing Committee has launched a new approval system in February 2007 to facilitate faster replies for the applications submitted to BOCOG. Many similar efforts have been taken by the Organizing Committee to ease the sponsorship process. See http://english.ipr.gov.cn/ipr/en/info/Article.jsp?a_no=55149&col_no=926&dir=200702,

accessed 2 May 2007.

80. See Art. 10 of the Regulation.

81. Ibid.

82. Ibid.

83. Ibid.

84. Ibid.

85. See http://news.xinhuanet.com/english/2007-06/14/content_6242374.htm, accessed 22 June 2007.

86. Ibid.

87. Ibid.

88. In such situations, the concerned party is given a right to institute legal proceedings in a People's Court within 15 days from the date of receipt of the notification of the disposition in accordance with the Administrative Procedure Law of the People's Republic of China and only when the infringer fails to institute legal proceedings or fails to carry out the disposition within the expiry of that time limit, the Department will apply for compulsory execution. See Art. 10 of the Regulation.

89. See Art. 10 of the Regulation.

90. Ibid.

91. See Art. 12 of the Regulation. According to this provision, in situations wherein any import or export goods are suspected to be infringing the exclusive rights of Olympic symbols, the Customs shall investigate into and deal with the case in accordance with the powers and procedures laid down under the Customs Law of the People's Republic of China and the Regulations of the People's Republic of China on the Customs Protection of Intellectual Property. Similar provisions can also be seen in the Sydney 2000 Games Act. Secs 32 and 33 of the Sydney 2000 Games Act deals with such issues and those provisions empowers the Chief Executive Officer of Customs in confiscating such goods. Also see Para 14 in Schedule 3 of the London Olympics Act which discusses about the powers of HMRC officers in preventing the entry of OSPA infringing goods into the territory of UK. In April 2006, the Beijing Customs seized around 26 boxes of cigarette in accordance with the procedures laid down under this provision as they had without authorization, used the words 'Beijing 2008' and Chinese seal of 'Dancing Beijing'. See www.ipr.gov.cn/ipr/en/info/Article.jsp?a_no=6309&col_no=926&dir=200606, accessed 20 December 2006.

92. See Art. 13 of the Regulation.

93. Ibid.

94. Ibid.

95. Ibid.

96. For example, see www.ipr.gov.cn/ipr/en/info/Article.jsp?a_no=10472&col_no=99&dir=200608, accessed 12 January 2007. Also see www.ipr.gov.cn/ipr/en/info/Article.jsp?a_no=8861&col_no=99&dir=200607, accessed 19 December 2006 and http://english.ipr.gov.cn/ipr/en/info/Article.jsp?a_no=3004&col_no=893&dir=200604, accessed 19 December 2006.

97. See generally, *ICC Development (International) Ltd.* v. *Arvee Enterprises and Anr.* [2003 (26) PTC 245 (Del)] and *ICC Development (International) Ltd.* v. *Ever Green Service Station* 2003 (26) PTC 228 (Del) discussed in detail in chapters 2 and 3.

98. In *ICC Development (International) Ltd.* v. *Arvee Enterprises and Anr.* [2003 (26) PTC 245 (Del)], discussed in detail in in chapters 2 and 3, the plaintiff argued by focusing on passing off action. In *ICC Development (International) Ltd.* v. *Ever Green Service Station* [2003 (26) PTC 228 (Del)], the plaintiff relied on both copyright infringements as well as passing off. In this case, the Court rejected the argument on passing off, but upheld the argument of copyright infringement as there was direct infringement. The third one was settled out of Court.

99. See *ICC Development (International) Ltd.* v. *Arvee Enterprises and Anr.* 2003 (26) PTC 245 (Del), Para 10.

100. Ibid.

101. For example, see the media attention given to the ambush marketing related dispute between Reliance Telecom and Hutch Telecom over the advertisements figuring Sachin Tendulkar during the ICC Cricket World Cup in 2007. Hutch was one of the official sponsors. Despite the strong anti-ambush marketing efforts from the side of ICC, Sachin Tendulkar endorsed the advertisements of Reliance Telecommunications during the event. Hutch has taken the matter to ICC and in all probabilities ICC may have to pay back at least some part of the sponsorship amount to Hutch for its failure in maintaining the exclusivity of sponsorship. The Indian media, especially the financial magazines and newspapers have been following up this dispute curiously. Although in a context entirely different from that of sponsorship and events, the Indian media made the term 'ambush marketing' quite popular when it highlighted a recent advertisement campaign of Kingfisher Airlines, one of the recent entrants and major players in the Indian domestic aviation sector. As part of a brand-refreshing programme, Jet Airways, another major player in the Indian aviation sector, had earlier issued a series of advertisements with the caption 'We have changed' in various media, including advertisement hoardings. But capitalizing on the same, Kingfisher Airlines posted an advertisement hoarding with the caption 'We Made Them Change' against Jet's hoarding with the caption 'We Have

Changed'. The photograph of these hoardings standing side by side was circulated throughout the world by the Indian media with the caption 'Ambush Marketing' and it has really helped the term 'ambush marketing' reach a wider audience.

5

Boundaries of Anti-Ambush Marketing
The Role of Constitutional and Competition Law

While our discussion in chapter 3 on the appropriateness of traditional legal measures in fighting ambush marketing exposed their serious limitations in combating sophisticated ambush marketing methods, chapter 4 pondered the contemporary approach of the use of event-specific legislation in countering ambush marketing. Chapter 4 also elucidated the acceptance of event-specific regulations from both the developing countries and the developed countries, irrespective of their divergent economic and social conditions. Though event-specific legislation has been successful to a great extent in threatening the ambush marketers, it has brought with it some serious public concerns also.

One of the most important arguments against the event-specific legislation is that it places unnecessary and unjustifiable restrictions on symbols and words in public domain. For example, we saw the Sydney 2000 Games Act placing restrictions on common words like 'Games City', 'Sydney 2000', 'Bronze', 'Games', 'Gold', 'Green and Gold', 'Medals', 'Millennium', 'Silver', 'Spirit', 'Sponsor', 'Summer', 'Sydney', 'Two Thousand', '2000', 'Olympian', 'Olympics', etc. It also placed restrictions on many common phrases like 'Share the Spirit', 'Summer Games', 'Team Millennium'. Majority of them are words which the public use unreservedly. Where the symbol or words are widespread, the restrictions on such symbols or words are expected to invite serious apprehensions among the people. For example, if a former medal winner like P.T. Usha promoted an athletic school during the Sydney Olympics with brochures describing her as a 'Gold Olympian' and if it was shown that such usage suggested her association with the 2000 Games, she would have been in breach of the provisions of Sydney 2000 Games Act. If strictly enforced, most of these event-specific legislation would limit the freedom of individual athletes to exploit their successes. It would be an injustice to the athletes and their personal sponsors if they are prevented from cashing in on their glory at the moment of their greatest achievements and marketability.[1] Another commonly heard argument is that these event-specific legislation will result in deviation of the basic objective of events like Olympics, which was to foster athletes and sports.

The imputation of criminal liability over ambush marketing practices, as seen in the London Olympics Act, is also a debatable issue. There is a considerable segment of public who prefers to view ambush marketing as just a creative form of advertisement which feeds on the unnoticed spaces in the organizing of an event and according to them the question of criminal liability is totally unjustifiable. Also consider the example of the effect of event-specific legislation on the right of people to choose consumer products of their choice. When an event organizer forces a genuine spectator to drop at the event entrance a non-sponsor's cola bottle or a T-shirt with the logo of a non-sponsor, serious questions about personal liberty and consumer choice arise.

This chapter pursues some of the arguments levelled against these event-specific statutes. This will be done mainly by examining the incidental effects of these statutes on the freedom of speech and expression guaranteed under the Constitution. This examination of Constitutional validity of the restrictions on advertisements in the first part of this chapter necessitates a discussion as to whether advertisements can be considered as 'commercial speech' and if so, whether the ambush marketing advertisements are within the purview of that protection. The second part of this chapter focuses on the issue from a completely different perspective. This part attempts to analyse the areas of interface of anti-ambush marketing efforts with competition law. The possibility of event-specific legislation in the creation of an anti-competitive atmosphere is a serious issue to be analysed in this context. This part will also examine the question of whether an abuse of a dominant position is happening blatantly in the name of anti-ambush marketing efforts.

CONSTITUTIONAL VALIDITY OF RESTRICTIONS ON ADVERTISEMENTS

Freedom of speech and expression is one of the most important fundamental right present in Constitutions across the world. For example, in India, Article 19 (1)(a) of the Constitution assures freedom of speech and expression. Whether the advertisements come within the literal terms of this broad protection was examined in detail by the Indian judiciary in many instances. One of the landmark Indian cases in this regard was *Tata Press Ltd.* v. *Mahanagar Telephone Nigam Limited.*[2] Even though the facts of this case are irrelevant to our discussion on ambush marketing, we see that the core issue to be determined here also was whether a simple 'commercial advertisement' is something within the concept of 'freedom of speech and expression' guaranteed under Article 19(1)(a) of the Constitution of India.[3]

The main argument of the Counsel for the Appellant in this case was that 'commercial speech' is protected under Article 19(1)(a) read with Article 19(2) of the Constitution and the defendant tried to rebut this by arguing that a purely commercial advertisement is meant for furtherance of trade or commerce and as such is outside the concept of freedom of speech and expression. In this landmark case, the Court was of the view that 'commercial speech' cannot be denied the protection under Article 19(1)(a) of the Constitution merely on the ground that the same was issued by businessmen.[4] In this case we can see the Court moving even to the extent of referring to advertising as the cornerstone of an economic system and as the life blood of free media.[5]

According to the Court, advertisement as a 'commercial speech' had two facets.[6] The advertisement was a commercial transaction as well as a mode for dissemination of information regarding the product advertised. The Court considered the fact that the public benefited from the information made available through advertisements. The Court pointed out that in a democratic economy, free flow of commercial information is indispensable and there cannot be honest and economical marketing by the public at large, without being educated by the information disseminated through advertisements.[7]

It is interesting to see the observation of the Supreme Court in this case that the economic system in a democracy would be handicapped without there being freedom of 'commercial speech'.[8] In the light of these observations the Court came to the conclusion that the public at large has a right to receive 'commercial speech' and Article (19)(1)(a) guarantees not only the freedom of speech and expression, but also protects the rights of an individual to listen, read, and receive the said speech.[9] This final observation of the Court is of vital value in invoking our thoughts on the constitutionality of restrictions imposed through event-specific legislation, as event-specific legislation is wiping out a substantial number of advertisements which the public would have received in the absence of restrictions through event-specific legislation.

The importance of advertisements was highlighted by the Supreme Court once again in *Hindustan Times* v. *State of UP*.[10] In this case we can see the Court preventing the state from acting arbitrarily in a manner which directly or indirectly affects the advertisements.[11] A similar approach can be seen in *Sakal Papers (P) Ltd.* v. *Union of India* also.[12] In this case we can see the Court taking a view that the restrictions on the advertising spaces in a newspaper through a law would be a direct interference with the right of freedom of speech and expression guaranteed under Article 19(1) (a).[13]

The US Courts also adopt a similar approach with regard to advertisements. By virtue of the first amendment rights we see that commercial speech, unrelated to any illegal activity, is given full protection in US. When we look at the history of commercial speech protection in the US, we see that the Courts were initially of the view that 'commercial speech' was absolutely unworthy of protection.[14] The Courts employed a balancing test to determine whether the speech contained material of sufficient public interest in such that the benefits of its free circulation outweighed the state's police power interest in suppression.[15] But later we can see the Courts shifting to a position that truthful and non-misleading commercial speech is entitled to undiluted first amendment protection.[16]

This shift in the approach of American Judiciary was from the time of the decision of the Court in *Virginia State Board of Pharmacy* v. *Virginia Citizens Consumer Council, Inc.*[17] Rejecting the views that existed before, the US Supreme Court took a radical view that society may have a strong interest in the free flow of commercial information and pointed out that even if an individual advertisement is entirely 'commercial', it may be of general public interest.[18] The Court further explained this argument by pointing out that even if the advertisements were tasteless and excessive, they would nonetheless disseminate information as to who is producing and selling what product, for what reason, and at what price. The Court was of the view that as long as we preserve a predominantly free enterprise economy, the allocation of resources in a large measure will be made through numerous private economic decisions and it is a matter of public interest that those decisions, in the aggregate, be intelligent and well informed. To this end, the Court considered the free flow of commercial information as indispensable.[19] Thus the case marked a turning point in the history of protection of advertisements and later this approach was seen in cases like *Bates* v. *State Bar of Arizona* also.[20]

Another US case worth mentioning in the context of our discussion on constitutionality of restrictions imposed through event-specific legislation is *Central Hudson Gas & Electric Corporation* v. *Public Service Commission of New York*.[21] In this case, the constitutionality of a regulation made by the Public Service Commission of the State of New York, banning all advertisements that promote the use of electricity was questioned. In this case the Court was of the view that even where advertising communicates only an incomplete version of the relevant facts, the First Amendment will presume that some accurate information is better than no information at all.[22] The court reasoned by showing that First Amendment's concern for commercial speech is based on the informational function of advertising.[23] But at the same time it is of importance for us to see the observation of the Court that the government may ban forms of communication which are more likely to deceive the public than to inform it and also when the commercial speech is related to an illegal activity.[24]

In this case the Court put forward a four-part analysis to help in determining whether restrictions on commercial speech can be allowed.[25] The first step is to determine whether the expression is protected by the First Amendment. For commercial speech to come within that provision it must be concerned with a lawful activity and not be misleading. In the second step, the question to be answered is whether the asserted governmental interest is substantial. If both inquiries yield positive answers, the third question of whether the regulation directly advances the governmental interest asserted, has to be asked. Finally, it has to be ensured that it is not more extensive than is necessary to serve that interest.[26] This test, which is commonly referred to as the Central Hudson Test has played a major role in protecting the interests of advertisers in US.

The analysis of the question of protection of advertisements as commercial speech in these two jurisdictions indubitably takes us to the conclusion that advertisements receive protection as 'commercial speech'. Now the second question comes into play. The second question is whether the type of advertisements which the ambush marketers engage in comes within the purview of that protection.

Though almost all jurisdictions like those in India and the US protect 'commercial speech', they also place reasonable restrictions on such freedoms. For example, when we look at the Indian position, we see that the Indian Constitution, through Article 19(2), lays down certain restrictions which can be imposed on the fundamental rights guaranteed under Article 19(1) (a) of the Constitution. Even though 'commercial speech' is protected in India, a 'commercial speech' which is deceptive, unfair, misleading, and untruthful would be hit by Article 19(2) of the Constitution and can be regulated/prohibited by the State.[27]

A similar approach can be seen in the US also. Although the United States' jurisprudence has historically recognized commercial speech as valuable, it does not extend such protection to false advertisements.[28] While expanding the ambit of commercial speech protection, the US also ensured a balance by permitting reasonable restrictions under certain circumstances.[29] In cases like *Bates* v. *State Bar of Arizona*[30] and *Central Hudson Gas & Electric Corporation* v. *Public Service Commission of New York*[31] we can see the courts repeatedly stressing the point that the government can ban forms of communication which are likely to deceive the public, than to inform them.[32] In *Bates* v. *State Bar of Arizona* it was explicitly held that advertisements, if false, deceptive, or misleading, would continue to be restrained and that, as with other varieties of speech, such advertisements could be made subject to reasonable restrictions on the time, place, and manner of such advertising.[33] The state can also regulate commercial speech relating to illegal activities.[34]

The ambush marketing advertisements are mainly aimed at deceiving or misleading the public rather than conveying some information to the public. The attempt of the ambush marketer is to mislead the people to believe that he is associated with the event and not to convey any true information. If we are to take the example of New Zealand Telecom advertisement 'With Telecom mobile you can take your own phone to the Olympics' in the factual contexts discussed in chapter 2, we find that the intention of the advertisement was to mislead the viewers by creating a false impression that it was associated with the Olympics, rather than conveying the information about the possibility of use of that telecom service at the event venue.[35] Or take the example of advertisements offering tickets to events as prizes in some contests. What we find in such advertisements also are attempts to capitalize on the goodwill of an event and to use the advertisements for misleading the viewers regarding the relationship of advertiser with the event organizer, who owns such goodwill.

Since misleading and false advertisements have been specifically taken out of the purview of commercial speech protection, the ambush marketers cannot plead for commercial speech protection. There is no reason for the limitations over commercial speech protection not to apply to ambush marketing advertisements. But if the ambush marketing company can prove through proper evidence that it was merely conveying some information through the advertisements, it may escape liability. But in the context of ambush marketing it is highly unlikely on the part of Courts to accept such arguments.

The inevitable result of bringing the ambush marketing advertisements outside the purview of protection of commercial free speech is that a legislation aimed at combating ambushing will not be considered as unconstitutional on the ground of being violative of commercial speech protection. Hence, most of the event-specific legislation including the Sydney 2000 Games (Indicia and Images) Protection Act 1996 and the London Olympic Games and Paralympic Games Act 2006 is likely to overcome constitutionality challenges on the ground of restrictions on freedom of speech and expression.

ANTI-AMBUSH MARKETING MEASURES AND COMPETITION LAW

Another area of law that has got certain significant interfaces with ambush marketing related restrictions is competition law. The primary objective of competition law is to ensure competition without undermining the interests of consumers in a market economy.[36] In the pursuit of maximization of profits in a free market, traders often engage in anti-competitive practices and a competition authority may have to interfere many a times to assure fair competition.[37] Competition law assumes greater significance at this juncture as recent years witnessed the transformation of many national economies from regulated to market based economies. Though different schools of thought seem to differ on the nature and extent to which competition laws are to be made applicable, the fundamental aim of all of them is to ensure fair play in a market driven economic system without bypassing the concerns of the consumer.[38]

The growth of competition law owes much to the dynamics in the US, the cradle of market economy. The two landmark legislation from US, the Sherman Act of 1890 and the Clayton Act of 1914, have played an instrumental role in the evolution of competition jurisprudence across the world. In Europe, the Treaty of Rome in 1957, which established the European Economic Community, provided the key provisions for assuring competition.[39] In India, the legislation currently dealing with competition related issues is Competition Act of 2002.[40] Our discussion here will primarily be from the point of view of the Indian Competition law and policy, at times reinforced by the US and EC competition jurisprudence.

The increasing significance of competition law across the world has also resulted in different kinds of discordance between competition law and other legislation. The frequent friction between competition law and legislation aimed at protecting intellectual property rights is a classic example in this regard. While competition law attempts to ensure competition in the market-place by giving fair chance to everyone to compete, intellectual property rights tries to forestall others from interfering in the rights of intellectual property owners.[41] Inspite of the differences in approaches, a substantial segment of scholars argue that intellectual property rights and competition law should be seen as working together in a complementary way to the ultimate goal of consumer welfare, though they do travel in conflicting ways at certain contexts.[42] The same friction and attraction can also be seen in the case of anti-ambush marketing measures, including event-specific legislation, which try to protect the intellectual property rights associated with an event.

It is pertinent to ask why the competition authorities intercede in the organizing of events related to sports and games which have many unique characteristics of its own and does not fall under the laws of market per se. The answer for this question, as one could gauge from the decisions and discussions from various jurisdictions like US and EC lies in the increasing economic activities generated by sports related events. As explained in chapter 1, sports have an intricate connection with contemporary economic and marketing strategies and nowadays it is almost considered as an economic activity by itself. The moment event organizers engage in economic activities, the competition authorities will receive the locus standi to oversee them to ensure fair competition and to protect the interests of consumers.[43] As many provisions of the event-specific legislation against ambush marketing contain elements of imposed exclusivity, they have to pass through the tests laid down by competition laws to assure fair competition in the market.

But it is a fact that most of the cases and discussions that have come up on the subject so far have focused primarily on the exclusive broadcasting rights of events and the rights of players to move from one organization to another.[44] Sponsorship and exclusive supply of goods were the other subjects that have come under scrutiny in the European forum. Even such discussions on the exclusive supply of goods have been limited to restrictions in the supply of sports goods for the event.

The discussion on the interface of competition law with anti-ambush marketing measures can broadly focus on two types of issues—those relating to the restrictions on advertisements and those relating to the restrictions on products and services in and near the venue. According to the scholars supporting the first issue, when advertisement acts as a medium of building trust, familiarity, and brand royalty and when they have the potential to establish and maintain a monopoly market, the competition law and policy should play a crucial role to ensure level playing field for all competitors in the market.[45] They consider the insistence of a sponsor to prevent rivals' advertisement during the broadcasting of an event as a strategy to avoid competition interface in their favour.[46] This argument is reinforced by the fact that most of the event organizers prefer long term contracts and thereby want to effectively prevent others from associating themselves with the event.[47] This provides scope for an argument that the restrictions on advertisement through an event-specific legislation encourage anti-competitive behaviour. In furtherance of the second issue, i.e, restrictions on the consumer choice over products and services in and near the venue, it may be argued that such restrictions necessarily lead to the creation of an anticompetitive market in and near the venue. As the extent of consequences on market is apparently different in both the issues, we may have to consider them slightly more in detail.

It is a fact that most of these arguments for the intervention of competition authorities in advertisement related issues are on the same logical path of arguments questioning the constitutional validity of event-specific legislation on the ground of restrictions on freedom of speech and expression, discussed in detail in the earlier part of this chapter. But even the pro-competition bloc would appreciate the restrictions which seem reasonable in the light of the economic investments made by the sponsors and in the necessity of defending the sponsorship value of an event. It is also essential not to overlook the very fact that most of the sponsorship contracts are awarded through a process of open bidding. Moreover, competition law by itself permits restrictions on false and misleading advertisements.[48] As seen in the preceding chapters, the ambush marketing advertisements are those which create a misleading association with a sponsored event. If ambush marketing advertisements are considered as misleading advertisements, the regulations on such advertisements shall not fall within the purview of competition law. Hence, the focus of our discussion in this part will be on the possible conflict of competition law with the restrictions on consumer choice over the goods and services of non-sponsors in and near an event venue. This focused and narrowed down approach is also based on the evidence of public outcry against such restrictions on consumer choice during most of the recent events, including the FIFA World Cup 2006 and the ICC Cricket World Cup 2007.

Across the jurisdictions, there are three common situations wherein competition laws interfere. Firstly, to prevent anti-competitive agreements having the objective of preventing, restricting, or distorting competition. The second is to prevent the abuse of a dominant position in a market. The third is the regulation of anti-competitive mergers and acquisitions.[49] For our discussion on the interface of anti-ambush marketing measures with competition law, the first two, i.e., anti-competitive agreements and abuse of a dominant position are the relevant ones. So our discussion can move further by seeking answers to two questions: Firstly, whether the event-specific legislation and other regulations against ambush marketing are anti-competitive in nature.[50] Secondly, whether the anti-ambush marketing measures and legislations pave way for the abuse of a dominant position by the event organizers. This discussion assumes specific significance as even the TRIPS Agreement recognize the right and duty of the member countries to control anti-competitive practices in contractual licenses.[51]

Anti-competitive Nature of Anti-Ambush Marketing Efforts

Competition law prohibits agreements, decisions, and practices that are considered as anti-competitive.[52] The agreements that have an anti-competitive nature are consequently treated as void under the present competition law.[53] For analysing whether the event-specific legislation and contracts against ambush marketing are in effect anti-competitive in nature, we need to understand what kind of agreements are considered as anti-competitive by the current competition regime. The concept of 'agreement' is used in a very broad sense under the Competition Act, so as to include even informal understandings or concerted actions between two persons or enterprises or associations of enterprises or persons.[54]

As pointed out in the previous chapter, the ambush marketing related restrictions are brought in by the organizing bodies and the host governments. As the concept of 'person' too is accorded a very broad definition under the present Competition Act, the organizing committees come within the meaning of the term 'person' and hence subject to the scrutiny of competition law. As only the sovereign functions of a government are exempted from the scrutiny of competition law, the acts of a government during the organizing of an event may also come within the scrutiny of the competition authorities.[55]

As the manoeuvres of an organizing committee or the government during the organizing of an event may become a subject for scrutiny before the competition authorities, we may move further to explore the kinds of acts prohibited under competition law. In the broader sense, competition law prohibits all agreements in the production, supply, distribution, storage, acquisition, and control of goods or services that cause or are likely to cause an adverse effect on competition.[56] In order to ascertain the effect on competition, the courts and the competition authorities have to first identify the market where competition has been allegedly adversely affected.[57] The market to be taken into consideration, in a technical sense, is known as relevant market, which in turn is based on determination of relevant product market and relevant geographic market.[58] Relevant geographic market is the market comprising a particular geographical area in which the conditions of competition for supply of goods or provision of services, or demand for goods or services are distinctly homogenous and can be apparently distinguished from the conditions prevailing in the neighbouring areas.[59] For instance, while determining the legality of anti-ambush marketing restrictions on the flow of goods and services in and near the venue during an event like the FIFA world cup, we would consider the stadium and its surroundings as the relevant geographical market. This delineation is made on the bare fact that the conditions of marketing prevailing inside the stadium and that outside are significantly different. On the other hand, relevant product market is determined by looking at all the products or services that are considered by a consumer as interchangeable or substitutable.[60] For example in the soft drinks market, Coke and Pepsi might be considered as interchangeable products. Or in the case of food services, Pizza Hut and Dominos might be considered as business houses with interchangeable food services.[61]

The next step is the determination of the adverse effect on competition. To put it more precisely, the task is to find whether the arrangement or understanding or action in concert is of such a nature that it can significantly reduce the level of existing competition. In cases wherein the existing competition is totally and explicitly eliminated, it is presumed that there is an adverse effect on competition, calling no further proofs to ascertain the negative consequence.[62] When one of the producers is denied market access in the name of anti-ambush marketing measures, the question of adverse effect on competition certainly arises. In a landmark judgement, the Indian Supreme Court detailed the factors to be taken into consideration while determining the issue of 'effect on competition'.[63] They are, (1) facts peculiar to the business to which the restraint is applied, (2) the conditions before and after the imposition of restraint, and (3) nature of restraint and its actual and probable effects. When the anti-ambush marketing measures are limited to restrictions relating to advertisement, they pass the test. But when these measures are extended to limit the choice of consumers regarding the products or services within or near the venue, it would come under the scanner of competition authorities. While determining the first issue, i.e., the facts peculiar to the business to which the restraint is applied, the competition authorities have to take into consideration, along with other factors, the duration of the event and the marketing potential in and near the venue. The second factor pointed out by the Supreme Court was the difference in condition before and after the imposition of restraint. This factor may not go in favour of the event organizers as the conditions before and after the proposed restrictions would be totally different. Before imposing restrictions, there is a free flow of goods and services. But once the ambush marketing related restrictions are placed, only the sponsor's goods or service can enter the venue. So the conditions before and after the restraint are entirely different. The third factor to be taken into consideration is the nature of the restraint and its actual and probable effect. The nature of restraint in the situations mentioned here is total restraint and its consequent effect would be a complete barrier to a potential market. It is certain that the restriction on sale of goods other than that of an official sponsor will severely limit the consumer choice. Even if a person does not like the taste of Pepsi, he may have to consume it during an event to quell his thirst, if Pepsi is the official sponsor and Coke is restrained from selling its products in and near the venue. It can be recalled that in the recently held ICC Cricket World Cup 2007 and FIFA World Cup 2006, the organizers had directed the spectators arriving at the venue to leave the bottles of non-sponsors, as a precondition for gaining entry into the venue.

But these factors needs to be juxtaposed with some of the specific and significant exceptions provided under competition law, which include reasonable measures adopted by owners of intellectual property rights to protect the rights conferred under respective intellectual property statutes.[64] As anti-ambush marketing efforts are basically directed towards the protection of intellectual property rights associated with the organizing of an event, the event organizers may take shelter under this provision to a great extent to save themselves from the clutches of competition law. But an in-depth analysis of this provision, which saves the reasonable measures adopted by owners of intellectual property rights, shows some important qualifying limitations in the Indian context. The most important limitation is that these exceptions for intellectual property rights are corresponding to the statutes specifically mentioned under Sec. 3 (5) of the Indian Competition Act. Hence, Sec. 3 (5) may first have to be amended to include an event-specific legislation, if it is to get the privilege of exception under the Competition Act.[65] The second important limitation towards the application of this exception provision is that the owner of an intellectual property right can impose only those reasonable conditions that are necessary towards protecting any of the rights conferred on him/her.[66] Any measure that travels beyond the ambit of 'reasonableness' shall not have the protection of this exception clause and this was recognized even under the TRIPS Agreement.[67] Whether the ambush marketing related restrictions on the flow of products and services in and near the venue are reasonable may be answered in the negative, when we take into consideration the serious impacts made by those restrictions.

Before giving a final ruling on the issue of effect on competition, the competition authorities will also have to see whether the restrictions have any positive results like accrual of benefits to consumers and improvements in production or distribution of goods or provision of services. The result on promotion of technical, scientific, and economic development by means of production or distribution of goods or provision of services too have to be taken into consideration.[68] It is apparent that restrictions on the choice of foods or drinks in and near the location of the event in the name of ambush marketing related measures might not necessarily lead to an accrual of benefits to consumers. On the other hand, in most of the cases, the exclusive service providers are seen charging the goods above the normal market prices, taking undue advantage of the monopoly conferred. The second factor is the question of improvement in production or distribution of goods or provision of services. The restriction on choice of foods or drinks by conferring the rights to a single player would not improve the efficiency in either production or distribution. Thus, the first two factors may not go in favour of the event organizers. But the direction of leniency of the third factor may go in favour of the event organizers, if the event organizers are able to prove before the Competition Authority that the restrictions have resulted in the promotion of technical, scientific, and economic development. They may prove it by explaining the importance of exclusivity to attract sponsorships and the necessity of sponsorships for the organizing of major events. Taking into consideration all these aspects, the Competition Authorities may either permit to maintain the status quo or direct the event organizers to make necessary changes. The chances are more for a direction to the event organizers to correct themselves in such a way as to protect the interests of consumers and the public at large.

Ambush Marketing Related Restrictions and the Question of Abuse of a Dominant Position by Event Organizers

It may be meaningful to analyse the interface of competition law with anti-ambush marketing efforts also from a totally different dimension—abuse of a dominant position by the event organizers. It is true that the conduct of many of the prominent sports event organizers in the recent past has raised weighty doubts as to whether abuse of a dominant position of event organizers, within the meaning of competition law, is taking place blatantly during the organizing of many of the major events. This is happening even when Competition laws give wide power to the competition authorities to interfere in cases where abuse of dominant position occurrs.[69]

We can examine this dimension of the problem by taking the ICC Cricket World Cup as an example scenario.[70] In order to prevent ambush marketing ICC usually takes a number of measures in and near the venue. This also includes a restriction on carrying consumable drinks and foods manufactured by non-sponsors to the venue.[71] Spectators arriving at an event venue are often asked to leave the non-sponsor's bottle at the gate and many volunteers and staff are posted at the gateways to monitor this. These intrusive restrictions imposed by the event organizers have caused public anger in most of the recent events and the legality of such acts would really be an important issue to be examined also from the angle of abuse of a dominant position by event organizers. This is particularly important for countries like China and India that are expected to host some major events in the near future.

In order to scrutinize the occurrence of abuse of a dominant position, the Courts generally search for three elements even though depending on the jurisdiction, the content and application of these elements may differ.[72] The first step is establishing the existence of a dominant position. Second, is to identify the practices that are harmful to competition and the third is to find out the overall effects in the relevant market.

The dominant position of a firm is something to be determined on the basis of facts pertaining to each case. According to Competition law, the elements that constitute a dominant position are a position of strength, being enjoyed in a relevant market (both product and geographical markets), which enables it to 'operate independently of competitive forces in the relevant market' or affect its competitors or consumers or relevant market in its favour.[73] If we take the example of ICC Cricket World Cup, we can see that ICC satisfies all the three criteria in India. ICC has a position of strength in the organizing of cricket tournaments and so far no association of such strength and reputation has come up in the organizing of cricket related events. This also shows its position in the relevant sports related market in India. It is also in a position to disregard market forces and impose trading conditions, which is something quite evident from the high sponsorship fees imposed by ICC on sponsors.[74] But it is the question of ability of an event organizer to 'affect the consumer', which substantially proves the dominant position of event organizers like ICC and also the importance of our examination of the issue from the slightly radical view of abuse of dominant position by event organizers.

Certain scholars believe that a firm's dominant position in a relevant market can also be identified by an assessment of its market share and the entry conditions.[75] With respect to our previously mentioned example of cricket competitions, this criterion may also get satisfied as ICC presently has a monopoly in the area of organizing of cricket competitions. One of the main reasons behind the entry barriers to other players in this area is the exclusionary contractual provisions and tying requirements that ICC has made with regional cricket organizations.[76] It is a fact that it is not easy for another international organization to come up with organizing of international cricket tournaments in this scenario. Another supportive method of identification of a dominant position is the direct evidence in terms of abnormally high profits or prices.[77] But it needs to be remembered at this point that enjoying a dominant position by itself is not against Competition law, which is concerned only with the abuse of such a dominant position.[78] So the identification of practices that are harmful to competition comes as the next step.

Before moving to the identification of such practices that are harmful to competition, an important clarification regarding the focus of such search needs to be specifically mentioned here. The question of 'abuse of dominant position' by the event organizers in the context of anti-ambush marketing efforts needs to be analysed from the angle of elimination of competition, rather than elimination of competitors, even though competition law considers both with equal significance. The significance of the difference in approach lies in the fact that in most cases an event organizer is not engaged in abusive practices that eliminates its competitors, but in eliminating competition in a market place. For an event organizer, a competitor is another event organizer. An example of an abusive practice of eliminating competitors can be seen in the exclusionary contracts BCCI has made with players through its dominant position, which in effect prevents its players from joining rival organizations like Indian Cricket League. Such actions threaten even the chances of formation of a good sports organization and recently the MRTP Commission of India has initiated an enquiry against BCCI on similar counts. But for our discussion on the question of abuse of a dominant position in the context of ambush marketing related measures, our focus of search will be on abusive practice by the event organizers in the name of anti-ambush marketing efforts that ultimately result in the elimination of competition in a market place. Examples are plenty in this regard and an event organizer's conduct in imposing rigorous anti-ambush marketing efforts like preventing the entry of non-sponsor's product within and near the venue is one of the best examples of eliminating or lessening competition in a relevant market. The public outcry against such severe restrictions in most of the recent events adds more importance to this focus of discussion.

Three economic standards that are useful in analysing the abuse of a dominant position are 'sacrifice test', 'efficient competitor test', and 'consumer harm test'.[79] According to the 'sacrifice test', any behavior of a dominant firm that would be profitable, or makes business sense, but has a tendency to eliminate or lessen competition amounts to abuse. Under this test, the intention to eliminate or lessen competition is the most important factor. In our illustrated example of excluding non-sponsors product or service within and near the event venue, the intention to lessen or eliminate competition is clearly visible and hence may qualify as abuse of dominant position under the 'sacrifice test'. According to the 'as efficient competitor test', only those practices which eliminates an equally efficient rival would be considered as an exclusionary abuse. In our illustrated example of ICC Cricket World Cup, the probability of excluding an equally efficient competitor exists in most of the situations. Coke and Pepsi can be considered as equally efficient competitors. Through the intervention of the event organizers, one of the efficient competitors is getting eliminated from the relevant market and hence may be considered as abuse of a dominant position under this test. The last one, 'consumer harm test', says that exclusion of rivals whose presence enhances consumer welfare shall be an abuse of dominant position.

The effect of the abusive practices of event organizers is harm to competition in the relevant market. The elimination of a product from an event venue is against consumer welfare as it reduces his choice and also increases the possibility of exorbitant prices. Even though the event organizers may not be preventing a rival event organizer through its dominant position, it is certainly paving the way for preventing a non-sponsor and thereby facilitating harm to competition.

Certain practices that are considered specifically as abuse of a dominant position under the Indian Competition law are directly or indirectly imposing unfair or discriminatory trading conditions in the supply of goods or services, unfair or discriminatory prices in the supply of goods or services including charging predatory prices, limiting or restricting the supply of goods or services or a market for goods or services or limiting technical or scientific development relating to goods or services, denial of market access, imposing on other contracting parties obligations not related to the basic contract with them, and using an existing dominant position in one market to gain entry into another market or to protect the other market.[80]

Among these specifically illustrated practices of abuse of a dominant position, at least two often figures through the anti-ambush marketing related restrictions imposed by event organizers. They are denial of market access and limiting or restricting the supply of goods or services. In situations of denial of market access, the competition authorities will have to take into consideration the market power of the firm, rationale behind the refusal and the resulting competitive harm.[81] So in a typical situation of denial of market access to Coke or Pepsi during a cricket world cup organized by ICC, instead of resorting unilinear conclusions, one has to take stock of all these three factors before forming a conclusive judgment. The economic power of ICC is an apparent and undisputed reality. But while scrutinizing the economic rationale behind the denial of market access, the necessity for exclusivity to attract sponsorships comes into the forefront of contemplation. Event organizers may make a very strong argument at this point that only exclusivity can bring in sponsorships and without sponsorships the organizing of mega events would not be possible at all, given the magnitude of the expenses involved. Though in different contexts, this argument for the need for exclusivity can be seen in most cases of interface of competition law with intellectual property rights and the US and EC has taken divergent views in this regard.[82] The event organizers may also foreground the fact that the sponsorship contracts are finalized after an open bidding process. Another possible argument may be that most of the event organizers are not engaged in profit making and all the money they are earning is spent on protecting the long term interests of the game. The competition authorities should take a careful approach on these issues before either justifying or rejecting the economic rationale behind anti-ambush marketing strategies imposed by the event organizer. As far as the third question of competition harm is concerned, it is apparent that unjustifiable ambush marketing related restrictions imposed by an event organizer predictably results in restricting competition and thereby consumer choice too. Hence, we arrive at the conclusion that the competition authorities may successfully invoke the provisions of competition law relating to abuse of dominant position to restrain the event organizers from abusing their dominant position to bring in unjustifiable anti-ambush marketing measures which harm competition. So far no case law has come up on these issues before any of the competition authorities and the Indian Competition Commission may take a good initiative in this regard as and when the Indian Parliament proposes an event-specific anti-ambush marketing legislation. Recent trends in Competition law are a positive signal in this regard.[83]

The analysis of the legality of anti ambush marketing efforts from the perspective of Constitutional law and Competition law in this chapter shows that, in the name of combating ambush marketing, if the event-specific legislation or the event organizers resort to bringing in unjustifiable restrictions that harm public interests, they are likely to be defeated in court. At least the conduct of some of the event organizers shows the probability of interesting legal battles in this regard. We may get a clear demarcation of the legally justifiable boundaries of the anti-ambush marketing efforts as and when such matters come up before the courts and competition authorities.

NOTES

1. See Graeme Orr, 507–8.
2. *Tata Press Ltd.* v. *Mahanagar Telephone Nigam Limited* AIR 1995 SC 2438. This case came as an Appeal from the judgment of the Bombay High Court which decreed that Mahanagar Telephone Nigam Limited (MTNL) and the Union of India alone had the right to print/publish the list of telephone subscribers and that the same cannot be printed or published by any other person without express permission from the company or Union of India. The High Court judgment had restrained the Tata Press Limited from printing, publishing and circulating the compilation which is commonly referred to as 'Tata Press Yellow Pages'. By way of Special Leave, the Tata Press appealed to the Supreme Court.
3. AIR 1995 SC 2438, para 11.
4. Ibid., at para 21.
5. Ibid., at para 22.
6. Ibid., at para 25.

7. Ibid.

8. Ibid.

9. The Court substantiated this view by citing the example of advertisements of life saving drugs. It was observed by the Court that an advertisement giving information regarding a life saving drug was of much more importance to the general public than to the advertiser who may be having a purely trade consideration. See AIR 1995 SC 2438, para 26. In this case, the Court finally permitted Tata Yellow Pages to continue the publication of yellow pages. But at the same it also held that it cannot publish any "list of telephone subscribers" without the permission of the telegraph authority. (para 32).

10. *Hindustan Times* v. *State of UP*, AIR 2003 SC 250. In this case the petitioners were challenging an order issued by the Special Secretary of the Government of Uttar Pradesh, wherein a direction had been issued to the effect that at the time of payment of bills for publication of government advertisements in newspapers having a circulation above 25,000 copies, 5 per cent of the amount, forming part of a fund for the purpose of granting pension to the working journalists, would be deducted. Here also the Court dealt with the issue of advertisements in detail. One of the main issues in this case was whether the newspapers were at liberty to not accept the advertisements made by the Government.

11. See *Hindustan Times* v. *State of UP*, AIR 2003 SC 250, para 38 and 39.

12. *Sakal Papers (P) Ltd.* v. *Union of India* AIR 1962 SC 305. In this case the petitioners who were publishing daily and weekly newspapers in Marathi named 'Sakal' from Poona challenged the constitutionality of the Newspaper (Price and Page) Act, 1956 and the Daily Newspaper (Price and Page) order, 1960. These legislations were aimed at regulating the number of pages according to the price charged and they also prescribed the number of supplements to be published and prescribed the sizes and area of advertising matter in relation to the other matters contained in a newspaper.

13. *Sakal Papers (P) Ltd.* v. *Union of India* AIR 1962 SC 305, para 37.

In this case, the Court held that this controversial legislation was unconstitutional.

14. See *Valentine* v. *Chrestensen*, 316 US 52 (1942). In this case, the respondent was the owner of a former United States Navy submarine and he was exhibiting it for profit. But when he tried to advertise it by distributing advertisement handbills in the city streets, he was told by the petitioner, who was a Police Commissioner, that his activity was violative of Sec. 318 of the Sanitary Code, which forbidded the distribution of commercial and business advertising matter in the streets. The main question in this case was whether the application of the ordinance to the respondent's activity was an unconstitutional abridgement on his freedom of speech. In this case

the Court was of the view that Constitution imposes no restrains on government with respect to purely commercial advertising.

15. For a detailed discussion, see Jonathan Weinberg, 'Constitutional Protection of Commercial Speech', 82 *Colum. L. Rev.* 720, 722 (1982).

16. Ibid.

17. *Virginia State Board of Pharmacy* v. *Virginia Citizens Consumer Council, Inc.*, 96 S. Ct. 1817 (1976). In this case, consumers of prescription drugs challenged the validity of a Virginia statute which prohibited licensed pharmacists from advertising the prices of prescription drugs.

18. 96 S. Ct. 1817, 1827.

19. Ibid.

20. *Bates* v. *State Bar of Arizona* 433 US 350 (1978). In this case, two attorneys who were licensed to practice law in Arizone made an advertisement stating that they offered 'legal services at very reasonable fees' and also listed their fees for various matters. As the advertisement was against the disciplinary rules of the Supreme Court of Arizona which prohibited Arizona lawyers from publicizing by 'commercial means', they were given one week suspension as a punishment. When they sought review of this punishment in the Supreme Court of Arizona, it was rejected. But when the matter came as appeal before the United States Supreme Court, it reversed the judgment of the Supreme Court of Arizona on the ground of violation of First Amendment rights. The Supreme Court held that the advertisement was not misleading and therefore fell within the scope of First Amendment's protection. The court was of the view that blanket suppression of advertising by attorneys would violate the free speech Clause of First Amendment.

21. *Central Hudson Gas & Electric Corporation* v. *Public Service Commission of New York* 100 S. Ct. 2343 (1982).

22. Ibid., at 2349.

23. Ibid., at 2350.

24. Ibid.

25. Ibid., at 2351.

26. Based on these four factors, the Commission's ban on promotional advertisement was held violative of First Amendment Protection.

27. See *Tata Press Ltd.* v. *Mahanagar Telephone Nigam Limited* AIR 1995 SC 2438, para 19.

28. For a detailed discussion on this aspect, see Jodie Sopher, 'Weight-Loss Advertising Too Good To Be True: Are Manufacturers Or The Media To Blame?', 22 *Cardozo Arts and Ent. L.J.* 933, 958 (2005).

29. A very good example of commercial speech restriction in US can be the case of tobacco advertisements. The FDA sought harsh advertising and promotion restrictions over tobacco and now the tobacco companies have

to adhere to many restrictions. The restrictions includes prohibition from marketing or selling products to young people, sponsoring events having a significant presence of teenagers, advertising on billboards or public transportation, using cartoon characters in advertisements, and selling clothing with logos. Similar advertising restrictions can be seen in India also.

30. *Bates* v. *State Bar of Arizona* 433 US 350 (1978).

31. *Central Hudson Gas and Electric Corporation* v. *Public Service Commission of New York* 100 S. Ct. 2343.

32. See *Central Hudson Gas and Electric Corporation* v. *Public Service Commission of New York* 100 S. Ct. 2343, 2350.

33. See *Bates* v. *State Bar of Arizona* 433 US 350, 383–4 (1978).

34. See *Central Hudson Gas and Electric Corporation* v. *Public Service Commission of New York* 100 S. Ct. 2343, 2350.

35. *The New Zealand Olympic and Commonwealth Games Association Inc.* v. *Telecom New Zealand Limited* [1996] FSR 757 (New Zealand HC).

36. This question of basic objective of competition law has been a subject matter of debate for a long time. Whether it is for protecting competitors from being kept out of the market, or to increase efficiency or to augment total welfare has been a matter of serious contention. Some experts prefer measuring welfare as consumer surplus, which is the difference between consumer's valuation of a good/service and the price s/he pays for producing it. Greater will be the surplus if the price is lower, while other factors remain unchanged. But this doesn't mean that ensuring the lowest price for products is the aim of competition law. The issue became complicated as the once held absolute polarity between consumers and sellers is getting transfigured in the contemporary market dynamics as a result of the growing participation of consumer segment in the management of companies through buying of shares, mutual funds, etc. Therefore competition law has to address this duality of concerns to ensure the overall efficiency, which is the maximization of both consumer surplus and producer surplus. It is also important to note that the concerns of competition law is neither similar nor its emphasis equal across the globe. The competition law in the United States focuses more on harm caused on the consumers and not competitors, while European competition law gives equal importance to consumers and competitors. See Valentine Korah, 'Competition Law and Intellectual Property Rights' in Vinod Dhall (ed.), *Competition Law Today—Concepts, Issues and the Law in Practice* (New Delhi: Oxford University Press, 2007), 132–3; Amit Bubna and Shubhashis Gangopadhyay, 'The Economics of Competition Law' in Vinod Dhall (ed.), *Competition Law Today—Concepts, Issues and the Law in Practice* (New Delhi: Oxford University Press, 2007), 440 and Alfred E Kahn, 'Standards for Anti trust Policy', 67 *Harv. L. Rev.* 28, 32–3, (November 1953).

37. It is pertinent here to note an observation of Adam Smith, the prophet of free market, way back in 1776 in his treatise *An Inquiry into the Nature and Causes of Wealth of Nations.* He made the interesting observation that '[P]eople of the same trade seldom meet together, even for merriment and diversion, but the conversation ends in a conspiracy against the public, or in some contrivance to raise prices. It is impossible indeed to prevent such meetings, by any law which either could be executed, or would be consistent with liberty and justice. But though the law cannot hinder people of the same trade from sometimes assembling together, it ought to do nothing to facilitate such assemblies, much less to render them necessary.' See Adam Smith, *An Inquiry into the Nature and Causes of Wealth of Nations,* Book 1, chapter X, at Part 2. The same is available online at http://www.adamsmith.org/smith/won/won-b1-c10-pt-2.html, accessed 1 August 2007.

38. The competition law and policy in US was mainly influenced by two schools of thought. The Harvard school of thought that developed the structure-conduct-performance concept in the 1950s advocated a strong interventionist role for competition authorities on the argument that market structure influences conduct, which in turn, influences performance. On the other hand, the Chicago School of thought developed in 1970s and 1980s advocated a less interventionist role for competition authorities as it considered pursuit of efficiency as the sole goal of anti-trust laws. According to them, most markets are competitive in nature and entry barriers are more imagined than real and firms are rational in their pursuit of profit maximization. These two schools of thought were described by some scholars as the double helix shaping the intellectual DNA of modern US anti trust law. The European competition law on the other hand was influenced by German ordo-liberal school of thought, which believed that competition is necessary for economic welfare and economic freedom is necessary for political freedom. This school of thought advocated the dispersal of private economic power in such a way as not to influence political power. See for a detailed discussion, Wanda Jane Rogers, 'Beyond Economic Theory: A Model for Analyzing the Antitrust Implications of Exclusive Dealing Arrangements', 45 *Duke L.J.* 1009 where the author analyses the divergent approaches of different schools of thought in the context of exclusive dealing related anti-trust cases. Also see William E. Kovacic, 'The Intellectual DNA of Modern US Competition Law for Dominant Firm Conduct: The Chicago/Harvard Double Helix', 2007 *Columbia Bus. L. Rev.* 1 (2007).

39. Articles 81 to 86 of this Treaty apply to undertakings and Articles 87 to 89 deals with aids granted by states.

40. The basic objective behind the legislation of Competition Act 2002 was to prevent practices having adverse effect on competition, to promote

and sustain competition in markets, to protect the interests of consumers and to ensure freedom of trade carried on by other participants in markets in India. See the Preamble of the Competition Act 2002. This Act was to replace the Monopolies and Restrictive Trade Practices Act, 1969, which became obsolete in many points as a result of the changes that happened in the Indian economy through the economic liberalization in 1990s.

41. While addressing the issues of friction between competition law and different types of intellectual property rights the same yardsticks shall not be used for every form of intellectual property. There are many authors who point out that the term 'intellectual property' means only a collection of disparate legal systems like patents, copyright, trade marks etc. and competition authorities should not see all of them on the same footing and should be aware of the differences in the economic rationale behind each of them while approaching competition law related issues. For example, see Ignacio De Leon, 'The Enforcement of Competition Policy on Intellectual Property and its Implications on Economic Development: The Latin American Experience', available online at http://papers.ssrn.com/sol3/papers. cfm?abstract_id=270730#PaperDownload, accessed 21 July 2007.

42. A monopoly conferred through an *ex post* intellectual property right serves as an *ex ante* incentive for necessary investment and public disclosure. The competition law on the other hand plays a vital role in ensuring that new technologies, products and services are bought, sold and licensed in a competitive environment. See Amit Bubna and Shubhashis Gangopadhyay, 'The Economics of Competition Law', 446 and U.S. Department of Justice and Federal Trade Communion, 'Antitrust Enforcement and Intellectual Property Rights: Promoting Innovation and Competition (2007)', available online at http://www.usdoj.gov/atr/public/hearings/ip/intro.pdf, accessed 18 June 2007.

43. For a detailed discussion about the European position in this regard, see Alexander Schaub, 'EC Competition Policy and its Implications for the Sports Sector', available online at http://ec.europa.eu/comm/competition/speeches/text/sp1999_019_en.pdf, accessed 10 July 2007. A similar view can be seen expressed by European Commissioner for Competition, Mario Monti, 'Competition and Sport the Rules of the Game', available online at http://europa.eu/rapid/pressReleasesAction.do?reference=SPEECH/01/84&format= HTML&aged=0&language=EN&guiLanguage=en, accessed 10 July 2007.

44. For example see *Eurovision case* (Case IV, 32.150, May 10, 2000) and *Bosman case* (Case C-415/93, *Union Royale Belge des Societes de Football ASBL* v. *Bosman*) from EC and also the landmark decision of the US Supreme Court in *Baltimore Inc.* v. *National League of Professional Base Ball Clubs (1922)*. Also see Glaucio Scremin, 'Impact of Antitrust Laws on American Professional Team Sports', available online at http://www.thesportjournal.

org/2005Journal/Vol8-No1/SCJ_04_antitrust.asp, accessed 10 July 2007 and Alexander Schaub, 'EC Competition Policy and its Implications for the Sports Sector'.

45. See John A. Fortunato, 'Reconciling Sports Sponsorship Exclusivity With Antitrust Law', 8 *Tex. Rev. Ent. and Sports L.* 33, 40–5 (Spring 2007). The author establishes this point by arguing that the exclusivity agreements commonly associated with sports sponsorship creates an opportunity for a dominant brand to promote and sell products by making subordinate brands impotent in their effort to achieve equivalent familiarity and trust. This issue will be more dominant in cases wherein extended rights like naming of the stadiums with that of sponsor is allowed. This argument is further supported by the fact of high costs involved in sponsorship contracts, which make it unreachable for most of the companies.

46. Ibid., 42–4.

47. For example, in the case of the Olympic Partnership (TOP) programme, it is seen that most of the companies have made agreements with the IOC for TOP Programme up to the 2012 Olympics. If we take the example of retail food services, we see that McDonalds is the Olympic Partner in this segment for eight years from the year 2004. See http://www.olympic. org/uk/organisation/facts/programme/profiles_uk.asp, accessed 18 June 2007. ICC and FIFA also favour such long term sponsorship contracts. For example, FIFA has recently given VISA the 'FIFA Partner' status in the financial services segment up to the year 2014. See http://www.fifa.com/aboutfifa/marketingtv/releases/newsid=540450.html#visa+becomes+fifa+partner+period+through+2014, accessed 29 June 2007.

48. See Vinod Dhall, 'Key Concepts in Competition Law' in Vinod Dhall (ed.), *Competition Law Today—Concepts, Issues and the Law in Practice* (New Delhi: Oxford University Press, 2007), 8.

49. In India, Sec. 3 of the Competition Act 2002 deals with anti-competitive agreements. Sec. 4 of this Act discusses dominant position and Sec. 5 deals with combinations.

50. The term 'other regulations' used here should be considered in a wider perspective as to include contracts with players and contracts with national associations also.

51 See Art. 40 of the TRIPS Agreement.

52 For example, see Sec. 3 of the Competition Act 2002 of India. It may be useful to mention here that in the case of anti-competitive agreements, the Commission can initiate action on its own motion or on receipt of a complaint from any person, consumer or their association, or a reference made to it by the Central Government or State Government or a statutory authority. See Sec. 19 (1) of the Competition Act 2002.

53. See Sec. 3(2) of the Competition Act 2002.

54. *According to* Sec. 2 (b) of the Competition Act, *"Agreement" includes any arrangement or understanding or action in concert,—*

(i) whether or not, such arrangement, understanding or action is formal or in writing; or

(ii) whether or not such arrangement, understanding or action is intended to be enforceable by legal proceedings. The real amplitude of this definition clause will be visible when we apply it to Sec. 3 (1) of the Competition Act which says that *No enterprise or association of enterprises or person or association of persons shall* enter into any agreement in respect of production, supply, distribution, storage, acquisition or control of goods or provision of services, which causes or is likely to cause an appreciable adverse effect on competition within India. Sec. 2 (l) and 2 (h) of Competition Act defines the terms 'person' and 'enterprise' respectively and the term 'person' is defined in a very broad manner as to include individuals, companies, firms, association of persons, registered co-operative societies, local authorities, and all artificial judicial persons. The term 'enterprise' includes a person or department of government.

55. See Sec. 2 (h) of the Competition Act 2002 of India, which defines the term 'enterprise'. In this definition clause, the sovereign functions of the Government are taken out of the purview of Competition law. The specifically included sovereign functions in this clause are those relating to atomic energy, currency, defence, and space.

56. See Sec. 3 (1) of the Competition Act 2002. *Sec. 3 (1) No enterprise or association of enterprises or person or association of persons shall enter into any agreement in respect of production, supply, distribution, storage, acquisition or control of goods or provision of services, which causes or is likely to cause an appreciable adverse effect on competition within India.* Art. 81 of Treaty of Rome also show a similar position. In US, Sec. 1 of the Sherman Act makes every contract or conspiracy in restraint of trade or commerce among the several states or with foreign nations illegal. Sec.2 makes it an offence to monopolize, or conspire with any other person or persons to monopolize, any part of the trade or commerce among the several states or with foreign nations.

57. This question of identification of the relevant market is given prime importance by Courts across the world. For example, see *Tampa Electric Co.* v. *Nashville Coal Co.*, 365 US 320 (1961). In this case, the contract in question was relating to the exclusive supply of coal from the respondent for the petitioner's new electric power generating units. The respondent refused to perform the contract at a later stage by arguing that the agreement was an anti-competitive agreement in violation of the provisions of Clayton Act. In this case, while analyzing the merits of the appeal, the Court specifically

held that for a proper analysis of the substantiality of an argument on 'anti competitive' nature of an agreement, it is necessary to weigh the probable effect of the contract on the relevant area of effective competition taking into account the relative strength of the parties, the proportionate volume of commerce involved in relation to the total volume of commerce in the relevant market area, and the probable immediate and future effects that pre-empt the market share. According to the Court, mere showing that the contract itself involves a substantial number of dollars is ordinarily of little consequence. See 365 US 320, 329.

58. For a very good discussion on the issues relating to delineation of relevant geographic market and relevant product market in the backdrop of a case study, see Wanda Jane Rogers, 'Beyond Economic Theory: A Model for Analyzing the Antitrust Implications of Exclusive Dealing Arrangements', 1033–9.

59. See Sec. 2(s) of the Competition Act 2002, which defines the term 'geographic market'.

60. See Sec. 2(t) of the Competition Act 2002 for the definition of the term 'product market'.

61. One of the interesting cases that may help as a guideline in understanding some of the issues relating to interchangeability of products is *United States* v. *Dupont & Co.* 351 US 377 (1956). In this case, the appellant was the producer of cellophane, which was used as a flexible packaging material. Appellant had more than 75 per cent of the market share of total cellophane sold in US, but Cellophane constituted less than 20 per cent of the total flexible packaging material market. One of the major questions before the Court was whether the relevant product market was cellophane market or flexible packaging material market. In this case Supreme Court held that the relevant market was flexible packaging materials market as cellophane was interchangeable with numerous other flexible packaging materials.

62. The rules for determining the effect of agreements on competition can broadly be classified into per se rule and rule of reason. Under the per se rule, the acts or practices specified by an Act as deemed or presumed to have an adverse effect on competition are by themselves prohibited, whereas under the rule of reason, the effect on the competition is determined on the basis of facts of the case, market and the competition. See T. Ramappa, *Competition Law in India* (New Delhi: Oxford University Press, 2006), 75-81. The unique characteristics of sports events and sponsorship contracts may force the exclusive supply and distribution agreements to come under rule of reason in the Indian context.

63. *Tata Engineering and Locomotive Co. Ltd.* v. *Registrar of Restrictive*

Trade Agreement (1977) 47 Comp Cas 520 (Supreme Court). In this case, the main question was whether the agreement between TELCO and its dealers regarding strict allocation of areas of sale was a restrictive trade practice.

64. See Sec. 3 (5) of the Competition Act 2002 which exempts from the purview of Sec. 3 reasonable conditions imposed by owners of intellectual property for the protection of intellectual property rights. One of the case law that discuss issues relating to the exceptions given for the intellectual property rights under competition law is the decision of the Court of Justice in *Parke, Davis and Co.* v. *Probel, Reese, Beintema-Interpharm and Centrafarm,* [1968] ECR 81.

65. See Sec. 3 (5) of the Competition Act 2002. At present, this provision contains only six statutes and does not even include the Protection of Plant Varieties and Farmer's Rights (PPVFR) Act 2001.

66. See Sec. 3 (5).

67. See Art. 40 of the TRIPS Agreement which recognizes the right of member states to take measures to prevent abuse of intellectual property rights causing an adverse effect on competition in the market.

68. See Sec. 19 (3), which provides some guidelines to determine whether an agreement is having an adverse effect on competition.

69. For example, see Sec. 19 (1) of the Indian Competition Act 2002. According to this provision, if competition authorities finds any practice as constituting an abuse of dominance, the Competition Commission may either on its own motion or on the receipt of a complaint from any person, consumer, or their association or trade association or a reference made to it by the Central Government or a State Government or a statutory authority, can inquire into alleged contravention of the provisions.

70. Please note that ICC is chosen here only for example sake and it is not intended to imply any thing with their conducts in the present or past.

71. Such restrictions were found in FIFA World Cup in 2006 and ICC Cricket World Cup in West Indies in 2007.

72. See Robert D. Anderson and Alberto Heimler, 'Abuse of Dominant Position- Enforcement Issues and Approaches for Developing Countries' in Vinod Dhall (ed.), *Competition Law Today—Concepts, Issues and the Law in Practice* (New Delhi: Oxford University Press, 2007), 59.

73. See the Explanation part of Sec.4 of Indian Competition Act 2002. For further references on this explanation clause, see T. Ramappa, *Competition Law in India,* 140–1.

74. While the higher sponsorship prices imposed by a firm may act as a useful indicator of the position of a firm to disregard the market forces and impose trading conditions, this higher prices alone shall not establish an abuse of such dominant position, as is evident from the decisions across the

world. For example, see the decisions of the Court of Justice in *Parke, Davis and Co.* v. *Probel, Reese, Beintema-Interpharm and Centrafarm* [1968] ECR 81 and *Deutsche Grammophon Gesellschaft mbH* v. *Metro-SB-Großmarkte*, [1971] ECR 487.

75. See Robert D. Anderson and Alberto Heimler, 'Abuse of Dominant Position—Enforcement Issues and Approaches for Developing Countries', 64.

76. These entry barriers were very much visible in the difficulties faced by Essel group in establishing a new cricket league in India against BCCI. ICC has refused to give authorization for Indian Cricket League (ICL). See *Economic Times*, 'ICC Throws its Weight Behind BCCI, Won't Approve League', (Ahmedabad: August 29, 2007), 5.

77. See Robert D. Anderson and Alberto Heimler, 'Abuse of Dominant Position—Enforcement Issues and Approaches for Developing Countries', 65.

78. For a detailed discussion, see T. Ramappa, *Competition Law in India*, 143.

79. J. Vicker cited in Robert D. Anderson and Alberto Heimler, 'Abuse of Dominant Position—Enforcement Issues and Approaches for Developing Countries', 67.

80. See Sec. 4 (2) (a) to (e) of Competition Act 2002. These practices can broadly be classified as exclusionary abuses and exploitative abuses.

81. See Robert D. Anderson and Alberto Heimler, 'Abuse of Dominant Position—Enforcement Issues and Approaches for Developing Countries', 68.

82. While US authorities take a very favourable approach towards the IP owners by recognizing their right to determine or refuse to license, the European authorities do not show that much leniency. According to the European Court of Justice, a refusal to license will be treated as an abuse when (1) there is no actual or potential substitute for the IP protected product in the relevant market; (2) there is no business justification for the exclusion and (3) a new product is denied to the consumer as a result of such refusal. *For example* see *Radio Teefis Eireann (RTE) and Independent Television Publications Ltd (ITP)* v. *Commission (Magill)* [1995] ECR 743 and *IMS Health GmbH & Co OHG* v. *NDC Health GmbH and Co KG*, [2004] ECR I5039. A major issue involved in cases of interface of monopoly created by intellectual property rights with the need for protection of competition in market is the difficulty in estimating the compensation to the holder of intellectual property rights. Whether this should include the amount to compensate the loss of monopoly profit is the most contentious issue. For a detailed discussion on this issue of frequent interface between Intellectual Property Rights and Competition law, see Valentine Korah, 'Competition Law and Intellectual Property Rights', 129–48.

83. The Indian Competition Commission is seen taking a pro-active approach in recent times. The effective advocacy role played by the Competi-

tion Commission in arguing strongly against the Indian Government's proposal to monopolize postal services below 500gms in the name of saving Indian Postal Services is a clear pointer in this regard. Similar trends are also seen from the other Competition authorities across the world. The Statement of Objections sent by European Competition Commission against Intel on July 26, 2007 accusing it of abusing its dominant position in the computer processor market, with the aim of excluding its main rival AMD is another good example in this regard. Another positive trend seen in recent times is the better media coverage received for the actions of competition authorities and the same is really helpful in the dissemination of information about the active role competition authorities can play in protecting the interests of consumers.

Conclusion

Intellectual property is rightly considered as the most valuable asset of a company/ individual in the dynamics of the new information economy. The time has come where the power of a person is measured not primarily in terms of physical assets, but in relation to the quality and quantity of intellectual property under his/her possession. In recent times, we have witnessed some of the big players in the market pleading for mercy from tiny companies for their survival, when they were incriminated with intellectual property infringements. The best example would be the Blackberry Patent dispute in the US wherein even the very existence of Blackberry's mobile service was hanging in air when it was confronted with a patent litigation by a relatively small company named NTP. Such sturdy disputes indicate that as the power of intellectual property amplify in intensity, the necessity and anguish to protect it also increases.

As we have seen in the preceding pages, different forms of intellectual property are coupled with the conduct of an event. When a person engages in ambush marketing s/he is trying to take a free ride over the valuable intellectual assets associated with the event. Though the practice began as a creative form of advertisement, it later turned out to be a parasitic problem that could threaten the very occurrence of such spectacular events that draws heavily from sponsorship resources. The foregoing analysis of different forms of ambush marketing that occurred during the conduct of the major events in the past testifies to this reality. It is almost an impossibility to have fabulous events of wider spectatorship without eliciting sponsorships due to the mammoth costs involved in the accomplishment of the event. And as no sponsor will be ready to give 'free donations' for conducting an event that is frequently being ambushed, the event organizers are forced to deal with the issue of ambush marketing very seriously.

As seen in chapter 3, the traditional legal measures like trade mark infringement action, copyright infringement action and action for passing off were first resorted to by the event organizers to tackle with the ambush menace. But as these established legal measures were not framed with the precise aim of preventing ambush marketing, they turned out to be enormously ineffective in successfully wrestling with most of the situations discussed in chapter 2. Though few in number, the cases that came before various courts across the world illustrates this reality. It also reveals the pressing necessity to find out efficient counter measures to effectively tackle the ever evolving ambush marketing technologies.

In search of an appropriate remedy capable of dealing with the issues of ambush marketing, it is found that event-specific legislation would be the best possible mechanism. Through ground-breaking measures like provision for corrective advertisements, Sydney 2000 Games Act proved to be an inclusive and efficacious legislation for curbing ambush marketing. As a result, the 2000 Olympics got the reputation of a 'clean' event, which is considered by many as the worst ever game for ambush marketers. Taking a cue from the Sydney Games, UK has enacted the London Olympic Games and Paralympic Games Act 2006 with a view to combat the ambush threat during the upcoming 2012 Olympics. Though the Act leaves the issue of framing of advertisement regulations to secondary legislation, to create regulations according to requirements in 2012, nevertheless one can see a very comprehensive and aggressive scheme against ambush marketers in this Act as well. One such approach is making the contravention of the provisions of the Act, a criminally liable one. The Act is compendious enough, even dealing with issues like unauthorized sale of tickets and street trading. This dynamic approach in the drafting of event-specific legislation is not limited to developed countries. Developing countries have also began to approach the issue with a similar sense of rigour and the Regulation on the Protection of Olympic Symbols 2002, drafted by China in view of Beijing Olympics in 2008 is a remarkable example to the point. While maintaining firmness similar to the other two legislations, the Chinese Regulation introduced the possibility of settlement of disputes through mediation. These legislative interventions have exhibited to the world, how encyclopedic and impeccable legislation must be, when it comes to fighting ambush marketing.

Nonetheless, this legislation too has invited forceful criticisms from many quarters especially from the point of view of the spectators. For instance, in the case of the last ICC Cricket World Cup, a number of cricket fans complained that the event organizers' anti-ambushing concerns were becoming excessive, impairing the excitement and glory of the event. Most of the blogs relating to cricket world cup considered the sunset legislation as something that totally ruined the fun of cricket on the alluring landscape of the Caribbean islands. Consequently, today the major challenge before the event organizers is to safeguard the genuine commercial interests without contravening the fundamental delights and vivacity of the very event. It is essential to strike a balance between the legitimate rights of event organizers and sponsors on one side and the basic rights of the general public on the other. Exploring new possibilities like allowing foods and drinks of non-sponsors inside the venue in packages that does not reflect their identity needs to be given a serious thought in this context. Such small steps can reduce public criticisms and promote the cooperation of the public in addressing the menaces of ambush marketing.

It is also futile to believe that an all-embracing, simultaneously evenhanded, legal measure alone would serve the purpose of countering ambush marketing. Litigations are not only costly but also arduously lengthy. One of the most important steps to be taken is creating awareness among the public about the damaging consequences of ambush marketing. There is an alarming lack of awareness on the part of the general public towards this form of marketing. A persuasive rectification at this level would convince the consumers/spectators that ambush marketing would ultimately only devastate and erase out the event. An informed rejection on the part of the general public would resolve this problem once for all.

Another vital aspect that has to go in concurrence with awareness creation is professional management of public relations. This assumes special significance in the background of incidents like the serious charges raised against FIFA for being exceedingly harsh against the viewing public while pursuing its anti-ambush marketing strategy during the FIFA World

Cup 2006. Similar accusations were levelled against the ICC for its extreme anti-ambush marketing drive during Cricket World Cup 2007. The marketing heads of FIFA were realistic enough to openly accept this as the failure of properly managing its public relations. In the absence of proper public relations and a resultant rapport with the public, the media and ultimately the public will turn against the event organizers for the stringency factor. It is also important on the part of organizers to have strong and consistent vigil before, during, and after the event. A well-resourced investigation squad equipped with a proficient legal team can go a long way in ensuring a better event.

Nonetheless, as human ingenuity is as unlimited as their wants, ambush marketing can be expected in small or bigger quantum, in creative and unusual ways, in the future as well. A holistic approach, as suggested in the previous pages, will at least give a red card to those ambush marketers, who attempt to play a game within a game.

Appendices

1

Regulations on the Protection of Olympic Symbols

(Adopted at the 54th Executive Meeting of the the State Council on January 30,2002,promulgated by Decree No.345 of the State Council of the People's Republic of China on February 4,2002,and effective as of April 1,2002.)

ARTICLE 1

These Regulations are formulated for the purposes of strengthening the protection of Olympic symbols, safeguarding the lawful rights and interests of the right holders of Olympic symbols and maintaining the dignity of Olympic movement.

ARTICLE 2

For the purposes of these Regulations, "Olympic symbols" refer to:

(1) The five Olympic rings, Olympic flag, Olympic motto, Olympic emblem and Olympic anthem of the International Olympic Committee (IOC);
(2) Expressions such as Olympic, Olympiad, Olympic Games and their abbreviations;
(3) The name, emblem and symbols of the Chinese Olympic Committee;
(4) The name, emblem and symbols of Beijing2008 Olympic Games Bid Committee;

(5) Symbols such as the name and emblem of Beijing Organizing Committee for the Games of the XXIX Olympiad, the mascots, anthem and slogan of the 29th Olympic Games, 'Beijing2008', the 29th Olympic Games and its abbreviations;
(6) Other symbols related to the 29th Olympic Games laid down in the Olympic Charter and the Host City Contract for the Games of the XXIX Olympiad in the Year 2008.

ARTICLE 3

For the purpose of these Regulations, "right holders of Olympic symbols" refers to the International Olympic Committee, the Chinese Olympic Committee and the Beijing Organizing Committee for the Games of the XXIX Olympiad.

The division of rights among the International Olympic Committee, the Chinese Olympic Committee and the Beijing Organizing Committee for the Games of the XXIX Olympiad shall be determined in accordance with the Olympic Charter and the Host City Contract for the Games of the XXIX Olympiad in the Year 2008.

ARTICLE 4

The right holders of the Olympic symbols enjoy the exclusive rights of Olympic symbols in accordance with these Regulations.

No one may use Olympic symbols for commercial purposes (including potential commercial purposes, and the same below) without the authorization of the right holders.

ARTICLE 5

For the purpose of these Regulations, "use for commercial purposes" means the use of Olympic symbols for profit-making purposes in the following ways:

(1) The use of Olympic symbols in goods, packages or containers of goods or trade documents of good;
(2) The use of Olympic symbols in services;
(3) The use of Olympic symbols in advertising, commercial exhibition, profit-making performance and other commercial activities;
(4) Selling, importing or exporting goods bearing Olympic symbols;
(5) Manufacturing or selling Olympic symbols;
(6) Other acts that might mislead people to think there are sponsorship or other supporting relations between the doers and the right holders of Olympic symbols.

ARTICLE 6

The administrative authorities for industry and commerce under the State Council shall, in accordance with the provisions of these Regulations, be responsible for the protection of Olympic symbols throughout the country.

The administrative department for industry and commerce at or above the country level shall, in accordance with the provisions of these Regulations, be responsible for the protection of Olympic symbols within their respective administrative areas.

ARTICLE 7

The right holders of Olympic symbols shall submit their Olympic symbols for the record to the administrative department for industry and commerce under the State Council, which shall make a proclamation therefore..

ARTICLE 8

Anyone who are to use Olympic symbols for commercial purposes with the authorization of their right holders shall conclude a license contract with such holders; anyone who is to use the Olympic symbols set forth in Item (1) or (2)of Article 2 of these Regulations shall conclude a contract with the International Olympic Committee and institutions authorized or approved by it; anyone who is to use the Olympic symbols set forth in Item(3) of Article 2 of these Regulations shall conclude a contract with the Chinese Olympic Committee; anyone who is to use the Olympic symbols set forth in Item(4),(5)or(6) of Article 2 of these Regulations shall, before December 31, 2008, conclude a contract with Beijing Organizing Committee for the Games of the XXIX Olympiad. The right holders of the Olympic symbols shall submit the license contracts for the record to the administrative departments for industry and commerce under the State Council.

Where a license contract is concluded in accordance with to the preceding paragraph, the licensee may only use the Olympic symbols within the geographical coverage and the time period set forth in the contract.

ARTICLE 9

The Olympic symbols that have been lawfully used before the effective date of these Regulations may be continually used within the original scope.

ARTICLE 10

Where a dispute arises from the use of Olympic symbols for commercial purposes without the authorization of the right holders, that is, from the infringement upon the exclusive rights of Olympic symbols, it may be settled through consultation by the parties concerned; if the parties concerned are unwilling to consult or the consultation fails, the right holders of Olympic symbols or the interested parties may institute legal proceedings in a people's court or request the administrative department for industry and commerce to make a disposition; where the said administrative department for industry and commerce finds that an infringement is constituted, it shall order an immediate cease of the infringement, confiscate or destroy the infringing goods and the special tools for manufacturing the infringing goods or for manufacturing Olympic symbols for commercial purposes without the authorization; if there is illegal income, the administrative department for industry and commerce shall confiscate the illegal income and may concurrently impose a fine of not more than five times of the illegal income; if there is no illegal income, a fine of not more than 50,000 Yuan may be imposed concurrently. Where a party concerned refuses to accept the disposition, he may, in accordance with the Administrative Procedure Law of the People's Republic of China, institute legal proceedings in a people's court within 15 days from the date of receipt of the notification of the disposition where the infringer neither institute legal proceedings nor carry out the disposition upon the expiry of the time limit, the administrative department for industry and commerce may apply to the people's court for compulsory execution. Upon the request of the parties concerned, administrative department for industry and commerce may mediate on the amount of compensation for the loss caused by infringement of exclusive rights of Olympic symbols; if the mediation fails, any parties concerned may, in accordance with the Civil Procedure Law of the People's Republic of China, institute legal proceedings in a people's court.

Anyone who use Olympic symbols to conduct swindle or other illegal activities therefore violates the criminal laws shall, in accordance with the provisions of the criminal Laws on the crime of swindle or other crimes, be investigated for criminal liabilities.

ARTICLE 11

The administrative departments for industry and commerce have the rights to investigate into and deal with the acts that infringe the exclusive rights of Olympic symbols.

When the administrative departments for industry and commerce, on the basis of the obtained evidence or information on suspected illegal acts, investigate into and deal with suspected infringement upon the exclusive rights of Olympic symbols, they may perform the following powers:

(1) Inquiring relevant parties concerned and investigating into matters related to the infringement;
(2) Consulting or copying contracts, invoices, accounting books and other relevant materials related to the infringement;
(3) Conducting on-the-spot inspection on the places where the parties concerned conduct the suspected infringement;
(4) Inspecting the articles related to the infringement; sealing or seizing the articles where there is evidence to support that such articles infringe upon the exclusive rights of Olympic symbols.

The parties concerned shall assist and coordinate with the administrative departments for industry and commerce when such departments perform the powers laid down in the preceding paragraph, and shall not refuse or hinder such performance.

ARTICLE 12

Where import or export goods are suspected of infringing the exclusive rights of Olympic symbols, the Customs shall investigate into and deal with the case with reference to the powers and procedures laid down in the Customs Law of the People's Republic of China and the Regulations of the People's Republic of China and the Regulations of the People's Republic of China on the Customs Protection of Intellectual Property.

ARTICLE 13

The amount of compensation for the loss caused by infringement of the exclusive rights of Olympic symbols shall be determined on the basis of the loss that the right holder has suffered from the infringement or the profit that the infringer has obtained through the infringement, including the reasonable expenses paid for checking the infringement; where the loss suffered by the infringe or the profit obtained by the infringer are difficult to determine, the compensation shall be reasonably determined with reference to the licensing fees for using Olympic symbol.

Those who unknowingly sell goods infringing the exclusive rights of Olympic symbols and can prove that the goods are acquired lawfully and point out the supplier shall not bear any compensation liability.

ARTICLE 14

In addition to these Regulations, Olympic symbols are also protected according to provisions of other laws and administrative regulations such as the Copyright Law of the People's Republic of China, Trademark Law of the People's Republic of China, the Patent Law of the People's Republic of China and the Regulations on Administration of Special Symbols.

ARTICLE 15

These Regulations shall be effective as of April 1, 2002.

2

London Olympic Games and Paralympic Games Act 2006

PREAMBLE

An Act to make provision in connection with the Olympic Games and Paralympic Games that are to take place in London in the year 2012; to amend the Olympic Symbol etc. (Protection) Act 1995; and for connected purposes.

[30th March 2006]

Be it enacted by the Queen's most Excellent Majesty, by and with the advice and consent of the Lords Spiritual and Temporal, and Commons, in this present Parliament assembled, and by the authority of the same, as follows:—

INTRODUCTORY

1 Interpretation of principal terms

(1) In this Act "the London Olympics" means—
   (a) the Games of the Thirtieth Olympiad that are to take place in 2012, and
   (b) the Paralympic Games that are to take place in that year.

(2) A reference in this Act to the London Olympics includes a reference to any event which forms part of the Games specified in subsection (1)(a) or (b) including, in particular—

(a) an event, other than a sporting event, held in accordance with the Host City Contract, and
(b) an event which is to take place outside London.

(3) In this Act—

(a) "the British Olympic Association" means the company limited by guarantee registered with that name,
(b) "London Olympic event" means an event (whether or not a sporting event and whether or not held in London) held as part of the London Olympics,
(c) "the London Olympics period" means the period which—
    (i) begins four weeks before the day of the opening ceremony of the Games of the Thirtieth Olympiad that are to take place in 2012, and
    (ii) ends with the fifth day after the day of the closing ceremony of the Paralympic Games 2012,
(d) "the London Organising Committee" means the organising committee formed in accordance with section 2 of the Host City Contract as the company limited by guarantee registered as the London Organising Committee of the Olympic Games Limited (LOCOG),
(e) "the Host City Contract" means the Host City Contract, for the Games of the Thirtieth Olympiad that are to take place in 2012, signed at Singapore on 6th July 2005 and entered into by—
    (i) the International Olympic Committee,
    (ii) the Mayor of London (representing London), and
    (iii) the British Olympic Association,
(f) "the Paralympic Games" means the events known by that name and to be organised by the London Organising Committee in accordance with section 60 of the Host City Contract, and
(g) "the Olympic Charter" means the Olympic Charter of the International Olympic Committee.

....

THE OLYMPIC DELIVERY AUTHORITY

3 Establishment

(1) There shall be a body corporate known as the Olympic Delivery Authority.
(2) Schedule 1 (which makes provision about the Authority) shall have effect.

....

ADVERTISING

19 Advertising regulations

(1) The Secretary of State shall make regulations about advertising in the vicinity of London Olympic events.

(2) In making the regulations the Secretary of State—

(a) shall aim to secure compliance with obligations imposed on any person by the Host City Contract,

(b) shall have regard to any requests or guidance from the International Olympic Committee, and

(c) shall also have regard to amenity and public safety.

(3) The regulations shall specify, or provide criteria for determining—

(a) the places in respect of advertising in which the regulations apply,

(b) the nature of the advertising in respect of which the regulations apply, and

(c) what is, or is not, to be treated for the purposes of the regulations as advertising in the vicinity of a place.

(4) The regulations may apply in respect of advertising of any kind including, in particular—

(a) advertising of a non-commercial nature, and

(b) announcements or notices of any kind.

(5) The regulations may apply in respect of advertising in any form including, in particular—

(a) the distribution or provision of documents or articles,

(b) the display or projection of words, images, lights or sounds, and

(c) things done with or in relation to material which has or may have purposes or uses other than as an advertisement.

(6) The regulations shall specify, or provide criteria for determining, the period of time during which they apply; and—

(a) the regulations shall apply only for such time as the Secretary of State considers necessary for the purpose of securing compliance with obligations imposed on any person by the Host City Contract, and

(b) the regulations may apply during different periods in respect of different places.

(7) The regulations shall permit, subject to any specified conditions, advertising undertaken or controlled by—

(a) any person specified in the regulations as appearing to the Secretary of State to have responsibility in accordance with the Host City Contract for the control of advertising in relation to the London Olympics ("a responsible body"), or

(b) any person authorised by a responsible body (whether or not subject to terms and conditions and whether or not in accordance with a sponsorship or other commercial agreement).

(8) The regulations—

(a) may prohibit action of a specified kind or in specified circumstances,

(b) may impose obligations on persons who—

(i) take action in relation to an advertisement, or

(ii) have an interest in or responsibility for a product or service to which an advertisement relates,

(c) may impose obligations on persons who own, occupy or have responsibility for the management of land, premises or other property,

(d) may, in particular, impose on a person an obligation to take steps to ensure—

(i) that other persons do not take action of a particular kind;

(ii) that a situation is not permitted to continue, and

(e) shall have effect despite any consent or permission granted (whether before or after the commencement of the regulations) by any landowner, local authority or other person.

20 Regulations: supplemental

(1) Regulations under section 19—

(a) may, to a specified extent or for specified purposes, disapply or modify specified enactments relating to planning or the control of advertising,

(b) may apply (with or without modifications) or make provision similar to any enactment (including, but not limited to, provisions of Chapter III of Part VIII of the Town and Country Planning Act 1990 (c. 8) (control of advertising) and regulations under that Chapter)),

(c) may provide for exceptions (in addition to those referred to in section 19(7)) which may be expressed by reference to the nature of advertising, its purpose, the circumstances of its display or any other matter (which may include the consent of a specified person),

(d) may make provision for application, with any specified modifications or exceptions, to the Crown,

(e) may make provision which applies generally or only for specified purposes or in specified circumstances,

(f) may make different provision for different purposes or circumstances, and

(g) may apply in relation to advertising whether or not it consists of the result or continuation of activity carried out before the regulations come into force.

(2) Regulations under section 19—
  (a) shall be made by statutory instrument, and
  (b) may not be made unless a draft has been laid before and approved by resolution of each House of Parliament.

(3) Before making regulations under section 19 the Secretary of State shall consult—
  (a) such authorities, with responsibilities for planning in respect of places to which the regulations apply or may apply, as he thinks appropriate,
  (b) one or more persons who appear to the Secretary of State to represent interests within the advertising industry which are likely to be affected by the regulations,
  (c) such other persons, who appear to the Secretary of State to represent interests likely to be affected by the regulations, as he thinks appropriate,
  (d) the Olympic Delivery Authority, and
  (e) the London Organising Committee.

(4) If regulations under section 19 would be treated as a hybrid instrument for the purposes of the standing orders of either House of Parliament, they shall proceed in that House as if they were not a hybrid instrument.

21 Offence

(1) A person commits an offence if he contravenes regulations under section 19.

(2) I t shall be a defence for a person charged with an offence under subsection (1) to prove that the contravention of the regulations occurred—
  (a) without his knowledge, or
  (b) despite his taking all reasonable steps to prevent it from occurring or (where he became aware of it after its commencement) from continuing.

(3) A person guilty of an offence under subsection (1) shall be liable—
  (a) on conviction on indictment, to a fine, or
  (b) on summary conviction, to a fine not exceeding £20,000.

(4) A court by or before which a person is convicted of an offence under subsection (1) may require him to pay to a police authority or to the Olympic Delivery Authority sums in respect of expenses reasonably incurred in taking action under section 22(1) in relation to the matters to which the offence relates.

22 Enforcement: power of entry

(1) A constable or enforcement officer may—

(a) enter land or premises on which they reasonably believe a contravention of regulations under section 19 is occurring (whether by reason of advertising on that land or premises or by the use of that land or premises to cause an advertisement to appear elsewhere);
(b) remove, destroy, conceal or erase any infringing article;
(c) when entering land under paragraph (a), be accompanied by one or more persons for the purpose of taking action under paragraph (b);
(d) use, or authorise the use of, reasonable force for the purpose of taking action under this subsection.

(2) The power to enter land or premises may be exercised only at a time that a constable or enforcement officer thinks reasonable having regard to the nature and circumstances of the contravention of regulations under section 19.

(3) Before entering land or premises a constable or enforcement officer must take reasonable steps to—
(a) establish the identity of an owner, occupier or person responsible for the management of the land or premises or of any infringing article on the land or premises, and
(b) give any owner, occupier or responsible person identified under paragraph (a) such opportunity as seems reasonable to the constable or enforcement officer in the circumstances of the case to end the contravention of the regulations (whether by removing, destroying or concealing any infringing article or otherwise).

(4) The power to enter premises may be exercised in relation to a dwelling only in accordance with a warrant issued by a justice of the peace; and a justice of the peace may issue a warrant only if satisfied on the application of a constable or enforcement officer that—
(a) there are reasonable grounds to believe a contravention of regulations under section 19 is occurring in the dwelling or on land that can reasonably be entered only through the dwelling,
(b) the constable or enforcement officer has complied with subsection (3),
(c) the constable or enforcement officer has taken reasonable steps to give notice to persons likely to be interested of his intention to apply for a warrant, and
(d) that it is reasonable in the circumstances of the case to issue a warrant.

(5) The power to remove an article may be exercised only if the constable or enforcement officer thinks it necessary for the purpose of—
(a) ending the contravention of regulations under section 19,
(b) preventing a future contravention of the regulations,
(c) enabling the article to be used as evidence in proceedings for an offence under section 21, or

(d) enabling the article to be forfeited in accordance with section 143 of the Powers of Criminal Courts (Sentencing) Act 2000 (c. 6).

(6) An article removed—

(a) if removed by an enforcement officer, shall as soon as is reasonably practicable be delivered to a constable, and

(b) whether removed by or delivered to a constable, shall be treated as if acquired by the constable in the course of the investigation of an offence.

(7) Having exercised a power under this section a constable or enforcement officer—

(a) shall take reasonable steps to leave the land or premises secure, and

(b) shall comply with any provision of regulations under section 19 about informing specified persons of what the constable or enforcement officer has done.

(8) Regulations under section 19 shall include provision enabling a person whose property is damaged in the course of the exercise or purported exercise of a power under this section (other than a person responsible for a contravention of the regulations or for the management of an infringing article) to obtain compensation from a police authority or the Olympic Delivery Authority; and the regulations may, in particular, include provision—

(a) conferring jurisdiction on a court or tribunal;

(b) about appeals.

(9) A police authority or the Olympic Delivery Authority may recover from a person responsible for the contravention of the regulations, as if it were a debt, the reasonable costs of taking action under this section.

(10) In this section—

- "enforcement officer" means a person designated for the purposes of that subsection by the Olympic Delivery Authority (and paragraph 29(1)(a) to (d) of Schedule 1 shall apply to an enforcement officer whether or not he is a member of the Authority's staff), and
- "infringing article" means—

(a) an advertisement which contravenes regulations under section 19, and

(b) any other thing that constitutes a contravention of regulations under section 19 or is being used in connection with a contravention of the regulations.

23 Role of Olympic Delivery Authority

(1) The Olympic Delivery Authority shall make arrangements to have the effect of regulations made or expected to be made under section 19 brought to the attention of persons likely to be affected or interested.

(2) In exercising their function under subsection (1) the Authority shall—
   (a) aim to give two years' notice of the general nature of the regulations, and
   (b) aim to give six months' notice of the detailed provisions of the regulations.

(3) The Olympic Delivery Authority—
   (a) shall make available to persons who are or may be affected by regulations under section 19 advice about the effect or likely effect of the regulations, and
   (b) may give assistance (which may include financial assistance) in complying with or avoiding breaches of the regulations.

(4) The Olympic Delivery Authority may institute criminal proceedings in respect of an offence under section 21.

(5) Subsection (4) shall not apply in relation to the institution of proceedings in Scotland or Northern Ireland.

(6) The Olympic Delivery Authority shall—
   (a) prepare a strategy for the exercise of their functions under this section and under section 22,
   (b) submit the strategy to the Secretary of State,
   (c) revise the strategy until it obtains the Secretary of State's approval, and
   (d) publish the strategy as approved.

24 Local planning authorities

(1) The Secretary of State may by order require a specified local planning authority who grant advertising consent to a person to notify him of the effect of—
   (a) section 19(8)(e), and
   (b) any regulations under section 19.

(2) In subsection (1) "advertising consent" means consent of such kind as the order shall specify.

(3) An order under subsection (1)—
   (a) shall be made by statutory instrument, and
   (b) shall be subject to annulment in pursuance of a resolution of either House of Parliament.

TRADING

25 Street tradinZg, &c.

(1) The Secretary of State shall make regulations about trading in the vicinity of London Olympic events.

(2) In making the regulations the Secretary of State—
   (a) shall aim to secure compliance with obligations imposed on any person by the Host City Contract,
   (b) shall have regard to any requests or guidance from the International Olympic Committee, and
   (c) shall also have regard to amenity and public safety (including in each case the need to avoid congestion).

(3) The regulations shall specify, or provide criteria for determining—
   (a) the places in respect of which the regulations apply,
   (b) the nature of the trading in respect of which the regulations apply, and
   (c) what is, or is not, to be treated for the purposes of the regulations as trading in the vicinity of a place.

(4) The regulations may apply only in respect of trading which takes place—
   (a) on a highway, or
   (b) in another place—
      (i) to which the public have access (whether generally or only for the purpose of the trading), and
      (ii) which is not in any building other than one designed or generally used for the parking of cars.

(5) The regulations shall specify, or provide criteria for determining, the period of time during which they apply; and—
   (a) the regulations shall apply only for such time as the Secretary of State considers necessary for the purpose of securing compliance with obligations imposed on any person by the Host City Contract, and
   (b) the regulations may apply during different periods in respect of different places.

(6) The regulations shall permit, subject to any specified conditions, trading in accordance with an authorisation granted by—
   (a) the Olympic Delivery Authority, or
   (b) a person to whom the function of granting authorisations for the purpose of this subsection is delegated by the Authority (and the Authority may delegate the function to different persons in respect of different areas or activities).

(7) An authorisation may be subject to terms and conditions; in particular—
   (a) an authorisation may be subject to terms and conditions about the times at which trading is carried out or about steps to be taken in respect of congestion, litter or noise, and
   (b) an authorisation granted to a person may be subject to terms and conditions which are inconsistent with, or more onerous than, the terms and conditions of any other licence held by the person in respect of trading.

(8) The regulations shall include provision about the circumstances in which authorisations under subsection (6) may and may not be granted; and the regulations may, in particular—
  (a) stipulate that an authorisation be granted in respect of a place only if a specified kind of licence exists in respect of trading in that place;
  (b) stipulate that an authorisation be granted in respect of a place only if it is designated for a specified purpose in accordance with a specified enactment;
  (c) stipulate that an authorisation be granted to a person only if he holds a specified kind of licence in respect of trading;
  (d) stipulate that an authorisation may be granted for trading in the course of a fair or market (which the regulations may define) only where—
    (i) the fair or market is held in accordance with a specified kind of licence or right, and
    (ii) any other specified conditions are satisfied;
  (e) require the Authority to have regard to the provisions of the Host City Contract;
  (f) confer, subject to provisions of the regulations, an absolute discretion in respect of each application for authorisation.

26 Section 25: supplemental

(1) Regulations under section 25—
  (a) may, to a specified extent or for specified purposes, disapply or modify specified enactments relating to trading (which may include enactments conferring rights to conduct a fair or market),
  (b) may apply (with or without modifications) or make provision similar to any enactment (which may include provision conferring a right of appeal in respect of the refusal of an authorisation),
  (c) may provide for exceptions which may be expressed by reference to the nature of trading, its circumstances, the application of profits or any other matter (which may include the consent of a specified person),
  (d) may make provision which applies generally or only for specified purposes or in specified circumstances, and
  (e) may make different provision for different purposes or circumstances.

(2) Regulations under section 25—
  (a) shall be made by statutory instrument, and
  (b) may not be made unless a draft has been laid before and approved by resolution of each House of Parliament.

(3) Before making regulations under section 25 the Secretary of State shall consult—
  (a) such authorities, with responsibilities for the licensing of trading in respect of places to which the regulations apply or may apply, as he thinks appropriate,
  (b) such persons, who appear to the Secretary of State to represent interests likely to be affected by the regulations, as he thinks appropriate,
  (c) the Olympic Delivery Authority, and
  (d) the London Organising Committee.

(4) Regulations under section 25 shall have effect despite any licence granted (whether before or after the commencement of the regulations)—
  (a) by any landowner, local authority or other person, or
  (b) by or by virtue of any enactment, Charter or other document.

(5) If regulations under section 25 would be treated as a hybrid instrument for the purposes of the standing orders of either House of Parliament, they shall proceed in that House as if they were not a hybrid instrument.

(6) In section 25 and this section "licence" includes any kind of consent, certificate, permission or authority (by whatever name).

27 Offence

(1) A person commits an offence if he contravenes regulations under section 25.

(2) A person guilty of an offence under subsection (1) shall be liable—
  (a) on conviction on indictment, to a fine, or
  (b) on summary conviction, to a fine not exceeding £20,000.

28 Enforcement: power of entry

(1) A constable or enforcement officer may—
  (a) enter land or premises on which they reasonably believe a contravention of regulations under section 25 is occurring;
  (b) remove any infringing article;
  (c) when entering land under paragraph (a), be accompanied by one or more persons for the purpose of taking action under paragraph (b);
  (d) use, or authorise the use of, reasonable force for the purpose of taking action under this subsection.

(2) The power to remove an article may be exercised only if the constable or enforcement officer thinks it necessary for the purpose of—
  (a) ending the contravention of regulations under section 25,
  (b) preventing a future contravention of the regulations,
  (c) enabling the article to be used as evidence in proceedings for an offence under section 27, or

(d) enabling the article to be forfeited in accordance with section 143 of the Powers of Criminal Courts (Sentencing) Act 2000 (c. 6).

(3) An article removed shall be returned when retention is no longer justified by a matter specified in subsection (2)(a) to (d); but this subsection does not apply to perishable articles which have ceased to be usable for trade.

(4) An article removed—

(a) if removed by an enforcement officer, shall as soon as is reasonably practicable be delivered to a constable, and

(b) whether removed by or delivered to a constable, shall be treated as if acquired by the constable in the course of the investigation of an offence;

but this subsection is subject to subsection (3).

(5) Having exercised a power under this section a constable or enforcement officer—

(a) shall take reasonable steps to leave the land or premises secure, and

(b) shall comply with any provision of regulations under section 25 about informing specified persons of what the constable or enforcement officer has done.

(6) Regulations under section 25 shall include provision enabling a person whose property is damaged in the course of the exercise or purported exercise of a power under this section (other than a person responsible for a contravention of the regulations) to obtain compensation from a police authority or the Olympic Delivery Authority; and the regulations may, in particular, include provision—

(a) conferring jurisdiction on a court or tribunal;

(b) about appeals.

(7) A police authority or the Olympic Delivery Authority may recover from a person responsible for the contravention of regulations under section 25, as if it were a debt, the reasonable costs of taking action under this section.

(8) In this section—

- "enforcement officer" means a person designated for the purposes of that subsection by the Olympic Delivery Authority (and paragraph 29(1)(a) to (d) of Schedule 1 shall apply to an enforcement officer whether or not he is a member of the Authority's staff), and
- "infringing article" means—

(a) an article that is being offered for trade in contravention of regulations under section 25 or is otherwise being used in connection with a contravention of the regulations, and

(b) anything (other than a vehicle) containing an article to which paragraph (a) applies.

29 Role of Olympic Delivery Authority

(1) The Olympic Delivery Authority shall—
  (a) make arrangements to have the effect of regulations made or expected to be made under section 25 brought to the attention of persons likely to be affected or interested, and
  (b) work with persons likely to be prevented by regulations under section 25 from carrying out their habitual trading activities in attempting to identify acceptable alternatives.
(2) In exercising their function under subsection (1) the Authority shall—
  (a) aim to give two years' notice of the general nature of the regulations, and
  (b) aim to give six months' notice of the detailed provisions of the regulations.
(3) The Olympic Delivery Authority—
  (a) shall make available to persons who are or may be affected by regulations under section 25 advice about the effect or likely effect of the regulations, and
  (b) may give assistance (which may include financial assistance) in complying with or avoiding breaches of the regulations.
(4) The Olympic Delivery Authority may institute criminal proceedings in respect of an offence under section 27.
(5) Subsection (4) shall not apply in relation to the institution of proceedings in Scotland or Northern Ireland.
(6) The Olympic Delivery Authority shall—
  (a) prepare a strategy for the exercise of their functions under this section and under or by virtue of sections 25 and 28,
  (b) submit the strategy to the Secretary of State,
  (c) revise the strategy until it obtains the Secretary of State's approval, and
  (d) publish the strategy as approved.

30 Other authorities

(1) The Secretary of State may by order require specified persons to give information about the effect or likely effect of regulations under section 25 to persons falling within a specified class.
(2) In particular, the order may require a person who grants a consent, certificate, permission or authority (by whatever name) to inform the recipient of the effect of section 26(4).
(3) An order under this section—
  (a) shall be made by statutory instrument, and
  (b) shall be subject to annulment in pursuance of a resolution of either House of Parliament.

31 Sale of tickets

(1) A person commits an offence if he sells an Olympic ticket—

(a) in a public place or in the course of a business, and

(b) otherwise than in accordance with a written authorisation issued by the London Organising Committee.

(2) For the purposes of subsection (1)—

(a) "Olympic ticket" means anything which is or purports to be a ticket for one or more London Olympic events,

(b) a reference to selling a ticket includes a reference to—

(i) offering to sell a ticket,

(ii) exposing a ticket for sale,

(iii) advertising that a ticket is available for purchase, and

(iv) giving, or offering to give, a ticket to a person who pays or agrees to pay for some other goods or services, and

(c) a person shall (without prejudice to the generality of subsection (1)(a)) be treated as acting in the course of a business if he does anything as a result of which he makes a profit or aims to make a profit.

(3) A person does not commit an offence under subsection (1) by advertising that a ticket is available for purchase if—

(a) the sale of the ticket if purchased would be in the course of a business only by reason of subsection (2)(c), and

(b) the person does not know, and could not reasonably be expected to discover, that subsection (2)(c) would apply to the sale.

(4) A person does not commit an offence under subsection (1) (whether actual or inchoate) only by virtue of making facilities available in connection with electronic communication or the storage of electronic data.

(5) Where a person who provides services for electronic communication or for the storage of electronic data discovers that they are being used in connection with the commission of an offence under subsection (1), the defence in subsection (4) does not apply in respect of continued provision of the services after the shortest time reasonably required to withdraw them.

(6) A person guilty of an offence under subsection (1) shall be liable on summary conviction to a fine not exceeding level 5 on the standard scale.

(7) Section 32(2)(b) of the Police and Criminal Evidence Act 1984 (c. 60) (power to search premises) shall, in its application to the offence under subsection (1) above, permit the searching of a vehicle which a constable reasonably thinks was used in connection with the offence.

(8) Subsection (9) applies where a person in Scotland is arrested in connection with the commission of an offence under subsection (1).

(9) For the purposes of recovering evidence relating to the offence, a constable in Scotland may without warrant enter and search—
   (a) premises in which the person was when arrested or immediately before he was arrested, and
   (b) a vehicle which the constable reasonably believes is being used or was used in connection with the offence.

(10) Subsection (9) is without prejudice to any power of entry or search which is otherwise exercisable by a constable in Scotland.

(11) The London Organising Committee shall make arrangements for the grant of authorisations under subsection (1)(b); and the arrangements may, in particular—
   (a) make provision about charges;
   (b) enable the Committee to exercise unfettered discretion.

(12) In this section a reference to a London Olympic event includes a reference to an event held by way of a pre-Olympic event in accordance with arrangements made by the London Organising Committee in pursuance of paragraph 7 of the Bye-Law to Rule 49 of the Olympic Charter.

MISCELLANEOUS

32 Olympic Symbol etc. (Protection) Act 1995

Schedule 3 (which amends the Olympic Symbol etc. (Protection) Act 1995 (c. 32)) shall have effect.

33 London Olympics association right

Schedule 4 (which creates the London Olympics association right) shall have effect.

SCHEDULE 3
OLYMPIC SYMBOL PROTECTION

INTRODUCTION

1 The Olympic Symbol etc. (Protection) Act 1995 (c. 32) shall be amended as follows.

Olympics association right: proprietor

2 After section 1(2) (proprietor of Olympics association right) insert—
"(2A) An order under subsection (2) above—
(a) may appoint more than one person;
(b) may make different appointments for different purposes;
(c) may make provision for joint or concurrent exercise of rights;

(d) may apply (with or without modifications) or make provision similar to a provision of section 23 of the Trade Marks Act 1994 (c. 26) (co-ownership)."

Words similar to protected words

3 (1) At the end of section 3(1)(b) (infringement: similar symbols and mottos) add "or a word so similar to a protected word as to be likely to create in the public mind an association with the Olympic Games or the Olympic movement".

(2) In the application of section 4(11) to (14) (infringement: protection for existing use) to the Olympics association right as it has effect by virtue of sub-paragraph (1) above, a reference to the commencement of the Act shall be treated as a reference to the commencement of that sub-paragraph.

Olympics association right: limitations

4 For section 4(1) to (10) (infringement of Olympics association right: limitations) substitute—

"(1) A person does not infringe the Olympics association right (despite section 3) by the use of a controlled representation—

(a) in publishing or broadcasting a report of a sporting or other event forming part of the Olympic Games,

(b) in publishing or broadcasting information about the Olympic Games,

(c) as an incidental inclusion in a literary work, dramatic work, artistic work, sound recording, film or broadcast, within the meaning of Part I of the Copyright, Designs and Patents Act 1988 (c. 48) (copyright), or

(d) as an inclusion in an advertisement for a publication or broadcast of a kind described in paragraph (a) or (b).

(2) But the exceptions in subsection (1)(a) and (b) do not apply to advertising material which is published or broadcast at the same time as, or in connection with, a report or information.

(3) A person does not infringe the Olympics association right by using a controlled representation in a context which is not likely to suggest an association between a person, product or service and the Olympic Games or the Olympic movement; and for the purpose of this subsection—

(a) the concept of an association between a person, product or service and the Olympic Games or the Olympic movement includes, in particular—

(i) any kind of contractual relationship,

(ii) any kind of commercial relationship,
(iii) any kind of corporate or structural connection, and
(iv) the provision by a person of financial or other support for or in connection with the Olympic Games or the Olympic movement, but

(b) a person does not suggest an association with the Olympic Games or the Olympic movement only by making a statement which—
(i) accords with honest practices in industrial or commercial matters, and
(ii) does not make promotional or other commercial use of a protected word by incorporating it in a context to which the Olympic Games and the Olympic movement are substantively irrelevant.

(4) The Secretary of State may by order specify what is to be or not to be treated for the purposes of subsection (3) as an association between a person, product or service and the Olympic Games or the Olympic movement; and an order under this subsection—
(a) may include incidental, consequential or transitional provision (which may include provision amending subsection (3)(a) or (b)),
(b) shall be made by statutory instrument, and
(c) may not be made unless a draft has been laid before and approved by resolution of each House of Parliament.

(5) A person does not infringe the Olympics association right by using a controlled representation in relation to goods if—
(a) they were put on the market in the European Economic Area by the proprietor or with his consent,
(b) the representation was used in relation to the goods when they were put on the market, and
(c) the proprietor does not oppose further dealings in the goods for legitimate reasons (including, in particular, that the condition of the goods has been changed or impaired after they were put on the market)."

5 At the end of section 5 (Olympics association right: power to prescribe further limitations) add—

"(4) An order under this section shall be subject to annulment in pursuance of a resolution of either House of Parliament."

The Paralympics

6 After section 5 insert—

"The Paralympics association right

5A Creation

(1) There shall be a right, to be known as the Paralympics association right.

(2) The provisions of this Act shall apply in relation to the Paralympics association right as they apply to the Olympics association right; and for that purpose—

(a) a reference to the Olympic Games shall be treated as a reference to the Paralympic Games,

(b) a reference to the Olympic motto shall be treated as a reference to the Paralympic motto,

(c) a reference to the Olympic movement shall be treated as a reference to the Paralympic movement,

(d) a reference to the Olympic symbol shall be treated as a reference to the Paralympic symbol, and

(e) a reference to the commencement of this Act is a reference to the commencement of this section."

7 In section 18(1) (interpretation) after the definition of "Olympic symbol" insert—

""the Paralympic Games" means the events known by that name and organised by the International Paralympic Committee;

"Paralympic motto" means the motto of the International Paralympic Committee — "Spirit in Motion";

"Paralympic symbol" means the symbol of the International Paralympic Committee which the Secretary of State shall set out in an order made by statutory instrument (which shall be laid before Parliament after being made)."

8 For section 18(2) (protected words) substitute—

"(2) For the purposes of this Act—

(a) each of the following is a protected word in relation to the Olympics association right—

(i) Olympiad,
(ii) Olympiads,
(iii) Olympian,
(iv) Olympians,
(v) Olympic, and
(vi) Olympics, and

(b) each of the following is a protected word in relation to the Paralympics association right—

(i) Paralympiad,
(ii) Paralympiads,
(iii) Paralympian,
(iv) Paralympians,

(v) Paralympic, and
(vi) Paralympics."

9 At the end of section 18 add—

"(5) The Secretary of State may by order amend this section to reflect a change of motto or symbol of the International Olympic Committee or the International Paralympic Committee.

(6) An order under subsection (5)—

(a) may include incidental, consequential or transitional provision (which may include provision similar to section 4(11) to (14) above),
(b) shall be made by statutory instrument, and
(c) shall be subject to annulment in pursuance of a resolution of either House of Parliament."

Infringement

10 In section 7(3)(a) (orders in relation to infringing goods: "infringing material") for ", or for advertising goods or services," substitute ", for advertising goods or services or by being displayed,".

Penalties

11 (1) In respect of an offence under section 8 (infringement marketing of goods) committed during the period specified in sub-paragraph (2), the reference in section 8(5)(a) (maximum fine on summary conviction) to the statutory maximum shall be taken as a reference to £20,000.

(2) The period referred to in sub-paragraph (1)—

(a) begins at the end of the period of two months beginning with the date on which this Act receives Royal Assent, and
(b) ends with 31st December 2012.

Enforcement

12 (1) After section 8 add—

"8A Enforcement by trading standards authority

(1) A local weights and measures authority may enforce within their area the provisions of section 8.

(2) The following provisions of the Trade Descriptions Act 1968 apply in relation to the enforcement of that section as in relation to the enforcement of that Act—

(a) section 27 (power to make test purchases),
(b) section 28 (power to enter premises and inspect and seize goods and documents),
(c) section 29 (obstruction of authorised officers), and

(d) section 33 (compensation for loss, &c of goods seized).

(3) Subsection (1) above does not apply in relation to the enforcement of section 8 in Northern Ireland; but—

(a) the Department of Enterprise, Trade and Investment may enforce that section in Northern Ireland, and

(b) for that purpose the provisions of the Trade Descriptions Act 1968 specified in subsection (2) apply as if for the references to a local weights and measures authority and any officer of such an authority there were substituted references to that Department and any of its officers.

(4) Nothing in this section shall be construed as authorising a local weights and measures authority to bring proceedings in Scotland for an offence."

(2) The London Organising Committee may—

(a) make arrangements with a local weights and measures authority for the exercise of the authority's power under section 8 of the Olympic Symbol etc. (Protection) Act 1995 (as inserted by sub-paragraph (1));

(b) may make payments to a local weights and measures authority in respect of expenses incurred in the exercise of that power.

13 After section 8A (inserted by paragraph 12 above) insert—

"8B Arrest

(1) After paragraph 21 of Schedule 1A to the Police and Criminal Evidence Act 1984 (arrestable offences) add—

"Olympic Symbol etc. (Protection) Act 1995

21A An offence under section 8 of the Olympic Symbol etc. (Protection) Act 1995 (offences in relation to goods)."

(2) A constable in Scotland may arrest without warrant a person who the constable reasonably believes is committing or has committed an offence under section 8 of the Olympic Symbol etc. (Protection) Act 1995.

(3) Subsection (2) is without prejudice to any power of arrest which is otherwise exercisable by a constable in Scotland."

14 After section 12 (forfeiture) insert—

"2A Detention by Revenue and Customs

(1) The proprietor may give notice in writing to the Commissioners for Her Majesty's Revenue and Customs—

(a) stating that at a time and place specified in the notice, goods which are infringing goods, material or articles are expected to arrive in the United Kingdom—

(i) from outside the European Economic Area, or

(ii) from within the Area but not having been entered for free circulation,

(b) specifying the nature of the controlled representation by reference to which the goods are infringing goods, material or articles, and

(c) requesting the Commissioners to detain the goods.

(2) The Commissioners may detain goods to which a notice under subsection (1) relates.

(3) But the Commissioners may not detain goods—

(a) imported by a person for his private and domestic use, or

(b) to which section 89(3) of the Trade Marks Act 1994 applies (Council Regulation (EC) No. 1383/2003).

(4) If the Commissioners detain goods to which a notice under subsection (1) applies they shall as soon as is reasonably practicable—

(a) give written notice of the detention and the grounds for it to the person in whose name the goods were presented or declared to customs, and

(b) give the proprietor notice that the goods have been detained, specifying in respect of the goods such information as is available to the Commissioners about—

(i) the nature of the goods,

(ii) their number,

(iii) the place where they were manufactured,

(iv) the place from which they were sent,

(v) the name and address of the person by whom they were sent,

(vi) the name and address of the person mentioned in paragraph (a),

(vii) the name and address of the person to whom they were to be delivered, and

(viii) the name and address of the person who holds them during detention.

(5) The Commissioners may provide samples of detained goods to the proprietor on request, in which case he—

(a) may use the samples only for the purpose of determining whether they are infringing goods, material or articles,

(b) must return the samples to the Commissioners as soon as is reasonably practicable, and

(c) must inform the Commissioners as soon as is reasonably practicable whether the goods are infringing goods, material or articles.

(6) The Commissioners may permit the proprietor on request to inspect detained goods (in which case he must inform the Commissioners as soon as is reasonably practicable whether the goods are infringing goods, material or articles).

(7) The Commissioners shall release goods detained in pursuance of a notice under subsection (1) if—
   (a) the Commissioners think that initiating process in proceedings under section 6 in respect of the goods has not been served during the period of 10 working days, in the case of non-perishable goods, or 3 working days, in the case of perishable goods, beginning with the date on which the notice under subsection (4)(b) was received,
   (b) the Commissioners think that proceedings under section 6 in respect of the goods have been withdrawn, have lapsed or have terminated without an order being made in respect of the goods by virtue of section 7, or
   (c) the Commissioners are informed by the proprietor that the goods are not infringing goods, material or articles.

(8) The Commissioners may detain goods which they think, having regard to the nature of the goods and to information provided by the proprietor, may be infringing goods, material or articles; and if the Commissioners detain goods under this subsection—
   (a) they shall as soon as is reasonably practicable invite the proprietor to give the Commissioners a notice that the goods are infringing goods, material or articles,
   (b) they shall, when giving an invitation under paragraph (a), give in respect of the goods such information as is available to them about—
      (i) the nature of the goods,
      (ii) their number,
      (iii) the place where they were manufactured,
      (iv) the place from which they were sent,
      (v) the name and address of the person by whom they were sent,
      (vi) the name and address of the person in whose name the goods were presented or declared to customs,
      (vii) the name and address of the person to whom they were to be delivered, and
      (viii) the name and address of the person who holds them during detention,
   (c) they may provide samples of the goods to the proprietor on request in which case he —
      (i) may use the samples only for the purpose of determining whether they are infringing goods, material or articles,
      (ii) must return the samples to the Commissioners as soon as is reasonably practicable, and
      (iii) must inform the Commissioners as soon as reasonably practicable whether the goods are infringing goods, material or articles,

(d) they may permit the proprietor on request to inspect the goods (in which case he must inform the Commissioners as soon as reasonably practicable whether the goods are infringing goods, material or articles),

(e) if no notice is given in accordance with paragraph (a) within the period of 3 working days beginning with the date on which the invitation under that paragraph is received, the Commissioners shall release the goods, and

(f) if a notice is given in accordance with paragraph (a), the Commissioners shall proceed as if it were a notice given under subsection (1) above (and as if the goods were detained in pursuance of that notice), but—

 (i) subsections (4)(b), (5) and (6) shall not have effect, and

 (ii) subsection (7) shall have effect as if the reference to the notice under subsection (4)(b) were a reference to information under paragraph (b) above.

12B Section 12A: supplementary

(1) Section 90 of the Trade Marks Act 1994 (c. 26) (regulations as to form of notice, &c.) shall have effect in relation to a notice under subsection 12A(1) or (8)(a) above as in relation to a notice under section 89(1).

(2) A person who is or was an officer or employee of the proprietor, or who acts or acted on the proprietor's behalf, commits an offence if he discloses information provided in accordance with section 12A(4)(b) or 12A(8)(b) other than—

 (a) for the purpose of, or with a view to the institution of, proceedings under section 6,

 (b) for the purpose of complying with an enactment,

 (c) in pursuance of an order of a court,

 (d) in a form which ensures that the identity of no person to whom the information relates is specified or can be deduced,

 (e) with the consent of each person to whom the information relates, or

 (f) with the consent of the Commissioners for Her Majesty's Revenue and Customs;

and sections 19(3), (4), (7) and 55(1) of the Commissioners for Revenue and Customs Act 2005 (c. 11) (defences and penalties) shall have effect in relation to this subsection.

(3) Section 139(1), (2), (3), (4), (7) and (8) of the Customs and Excise Management Act 1979 (detention of goods: constables, &c.) shall apply in relation to goods liable to detention in accordance with section 12A above as in relation to things liable to forfeiture—

(a) with the substitution of a reference to this Act for a reference to the customs and excise Acts, and

(b) with any other necessary modifications.

(4) Section 144 of that Act (protection of officers) shall apply in relation to the detention of goods in accordance with section 12A above—

(a) with the substitution of a reference to proceedings under section 6 above for the reference in section 144(1) to proceedings for condemnation, and

(b) with any other necessary modifications.

(5) In section 12A "working day" means a day that is not a Saturday, a Sunday or a bank holiday (within the meaning of section 1 of the Banking and Financial Dealings Act 1971 (c. 80))."

SCHEDULE 4

LONDON OLYMPICS ASSOCIATION RIGHT

The right

1 (1) There shall be a right, to be known as the London Olympics association right, which shall confer exclusive rights in relation to the use of any representation (of any kind) in a manner likely to suggest to the public that there is an association between the London Olympics and—

(a) goods or services, or

(b) a person who provides goods or services.

(2) For the purposes of this Schedule—

(a) the concept of an association between a person, goods or a service and the London Olympics includes, in particular—

(i) any kind of contractual relationship,

(ii) any kind of commercial relationship,

(iii) any kind of corporate or structural connection, and

(iv) the provision by a person of financial or other support for or in connection with the London Olympics, but

(b) a person does not suggest an association between a person, goods or a service and the London Olympics only by making a statement which—

(i) accords with honest practices in industrial or commercial matters, and

(ii) does not make promotional or other commercial use of a representation relating to the London Olympics by incorporating it in a context to which the London Olympics are substantively irrelevant.

(3) The Secretary of State may by order specify what is to be or not to be treated for the purposes of sub-paragraph (2) as an association between a person, goods or a service and the London Olympics; and an order under this subsection—

(a) may include incidental, consequential or transitional provision (which may include provision amending sub-paragraph (2)(a) or (b)),
(b) shall be made by statutory instrument, and
(c) may not be made unless a draft has been laid before and approved by resolution of each House of Parliament.

Infringement: general

2 (1) A person infringes the London Olympics association right if in the course of trade he uses in relation to goods or services any representation (of any kind) in a manner likely to suggest to the public that there is an association between the London Olympics and—

(a) the goods or services, or
(b) a person who provides the goods or services.

(2) Sub-paragraph (1) is subject to the provisions of this Schedule.

Infringement: specific expressions

3 (1) For the purpose of considering whether a person has infringed the London Olympics association right a court may, in particular, take account of his use of a combination of expressions of a kind specified in sub-paragraph (2).

(2) The combinations referred to in sub-paragraph (1) are combinations of—

(a) any of the expressions in the first group, with
(b) any of the expressions in the second group or any of the other expressions in the first group.

(3) The following expressions form the first group for the purposes of sub-paragraph (2)—

(a) "games",
(b) "Two Thousand and Twelve",
(c) "2012", and
(d) "twenty twelve".

(4) The following expressions form the second group for the purposes of sub-paragraph (2)—

(a) gold,
(b) silver,
(c) bronze,

(d) London,
(e) medals,
(f) sponsor, and
(g) summer.

(5) It is immaterial for the purposes of this paragraph whether or not a word is written wholly or partly in capital letters.

(6) The Secretary of State may by order add, remove or vary an entry in either group of expressions.

(7) An order under sub-paragraph (6)—

(a) shall be made by statutory instrument, and
(b) may not be made unless a draft has been laid before and approved by resolution of each House of Parliament.

(8) An order under sub-paragraph (6) which adds or varies an entry in a group of expressions may be made only if the Secretary of State thinks it necessary in order to prevent commercial exploitation of the London Olympics.

(9) Before laying a draft order in accordance with sub-paragraph (7)(b) the Secretary of State shall consult—

(a) one or more persons who appear to him to have relevant responsibility for regulating the advertising industry (including enforcing standards of professional conduct),
(b) one or more persons who appear to him to represent the interests of the advertising industry,
(c) the London Organising Committee, and
(d) such other persons as he thinks appropriate.

Authorised use

4 (1) The London Olympics association right is not infringed by use of a representation in accordance with an authorisation granted by the London Organising Committee.

(2) The London Organising Committee shall make arrangements for the grant of authorisations; and the arrangements may, in particular—

(a) make provision about charges;
(b) enable the Committee to exercise unfettered discretion (subject to any direction under section 15 of the Olympic Symbol etc. (Protection) Act 1995 (c. 32) as applied by paragraph 10 below).

5 (1) The London Organising Committee shall maintain a register of persons, and classes of person, authorised for the purposes of paragraph 4.

(2) The register shall specify in respect of each authorised person—

(a) his name,
(b) his principal place of business,

(c) the goods or services to which the authorisation relates,
(d) the period in respect of which the authorisation has effect.

(3) The register shall specify in respect of each authorised class of person—

(a) the nature of the class,
(b) the goods or services to which the authorisation relates (including the circumstances in which it does or does not apply), and
(c) the period in respect of which the authorisation has effect.

(4) The London Organising Committee shall—

(a) ensure that a copy of the register is accessible to the public by use of the internet, and
(b) comply with a written request for a copy of the register or of an entry in the register.

(5) The London Organising Committee may require a request under sub-paragraph (4)(b) to be accompanied by a specified fee; and the Committee—

(a) may specify different fees for different purposes,
(b) may charge no fee, or waive a fee, in such cases as it thinks appropriate, and
(c) may not specify a fee which exceeds any maximum specified by order of the Secretary of State.

(6) An order under sub-paragraph (5)(c)—

(a) may make different provision for different purposes,
(b) may include transitional provision,
(c) shall be made by statutory instrument, and
(d) shall be subject to annulment in pursuance of a resolution of either House of Parliament.

(7) If a copy of the register or of an entry in the register issued by the London Organising Committee is certified on behalf of the Committee as an accurate copy, it shall be treated as accurate for all purposes (including for the purposes of legal proceedings) unless the contrary is proved.

(8) A request for a copy under sub-paragraph (4)(b) may require the copy to be certified in accordance with sub-paragraph (7).

Infringement: other exceptions

6 The London Olympics association right is not infringed by the use of a trade mark registered under the Trade Marks Act 1994 (c. 26) in relation to goods or services for which it is registered.

7 The London Olympics association right is not infringed by—

(a) the use by a person of his own name or address,
(b) the use of indications concerning the kind, quality, quantity, intended

purpose, value, geographical origin, time of production of goods or of rendering of services, or other characteristics of goods or services,

(c) the use of a representation which is necessary to indicate the intended purpose of a product or service;

provided, in each case, that the use is in accordance with honest practices in industrial or commercial matters.

8 (1) The London Olympics association right is not infringed by the use of a representation—

(a) in publishing or broadcasting a report of a sporting or other event forming part of the London Olympics,

(b) in publishing or broadcasting information about the London Olympics,

(c) as an incidental inclusion in a literary work, dramatic work, artistic work, sound recording, film or broadcast, within the meaning of Part I of the Copyright, Designs and Patents Act 1988 (c. 48) (copyright), or

(d) as an inclusion in an advertisement for a publication or broadcast of a kind described in paragraph (a) or (b).

(2) But the exceptions in sub-paragraph (1)(a) and (b) do not apply to advertising material which is published or broadcast at the same time as, or in connection with, a report or information.

9 The London Olympics association right is not infringed by the use of a representation in relation to goods if—

(a) they were put on the market in the European Economic Area in accordance with an authorisation granted by the London Organising Committee,

(b) the representation was used in relation to the goods when they were put on the market, and

(c) the London Organising Committee does not oppose further dealings in the goods for legitimate reasons (including, in particular, that the condition of the goods has been changed or impaired after they were put on the market).

Application of Olympic Symbol etc. (Protection) Act 1995

10 (1) The following provisions of the Olympic Symbol etc. (Protection) Act 1995 (c. 32) shall have effect (with any necessary modifications) in relation to the London Olympics association right as they have effect in relation to the Olympics association right—

(a) section 2(2) to (4) (effect of right),

(b) section 3(2) (infringement: specific cases),

(c) section 4(11) to (14) (infringement: protection for existing rights),

(d) section 5 (power to prescribe further limitations),
(e) section 6 (action for infringement),
(f) section 7 (orders in relation to infringing goods, &c.),
(g) section 15 (directions by Secretary of State), and
(h) section 16 (action for groundless threats).

(2) In the application of provisions of that Act by virtue of sub-paragraph (1)—

(a) a reference to a controlled representation is a reference to a visual or verbal representation (of any kind) likely to create in the public mind an association between the London Olympics and—
  (i) goods or services, or
  (ii) a provider of goods or services,
(b) a reference to the person appointed under section 1(2) as proprietor shall be taken as a reference to the London Organising Committee,
(c) a reference to the commencement of that Act shall be taken as a reference to the commencement of this Schedule, and
(d) a reference to the Olympic Games or the Olympic movement or to the Paralympic Games or the Paralympic movement shall be taken as a reference to the London Olympics.

(3) In each case, a reference in sub-paragraph (1) to a provision of that Act is to that provision as amended by Schedule 3 above.

3

Sydney 2000 Games (Indicia and Images) Protection Act 1996 No. 22, 1996

(Assented to 28 June 1996)

SYDNEY 2000 GAMES (INDICIA AND IMAGES) PROTECTION ACT 1996 NO. 22, 1996 - LONG TITLE

An Act to make provision for the regulation of the use for commercial purposes of the indicia and images associated with the Sydney 2000 Olympic Games and the Sydney 2000 Paralympic Games, and for related purposes

1 Short title

This Act may be cited as the Sydney 2000 Games (Indicia and Images) Protection Act 1996.

2 Commencement

This Act commences on the day on which it receives the Royal Assent.

3 Objects of Act

(1) The objects of this Act are:

(a) to protect, and to further, the position of Australia as a participant in, and a supporter of, the world Olympic and Paralympic movements; and

(b) to the extent that it is within the power of the Parliament, to assist in protecting the relations, and in ensuring the performance of the obligations, of the Sydney 2000 Games bodies with and to the world Olympic and Paralympic movements;

in relation to the holding of the Sydney 2000 Games.

(2) Those objects are to be achieved by facilitating the raising of licensing revenue in relation to the Sydney 2000 Games through the regulation of the use for commercial purposes of the indicia and images associated with the Games.

(3) The reference in paragraph (1)(b) to Sydney 2000 Games bodies is a reference to:

(a) SOCOG; and
(b) SPOC; and
(c) the Australian Olympic Committee Inc.; and
(d) the Australian Paralympic Federation; and
(e) the City of Sydney; and
(f) the Government of the State of New South Wales.

4 Act binds the Crown

This Act binds the Crown in all its capacities.

5 Application of Act

This Act extends to:

(a) Christmas Island; and
(b) Cocos (Keeling) Islands; and
(c) Norfolk Island; and
(d) the waters above the continental shelf of Australia; and
(e) the airspace above Australia and the continental shelf of Australia.

6 Additional operation of Act

In addition to its effect apart from this section, this Act also has the effect that it would have if each reference to use for commercial purposes were a reference to:

(a) use for commercial purposes by:
   (i) a foreign corporation within the meaning of paragraph 51(xx) of the Constitution; or
   (ii) a trading corporation (within the meaning of that paragraph) formed within the limits of the Commonwealth; or
   (iii) a financial corporation (within the meaning of that paragraph) so formed, including a body corporate that carries on as its sole or principal business the business of banking (other than State

banking not extending beyond the limits of the State concerned) or insurance (other than State insurance not extending beyond the limits of the State concerned); or
(iv) a body corporate incorporated in a Territory; or
(b) use for commercial purposes by any person in the course of:
(i) trade or commerce with other countries; or
(ii) trade or commerce among the States; or
(iii) trade or commerce within a Territory, between a State and a Territory or between the Territories; or
(iv) the supply of goods or services to the Commonwealth, a Territory, or to an authority or instrumentality of the Commonwealth or of a Territory; or
(v) the use of postal, telegraphic or telephonic services; or
(vi) the making of a broadcast; or
(c) use for commercial purposes by any person that detrimentally affects the rights conferred by or under this Act on a licensed user that is a corporation within the meaning of subparagraphs (a)(i) to (a)(iii).

7 General definitions

(1) In this Act, unless the contrary intention appears:
Australia includes the following external Territories:
(a) Christmas Island;
(b) Cocos (Keeling) Islands;
(c) Norfolk Island.
broadcast means a transmission by means of:
(a) a broadcasting service within the meaning of the Broadcasting Services Act 1992; or
(b) something that would be such a broadcasting service if the definition of broadcasting
service in subsection 6(1) of that Act were amended by omitting all the words from and
including "but does not include" to the end of the definition.
continental shelf has the same meaning as in the Seas and Submerged Lands Act 1973.
Federal Court means the Federal Court of Australia.
licensed user means a person in relation to whom a licence under section 14 is in force.
prescribed court means a court that is a prescribed court by virtue of section 50.
register means the register of licensed users established and maintained by SOCOG for the purposes of section 16.

Secretary means the Secretary of the Department.
SOCOG means the Sydney Organising Committee for the Olympic Games constituted by the Sydney Organising Committee for the Olympic Games Act 1993 of New South Wales.
SPOC means Sydney Paralympic Organising Committee Limited incorporated under the law of New South Wales.
Sydney 2000 Games means:
(a) the Sydney 2000 Olympic Games; and
(b) the Sydney 2000 Paralympic Games.
Sydney 2000 Games images means:
(a) common Sydney 2000 Games images; and
(b) Sydney 2000 Olympic Games images; and
(c) Sydney 2000 Paralympic Games images;
as defined in section 9.
Sydney 2000 Games indicia means:
(a) common Sydney 2000 Games indicia; and
(b) Sydney 2000 Olympic Games indicia; and
(c) Sydney 2000 Paralympic Games indicia;
as defined in section 8.
Sydney 2000 Olympic Games means the Games of the XXVII Olympiad in Sydney in the year 2000.
Sydney 2000 Paralympic Games means the Games of the XIth Paralympiad in Sydney in the year 2000.
this Act includes the regulations.
working day, in relation to the period within which an act is to be, or may be, done, means a day that is not:
(a) a Saturday or a Sunday; or
(b) a public holiday or a bank holiday in any place in which the act is to be, or may be,
done.

(2) The use in this Act of the words "indicia" and "images" is not intended to express a contrary intention for the purposes of section 23 of the Acts Interpretation Act 1901.
Note:Paragraph 23(b) of the Acts Interpretation Act 1901 provides that words in the plural number include the singular.

8 Sydney 2000 Games indicia

(1) For the purposes of this Act:
common Sydney 2000 Games indicia means:
(a) any of the following phrases:
(i) "Games City";

(ii) "Millennium Games";
(iii) "Sydney Games";
(iv) "Sydney 2000"; or

(b) any combination of the word "Games" and the number "2000" or the words "Two Thousand". Sydney 2000 Olympic Games indicia means:

(a) either of the following words:
(i) "Olympiad";
(ii) "Olympic"; or

(b) any of the following phrases:
(i) "Share the Spirit";
(ii) "Summer Games";
(iii) "Team Millennium"; or

(c) any combination of "24th", "Twenty-Fourth" or "XXIVth" and the word "Olympics" or "Games"; or

(d) any combination of a word in List A with a word, words, phrase or number in List B:

List A	List B
Olympian	Bronze
Olympics	Games
	Gold
	Green and Gold
	Medals
	Millennium
	Silver
	Spirit
	Sponsor
	Summer
	Sydney
	Two Thousand
	2000

Sydney 2000 Paralympic Games indicia means:

(a) either of the following words:
(i) "Paralympiad";
(ii) "Paralympic"; or

(b) any combination of "11th", "Eleventh" or "XIth" and the word "Paralympics" or "Games"; or

(c) any combination of a word in List A with a word, words, phrase or number in List B:

List A	List B
Paralympian	Bronze
Paralympics	Games
	Gold
	Green and Gold
	Medals
	Millennium
	Silver
	Spirit
	Sponsor
	Summer
	Sydney
	Two Thousand
	2000

(2) For the purposes of this Act, any Sydney 2000 Games indicia that are represented in a language other than English are to be taken to be Sydney 2000 Games indicia.

9 Sydney 2000 Games images

For the purposes of this Act:

Common Sydney 2000 Games images means any visual or aural representations that, to a reasonable person, in the circumstances of the presentation, would suggest a connection with the Sydney 2000 Olympic Games and the Sydney 2000 Paralympic Games.

Sydney 2000 Olympic Games images means any visual or aural representations that, to a reasonable person, in the circumstances of the presentation, would suggest a connection with the Sydney 2000 Olympic Games.

Sydney 2000 Paralympic Games images means any visual or aural representations that, to a reasonable person, in the circumstances of the presentation, would suggest a connection with the Sydney 2000 Paralympic Games.

10 Application of Sydney 2000 Games indicia and images

(1) For the purposes of this Act and without limiting the generality of the meaning of the expression, Sydney 2000 Games indicia and images are to be taken to be applied to goods or services if:

(a) in the case of goods, the indicia or images:

(i) are woven in, impressed on, worked into, or affixed or annexed to, the goods; or

(ii) are applied to any covering, document, label, reel or thing in or with which the goods are, or are intended to be, dealt with or provided in the course of trade; or

(b) in the case of goods or services, the indicia or images:

(i) are used on a signboard or in an advertisement (including a television or radio advertisement) that promotes the goods or services; or

(ii) are used in an invoice, price list, catalogue, brochure, business letter, business paper or other commercial document that relates to the goods or services.

(2) If:

(a) goods are imported into Australia for the purpose of sale or distribution by a person; and

(b) when imported, the goods have already had applied to them Sydney 2000 Games indicia or images; for the purposes of Divisions 2 and 3 of Part 4, the person is to be taken to have applied the indicia or images to the goods.

(3) In subparagraph (1)(a)(ii):

covering includes packaging, frame, wrapper, container, stopper, lid or cap.

label includes a band or ticket.

11 Use for commercial purposes

For the purposes of this Act, a person uses Sydney 2000 Games indicia and images for commercial purposes if:

(a) the person applies the indicia or images to goods or services of the person; and

(b) the application is for advertising or promotional purposes, or is likely to enhance the demand for the goods or services; and

(c) the application, to a reasonable person, would suggest that the first-mentioned person is or was a sponsor of, or is or was the provider of other support for:

(i) the Sydney 2000 Olympic Games, the Sydney 2000 Paralympic Games, or both Games; or

(ii) any event arranged:

(A) by SOCOG, the Australian Olympic Committee Inc., or the International Olympic Committee in connection with the Sydney 2000 Olympic Games; or

(B) by SPOC, the Australian Paralympic Federation, or the International Paralympic Committee in connection with the Sydney 2000 Paralympic Games.

12 Regulation of use of Sydney 2000 Games indicia and images

(1) A person, other than:
    (a) SOCOG; or
    (b) SPOC; or
    (c) a licensed user; must not use Sydney 2000 Games indicia and images for commercial purposes.

(2) SOCOG may only use the following Sydney 2000 Games indicia and images for commercial purposes:
    (a) common Sydney 2000 Games indicia;
    (b) Sydney 2000 Olympic Games indicia;
    (c) common Sydney 2000 Games images;
    (d) Sydney 2000 Olympic Games images.

(3) SPOC may only use the following Sydney 2000 Games indicia and images for commercial purposes:
    (a) common Sydney 2000 Games indicia;
    (b) Sydney 2000 Paralympic Games indicia;
    (c) common Sydney 2000 Games images;
    (d) Sydney 2000 Paralympic Games images.

(4) A licensed user may only use for commercial purposes the Sydney 2000 Games indicia and images that the person is licensed to use, and may only use those indicia and images in accordance with the licence.

(5) For the purposes of subsection (1), the use of indicia so closely resembling Sydney 2000 Games indicia as to be likely to be mistaken, by a reasonable person, for Sydney 2000 Games indicia is to be taken to be use of those Sydney 2000 Games indicia.

13 Use of Olympic insignia not regulated by this Act

The use of the Olympic insignia protected by the Olympic Insignia Protection Act 1987 is not regulated by this Act, and this Act is not intended to affect the operation of the Olympic Insignia Protection Act 1987.

14 Licensing by SOCOG and SPOC

(1) For the purposes of this Act, SOCOG may license a person to use all, or any one or more, of the following Sydney 2000 Games indicia and images for commercial purposes:
    (a) common Sydney 2000 Games indicia;
    (b) Sydney 2000 Olympic Games indicia;
    (c) common Sydney 2000 Games images;
    (d) Sydney 2000 Olympic Games images;

    in all circumstances or in specified circumstances, for a specified time or until this Act ceases to have effect.

Note: For when this Act ceases to have effect see section 55.

(2) For the purposes of this Act, SPOC may license a person to use all, or any one or more, of the following Sydney 2000 Games indicia and images for commercial purposes:

(a) common Sydney 2000 Games indicia;
(b) Sydney 2000 Paralympic Games indicia;
(c) common Sydney 2000 Games images;
(d) Sydney 2000 Paralympic Games images;

in all circumstances or in specified circumstances, for a specified time or until this Act ceases to have effect.

Note: For when this Act ceases to have effect see section 55.

(3) Nothing in this section is intended to affect the capacity of SOCOG or SPOC to determine the terms and conditions on which a person is licensed, including terms and conditions relating to the payment of money.

15 Registration

(1) Where SOCOG or SPOC licenses a person to use Sydney 2000 Games indicia or images, SOCOG or SPOC (as the case may be) must make an entry in the register of licensed users.

(2) Licensing takes effect when the entry is made in the register, and ceases on the day on which the licence ceases to be in force.

16 The register

(1) SOCOG must establish and maintain a register of licensed users.

(2) The register must:

(a) be kept by SOCOG at the principal place of business of SOCOG; and
(b) be open for inspection without charge by any person during the normal business hours of SOCOG.

(3) If the register is kept by the use of a computer, paragraph (2)(b) is satisfied:

(a) by arranging for inspection of a written copy of the particulars in the register; or
(b) by providing for access to a computer terminal from which the particulars in the register can be read.

(4) SOCOG must give a person a copy of the register (or part of the register) within 5 working days if the person:

(a) asks SOCOG for a copy; and
(b) pays any fee (up to the prescribed amount) required by SOCOG.

If the register is kept by the use of a computer and the person asks for the copy on a floppy disk, SOCOG must give the copy to the person on a floppy disk. The person is not, however, entitled to have the floppy disk formatted for an operating system preferred by the person.

17 Entry in register

(1) An entry in the register must contain the following particulars in relation to a licensed user:

(a) the name and principal place of business of the person;

(b) the Sydney 2000 Games indicia and images the person may use for commercial purposes, and the circumstances in which the person may use those indicia and images;

(c) if the licence is for a specified time-the date on which the licence ceases to be in force;

(d) the date on which the entry is made;

(e) any prescribed matters.

(2) If a licence is revoked, SOCOG or SPOC (as the case may be) must include in the entry in the register relating to the licence a note of the revocation of the licence and of the date of effect of the revocation.

18 Certified copy of entry in register

(1) If a person asks SOCOG to give the person a certified copy of the particulars contained in an entry in the register, SOCOG must, within 5 working days, give the person:

(a) if the register is kept by the use of a computer-a document certified to be a reproduction in writing of the particulars contained in the entry in the register; or

(b) in any other case-a document certified to be a copy of the particulars contained in the entry in the register.

(2) If the person referred to in subsection (1) is not the licensed user to whom the entry relates, the person must pay any fee (up to the prescribed amount) required by SOCOG.

(3) The reference in subsection (1) to a document certified to be a reproduction in writing or a copy of the particulars contained in an entry in the register is a reference to a document so certified by the Chief Executive Officer of SOCOG or by a person authorised in writing by the Chief Executive Officer for the purposes of subsection (1).

19 Effect and evidence of entry in register

(1) Subject to subsections (2) and (3), a person whose name appears in an entry in the register is to be taken to be a licensed user, for the purposes of this Act, of the Sydney 2000 Games indicia and images specified in the entry.

(2) If the entry includes a date specified for the purpose of paragraph 17(1)(c), the person is to be taken to be, or to have been, a licensed user until that date.

(3) If the entry includes a note for the purpose of subsection 17(2), the person is to be taken to be, or to have been, a licensed user until the date specified in the note as the date of effect of the revocation.

(4) A document certified in accordance with section 18 to be a reproduction in writing or a copy of the particulars contained in an entry in the register is evidence that the particulars set out in the document are contained in an entry in the register.

20 SPOC may authorise SOCOG to act on its behalf

(1) If SPOC asks SOCOG to make an entry, or include a note in an entry, in the register on SPOC's behalf, SOCOG must make the entry or include the note in an entry, as the case may be.

(2) For the purposes of sections 15 and 17, an entry made, or note included in an entry, in the register by SOCOG under subsection (1) is to be taken to have been made, or included, by SPOC.

21 Copy of register to be supplied by SOCOG to Secretary of Department

(1) SOCOG must give the Secretary a copy of the register as soon as practicable after the commencement of this Act. SOCOG must also give the Secretary a copy of any entry, or note in an entry, subsequently made in the register as soon as practicable after the entry is made or the note is included, as the case may be.

(2) If the register is kept by the use of a computer, SOCOG may, if the Secretary agrees, give the copy, and a copy of any subsequent entry or note, on a floppy disk.

22 Secretary to make copy of register available

(1) The Secretary must, as soon as practicable after the Secretary is given a copy of the register, make arrangements for a copy of the register to be available for inspection in an office located in each of the capital cities of the States and in Canberra.

(2) The Secretary must, as soon as practicable after the Secretary is given a copy of any subsequent entry, or note in an entry, make arrangements for the copy of the register to be updated to include the subsequent entry or note.

23 Public access to copy of register

(1) A copy of the register made available for inspection in accordance with section 22 must be open for inspection without charge by any person

during the normal business hours of the office in which it is available for inspection.

(2) Any person who inspects the copy of the register, or who asks the Secretary for a copy of it (or part of it), must be informed that the copy of the register that they are inspecting, or that they are to receive a copy of, may not necessarily be an up-to-date copy of the register.

(3) If the copy of the register is kept by the use of a computer, subsection (1) is satisfied:
   (a) by arranging for inspection of a written copy of the particulars in the copy of the register; or
   (b) by providing for access to a computer terminal from which the particulars in the copy of the register can be read.

(4) The Secretary must give a person a copy of the copy of the register (or part of the register) within 5 working days if the person:
   (a) asks the Secretary for a copy; and
   (b) pays the prescribed fee (if any).

If the copy of the register is kept by the use of a computer and the person asks for the copy on a floppy disk, the Secretary must give the copy on a floppy disk. The person is not, however, entitled to have the floppy disk formatted for an operating system preferred by the person.

24 Trade mark and design rights

Nothing in this Act is intended to affect the operation of the following Acts:
   (a) the Trade Marks Act 1995;
   (b) the Designs Act 1906;

or to affect any rights conferred, or liabilities imposed, by or under those Acts.

25 Provision of information

(1) In order to avoid doubt, it is declared that the use of Sydney 2000 Games indicia and images for the purposes of, or in connection with, the provision of information or for the purposes of criticism or review is not alone sufficient to suggest a sponsorship, or the provision of other support, for the purposes of paragraph 11(c).

(2) In subsection (1):
   (a) a reference to the provision of information includes a reference to the reporting of news and the presentation of current affairs; and (b) a reference to criticism or review includes a reference to criticism or review:
      (i) in a newspaper, magazine or similar periodical; or

(ii) in a broadcast; or
(iii) in a cinematograph film.

26 Consent of SOCOG or SPOC to giving of notices etc.

A licensed user may not:

(a) give a notice of objection to importation under section 32; or
(b) make an application for an injunction under section 43; or
(c) bring an action for damages under section 46;

except with the written consent of the body (the licensing body) that licensed the person to use the Sydney 2000 Games indicia or images to which the notice, application or action (as the case may be) relates.

27 Request for consent

If:

(a) a licensed user gives SOCOG or SPOC (whichever is the licensing body) a written request for consent under section 26; and
(b) the licensing body neither gives nor refuses that consent before the end of the working day following the day on which the request was given;

the licensing body is to be taken to have given the consent.

28 Consent must not be unreasonably refused

Consent under section 26 must not be unreasonably refused.

29 Definitions

In this Division, unless the contrary intention appears:

application period, in relation to seized goods, means:

(a) if there is only one objector to the importation of the goods-the period specified in the notice given to the objector under section 34 or, if that period is extended under subsection 34(5), that period as so extended; or
(b) if there is more than one objector to the importation of the goods-the period beginning on the earliest day on which a period specified in a notice given to an objector under section 34 commences and ending:
    (i) on the last day on which a period specified in such a notice ends; or
    (ii) on the last day on which such a period as extended under subsection 34(5) ends;

whichever is the later.

CEO means the Chief Executive Officer of Customs.

designated owner, in relation to goods imported into Australia, means the person identified as the owner of the goods in the entry made in relation to the goods under section 68 of the Customs Act 1901.

objector, in relation to seized goods, means the person by whom a notice in force under section 32 in relation to the goods was given.

seized goods means goods seized under section 33.

30 Copy of register to be supplied by SOCOG to CEO

(1) For the purposes of this Division, SOCOG must give the CEO a copy of the register as soon as practicable after the commencement of this Act. SOCOG must also give the CEO a copy of any entry, or note in an entry, subsequently made in the register as soon as practicable after the entry is made or the note is included, as the case may be.

(2) If the register is kept by the use of a computer, SOCOG may, if the CEO agrees, give the copy, and a copy of any subsequent entry or note, on a floppy disk.

31 Notice to CEO of imports by SOCOG and SPOC

(1) If:

(a) goods are to be imported by or for SOCOG; and

(b) any of the Sydney 2000 Games indicia and images specified in subsection 12(2) have been applied to the goods;

SOCOG must give the CEO a written notice specifying the indicia and images so applied and setting out particulars sufficient to enable the CEO to identify the goods.

(2) If:

(a) goods are to be imported by or for SPOC; and

(b) any of the Sydney 2000 Games indicia and images specified in subsection 12(3) have been applied to the goods;

SPOC must give the CEO a written notice specifying the indicia and images so applied and setting out particulars sufficient to enable the CEO to identify the goods.

32 Notice of objection to importation

(1) Subject to this section SOCOG, SPOC or a licensed user may give the CEO a written notice objecting to the importation, after the day on which the notice is given, of goods that have applied to them Sydney 2000 Games indicia or images that the designated owner of the goods is not authorised by, or licensed under, this Act to use for commercial purposes in relation to the goods.

(2) A notice:

(a) is to be given together with any prescribed document; and

(b) is to be accompanied by the prescribed fee (if any).

(3) SOCOG may only give a notice in relation to the following Sydney 2000 Games indicia and images:

(a) common Sydney 2000 Games indicia;
(b) Sydney 2000 Olympic Games indicia;
(c) common Sydney 2000 Games images;
(d) Sydney 2000 Olympic Games images.

(4) SPOC may only give a notice in relation to the following Sydney 2000 Games indicia and images:

(a) common Sydney 2000 Games indicia;
(b) Sydney 2000 Paralympic Games indicia;
(c) common Sydney 2000 Games images;
(d) Sydney 2000 Paralympic Games images.

(5) A licensed user may only give a notice in relation to the Sydney 2000 Games indicia and images the person is licensed to use.

(6) A notice given by SOCOG, SPOC or a licensed user may be revoked at any time by notice in writing given to the CEO by the person who gave the original notice.

(7) If a notice is not revoked under subsection (6), it ceases to have effect:

(a) in the case of SOCOG and SPOC-when this Act ceases to have effect; and
(b) in the case of a licensed user-when this Act ceases to have effect or, if the licence is for a specified time or is revoked, on the day on which the licence ceases to be in force, whichever is the earlier.

Note: For when this Act ceases to have effect see section 55.

33 CEO may seize goods

(1) This section applies to goods manufactured outside Australia that:

(a) are imported into Australia; and
(b) are subject to the control of the Customs within the meaning of the Customs Act 1901.

(2) If:

(a) goods to which this section applies have had applied to them Sydney 2000 Games indicia or images; and
(b) a notice in force under section 32 relates to the goods; and
(c) it appears to the CEO that the designated owner is not authorised by, or licensed under, this Act, to use the indicia or images for commercial purposes in relation to the goods;

the CEO must seize the goods unless the CEO has reasonable grounds for believing that section 12 of this Act would not be contravened by the use by the designated owner of the indicia or images for commercial purposes.

(3) The CEO may refuse to seize the goods unless the CEO has been given by the objector, or by one or more of the objectors, security in an amount that the CEO considers sufficient to reimburse the Commonwealth for the reasonable expenses that may be incurred by the Commonwealth if the goods were seized.

(4) Goods seized under this section must be kept in a secure place as directed by the CEO.

34 Notice of seizure

(1) As soon as practicable after goods are seized under section 33, the CEO must give the designated owner and each objector, either personally or by post, a written notice identifying the goods and stating that they have been seized under section 33.

(2) A notice under subsection (1) that is given to each objector must also:

  (a) specify:

    (i) the full name and address of the designated owner of the goods; and

    (ii) any information that the CEO has and that the CEO believes, on reasonable grounds, to be likely to help the objector, or objectors, to identify the designated owner; and

  (b) state that the goods will be released to the designated owner unless:

    (i) an application for an injunction under section 43 in relation to the goods is made by the objector, or by one of the objectors, within the period of 10 working days commencing on a specified day; and

    (ii) written notice of the making of the application is given to the CEO within that period.

(3) The day specified for the purpose of subparagraph (2)(b)(i) must not be earlier than the day on which the notice is given.

(4) An objector may, by written notice given to the CEO before the end of the period specified in a notice for the purposes of subparagraph (2)(b)(i), request that the period be extended.

(5) If:

  (a) a request is made in accordance with subsection (4); and

  (b) the CEO is satisfied that it is reasonable that the request be granted;

the CEO may extend the period by not more than 10 working days.

35 Forfeiture of goods-by consent

(1) The designated owner of any seized goods may, at any time before an objector makes an application for an injunction under section 43 in relation to the goods, consent to the goods being forfeited to the Commonwealth by giving a written notice to that effect to the CEO.

(2) If the designated owner gives such a notice, the goods are forfeited to the Commonwealth and must be disposed of as the CEO directs.

36 Release of goods-no application for injunction

(1) The CEO must release seized goods (not being goods forfeited to the Commonwealth under section 35) to their designated owner at the end of the application period unless, within that period, the objector, or one of the objectors, has:

(a) made an application for an injunction under section 43 in relation to the goods; and

(b) given to the CEO written notice of the application.

(2) The CEO must also release the seized goods to their designated owner if, before the end of the application period, the objector, or each of the objectors, has, by written notice given to the CEO, consented to the release of the goods.

(3) The CEO may release the seized goods to their designated owner at any time before the end of the application period if:

(a) the CEO, having regard to information that has come to his or her knowledge after the goods were seized, does not have reasonable grounds for believing that section 12 would be contravened by the importation of the goods; and

(b) the objector has not, or none of the objectors has, made an application for an injunction under section 43 in relation to the goods.

Note: In obtaining information for the purposes of this section, the CEO must comply with Principles 1, 2 and 3 in section 14 of the Privacy Act 1988.

37 Application for injunction-additional parties, relief etc.

(1) In this section, a reference to an application for an injunction under section 43 is a reference to such an application made, in relation to seized goods, by a person who is an objector in relation to the goods.

(2) A prescribed court in which an application for an injunction under section 43 is pending:

(a) may, on the application of a person having a sufficient interest in the subject-matter of the application, allow the person to be joined as a respondent to the application; and

(b) must allow the CEO to appear and be heard.

(3) In addition to any relief that the court may grant apart from this section, the court may:

(a) at any time, if it thinks it just, order that the seized goods be released to their designated owner subject to such conditions (if any) as the court thinks fit; or (b) order that the seized goods be forfeited to the Commonwealth.

(4) If:

(a) the court decides that an injunction should not be granted under section 43; and

(b) the designated owner of the goods, or any other respondent, satisfies the court that he or she has suffered loss or damage because the goods were seized;

the court may order the objector to pay to the designated owner or other respondent compensation, in the amount determined by the court, for any part of that loss or damage that is attributable to any period beginning on or after the day on which the application under section 43 was made.

(5) If, at the end of 3 weeks commencing on the day on which the application for an injunction under section 43 was made, there is not in force an order of the court preventing the goods from being released, the CEO must release the goods to their designated owner.

(6) If the court orders that the goods be released, the CEO must, subject to section 39, comply with the order.

38 Disposal of goods ordered to be forfeited

If the court orders under section 37 that goods be forfeited to the Commonwealth, the goods are to be disposed of as the CEO directs.

39 Power of CEO to retain control of goods

In spite of this Part, the CEO:

(a) must not release, or dispose of, any seized goods; or

(b) must not take any action in relation to the goods to give effect to any order of a court under section 37;

if the CEO is required or allowed to retain control of the goods under any other law of the Commonwealth.

40 Insufficient security

If security given under subsection 33(3) by the objector or objectors who gave notice under section 32 is not sufficient to meet the expenses incurred by the Commonwealth as a result of the action taken by the CEO under this Division because of the notice, the amount of the difference between those expenses and the amount of security:

(a) is a debt due by the objector, or by the objectors jointly and severally, to the Commonwealth; and

(b) may be recovered by action in any court of competent jurisdiction.

41 Commonwealth not liable for loss etc. suffered because of seizure

The Commonwealth is not liable for any loss or damage suffered by a person:

(a) because the CEO seized, or failed to seize, goods under this Division; or

(b) because of the release of any seized goods.

42 Modification in relation to Christmas Island etc.

The regulations may provide for the modification or adaptation of this Division in its application to:

(a) Christmas Island; or

(b) Cocos (Keeling) Islands; or

(c) Norfolk Island.

43 Injunctions

(1) If a person has engaged, is engaging, or is proposing to engage, in conduct in contravention of section 12, a prescribed court may grant an injunction restraining the person from engaging in the conduct.

(2) The power of the court to grant an injunction may be exercised:

(a) whether or not it appears to the court that the person intends to engage again, or to continue to engage, in conduct of that kind; and

(b) whether or not the person has previously engaged in conduct of that kind.

(3) An injunction under this section may only be granted on the application of SOCOG, SPOC or a licensed user.

(4) An injunction granted under this section on the application of SOCOG may only relate to conduct constituting use of Sydney 2000 Games indicia or images referred to in one or more of the following paragraphs:

(a) common Sydney 2000 Games indicia;

(b) Sydney 2000 Olympic Games indicia;

(c) common Sydney 2000 Games images;

(d) Sydney 2000 Olympic Games images.

(5) An injunction granted under this section on the application of SPOC may only relate to conduct constituting use of Sydney 2000 Games indicia or images referred to in one or more of the following paragraphs:

(a) common Sydney 2000 Games indicia;

(b) Sydney 2000 Paralympic Games indicia;

(c) common Sydney 2000 Games images;

(d) Sydney 2000 Paralympic Games images.

(6) An injunction granted under this section on the application of a person

who is a licensed user may only relate to conduct constituting a use of Sydney 2000 Games indicia or images to which the licence granted to the person under Division 2 of Part 3 relates.

(7) The court may discharge or vary an injunction granted under this section.

(8) The powers conferred on the court by this section are in addition to, and not in derogation of, any other powers of the court, whether conferred by this Act or otherwise.

(9) For the purposes of subsections (4), (5) and (6), the use of indicia so closely resembling the Sydney 2000 Games indicia referred to in those subsections as to be likely to be mistaken, by a reasonable person, for the Sydney 2000 Games indicia referred to, is to be taken to be use of the Sydney 2000 Games indicia referred to.

44 Interim injunctions

(1) A prescribed court may grant an interim injunction pending the determination of an application under section 43.

(2) For the purposes of subsection (1) of this section, a contravention of section 12 is to be taken to have caused immediate and irreparable damage to the applicant.

45 Corrective advertisements

Without limiting the generality of section 43 and whether or not relief is granted under that section, where, on the application of SOCOG or SPOC, a prescribed court is satisfied that a person has engaged in conduct constituting a contravention of section 12, the court may make an order requiring the person, by such means (including a broadcast) as the court thinks fit, at the person's own expense and at times specified in the order, to publish advertisements the terms of which are specified in, or are to be determined in accordance with, the order.

46 Damages

(1) If SOCOG, SPOC or a licensed user suffers loss or damage as a result of anything done by a person in contravention of section 12, the amount of the loss or damage may be recovered by action in a prescribed court.

(2) The action must be brought within 3 years after the day on which the contravention occurred. A request under section 27 for consent to the bringing of an action must be given not later than the day preceding the last working day before this Act ceases to have effect.
Note: For when this Act ceases to have effect see section 55.

(3) The grant of an injunction under section 43 does not prevent the award of damages under this section.

47 Other remedies

(1) The remedies provided under this Division are in addition to remedies provided by any law (whether a law of the Commonwealth or a law of a State or Territory) that confers any rights or powers on SOCOG, SPOC or a licensed user in relation to conduct of a kind that constitutes a contravention of section 12 of this Act.

(2) Without limiting the generality of subsection (1), the remedies provided under this Division are in addition to the remedies provided by the Trade Practices Act 1974 in relation to engaging in conduct that is misleading or deceptive (see section 52 of that Act) and, in particular, in relation to representations:

(a) that goods or services have sponsorship or approval that they do not have (see paragraph 53(c) of that Act); or

(b) that a corporation (as defined in that Act) has a sponsorship, approval or affiliation that it does not have (see paragraph 53(d) of that Act).

(3) The references in subsection (2) to particular provisions of the Trade Practices Act 1974 do not imply that other provisions of that Act do not apply in relation to conduct of a kind that constitutes a contravention of section 12 of this Act.

48 Groundless threats of legal proceedings

(1) If SOCOG, SPOC or a licensed user threatens to make an application, or bring an action, against a person (the threatened person) on the ground that the threatened person has engaged, is engaging, or is proposing to engage in conduct in contravention of section 12, any person aggrieved by the threat may bring an action in a prescribed court against SOCOG, SPOC or the licensed user (as the case may be).

(2) In an action under subsection (1), the court may:

(a) make a declaration that SOCOG, SPOC or the licensed user had no grounds for making the threat; and

(b) grant an injunction restraining SOCOG, SPOC or the licensed user from continuing to make the threat.

The court may also award damages for loss that the person aggrieved has suffered as a result of the making of the threat.

(3) An action may not be brought under this section if the person who made the threat has made an application, or brought an action, under Division 3 against the threatened person in relation to the act, or proposed act, to which the threat related.

(4) An action under this section may not be continued if the person who made the threat makes an application, or brings an action, under Division

3 against the threatened person in relation to the act, or proposed act, to which the threat related.

(5) It is a defence to an action under subsection (1) that the conduct of the threatened person, in relation to which the threat was made, constitutes a contravention of section 12.

49 Counterclaim in action on groundless threats

(1) If SOCOG, SPOC or a licensed user would be entitled to make an application, or bring an action, against a person for a contravention of section 12, SOCOG, SPOC or the licensed user may, in an action under section 48, make a counterclaim for any relief to which SOCOG, SPOC or the licensed user would be entitled under Division 3.

(2) The provisions of Divisions 1, 2 and 3 apply as if a counterclaim were an application or action made or brought by SOCOG, SPOC or a licensed user under Division 3.

50 Prescribed courts

Each of the following courts is a prescribed court for the purposes of this Act:

(a) the Federal Court;
(b) the Supreme Court of a State;
(c) the Supreme Court of the Australian Capital Territory;
(d) the Supreme Court of the Northern Territory;
(e) the Supreme Court of Norfolk Island.

51 Jurisdiction of Federal Court

The Federal Court has jurisdiction in relation to all matters arising under this Act.

52 Jurisdiction of other prescribed courts

(1) Each prescribed court (other than the Federal Court) has federal jurisdiction in relation to all matters arising under this Act.

(2) The jurisdiction conferred by subsection (1) on the Supreme Court of a Territory is conferred to the extent that the Constitution permits.

53 Transfer of proceedings

(1) A prescribed court in which an application has been made, or an action brought, under this Act may, on the application of a party made at any stage, by an order, transfer the application or action to another prescribed court having jurisdiction to hear and determine the application or action.

(2) When a court transfers an application or action to another court:
   (a) all relevant documents of record filed in the transferring court must be sent to the other court by the Registrar or other appropriate officer of the transferring court; and
   (b) the application or action continues in the other court as if:
      (i) it had been started there; and
      (ii) all steps taken in the transferring court had been taken in the other court.

54 Concurrent operation of State and Territory laws

It is the intention of the Parliament that this Act is not to apply to the exclusion of a law of a State or Territory to the extent that the law is capable of operating concurrently with this Act.

55 Cessation of operation of Act

If this Act is not repealed before the end of 31 December 2000, it ceases to have effect at that time.

Note: In relation to an Act that ceases to have effect, see section 8B of the Acts Interpretation Act 1901.

56 Regulations

The Governor-General may make regulations:
(a) prescribing matters required or permitted by this Act to be prescribed; or
(b) prescribing matters necessary or convenient to be prescribed for carrying out or giving effect to this Act.

Bibliography

BOOKS

Gutterman, Alan S. and Bently J. Anderson, *Intellectual Property in Global Markets*, London: Kluwer Law International, 1997.

Michaels, Amanda, *A Practical Guide to Trade Mark Law*, London: Sweet and Maxwell, 2002.

Issac, Belinda, *Brand Protection Matters*, London: Sweet and Maxwell, 2000.

Hoekman, Bernard, Aaditya Mattoo, and Philip English (eds), *Development, Trade and the WTO*, Washington D.C.: The World Bank, 2002.

Berman, Bruce (ed.), *From Ideas to Assets- Investing Wisely in Intellectual Property*, New York: John Wiley and Sons, 2002.

Pickering, C.D.G., *Trade Marks in Theory and Practice*, Oxford: Hatt Publishing, 1998.

Fink, Carsten and Keith E. Maskus (eds), *Intellectual Property and Development*, Washington D.C.: World Band and Oxford University Press, 2005.

Morcom, Christopher, Ashley Roughton, and James Graham, *The Modern Law of Trade Marks*, London: Butterworths, 1999.

Wadlow, Christopher, *The Law of Passing Off*, London: Sweet and Maxwell, 2004.

Kitchin, David, David Llewelyn, James Mellor, Richard Meade, and Thomas Moody Stuart, *Kerly's Law of Trade Marks*, London: Sweet and Maxwell, 2001.

Stallard, Hayley (ed.), *Bagehot on Sponsorship, Merchandising and Endorsement*, London: Sweet and Maxwell, 1998.

McCarthy, J. Thomas, *McCarthy on Trademarks and Unfair Competition*, Fourth Edition, 4 McCarthy on Trademarks and Unfair Competition Â§ 27:66 (4th edn).

McKeough, Jill, Kathy Bowrey and Philip Griffith, *Intellectual Property—Comments and Materials*, Pyrmont, NSW: Law Book Company, 2002.

Jeremiah, Joanna R, *Merchandising Intellectual Property Rights*, Chichester: John Wiley and Sons, 1997.

Idris, Kamil, *Intellectual Property—A Power Tool for Economic Growth*, Geneva: World Intellectual Property Organization, 2003.

Garnett, Kevin, Gillian Davies, and Gwilym Harbottle, *Copinger and Skone James on Copyright*, London: Sweet and Maxwell, 2005.

Jennewein, Klaus, *Intellectual Property Management*, Heidelberg: Physica–Verlag, 2005.

Bently, Lionel and Brad Sherman, *Intellectual Property Law*, New Delhi: Oxford University Press, 2003.

Wilkof, Neil. J. and Daniel Burkitt, *Trademark Licensing*, London: Sweet & Maxwell, 2005.

Narayanan, P., *Law of Trade Marks and Passing Off*, Kolkata: Eastern Law House, 2004.

Groves, Peter J., *Source Book on Intellectual Property Law*, London: Cavendish Publishing Limited, 1997.

Towse, Ruth and Rudi Holzhauer (eds), *The Economics of Intellectual Property-Volume III*, Glos: Edward Elgar Publishing Ltd, 2002.

Ramappa, T., *Competition Law in India*, New Delhi: Oxford University Press, 2006.

Ward, Thomas M., *Intellectual Property in Commerce*, MA: Thomson West, 2004.

Dhall, Vinod (ed.), *Competition Law Today—Concepts, Issues and the Law in Practice*, New Delhi: Oxford University Press, 2007.

Cornish, W.R., *Intellectual Property: Patents, Copyright, Trademarks and Allied Rights*, Delhi: Universal Law Publishing Co. Pvt. Ltd., 2003.

ARTICLES

A. G. Papandreou, 'The Economic Effect of Trademarks' in Ruth Towse and Rudi Holzhauer (eds), *The Economics of Intellectual Property- Volume III* (Glos: Edward Elgar Publishing Ltd, 2002).

Aarti Dua, 'Not a Flight of Fancy', *Businessworld* (April 2, 2007), 56.

Abram Sauer, 'Ambush Marketing: Steals the Show' available online at http://www.brandchannel.com/features_effect.asp?pf_id=98.

Alexander Schaub, 'EC Competition Policy and its Implications for the Sports Sector', available online at http://ec.europa.eu/comm/competition/speeches/text/sp1999_019_en.pdf .

Alfred E Kahn, 'Standards for Anti trust Policy', 67 *Harv. L.Rev.* 28, (November 1953).

Amit Bubna and Shubhashis Gangopadhyay, 'The Economics of Competition Law' in Vinod Dhall (ed.), *Competition Law Today – Concepts, Issues and the Law in Practice* (New Delhi: Oxford University Press, 2007).

Andrew Moss, 'The Olympics: A Celebration of Sport and the Role of Law', Ent. L.R. 2004, 15(8), (2004), pp. 237–42.

Anita M. Moorman and T. Christopher Greenwell, 'Consumer Attitudes of Deception and the Legality of Ambush Marketing Practices', 15 J. Legal Aspects Sport 183 (2005).

Anne M. Wall, 'Sports Marketing and the Law: Protecting Proprietary Interests In Sports Entertainment Events', 7 *Marq. Sports L.J.* 77 (1996).

Anne M. Wall, 'The Game Behind The Games', 12 *Marq. Sports L. Rev.* 557 (2002).

Askan Deutsch, 'Sports Broadcasting and Virtual Advertising: Defining the Limits of Copyright Law and the Law of Unfair Competition', 11 *Marq. Sports L. Rev.* 41 (2000)

Avril Martindale, 'Let the Sponsor Beware', *Ent. L.R.* 1993, 4(6), (1993), pp. 165–8.

Bill Wilson, 'Olympics Lining Up Financial Rewards' available online at http://news.bbc.co.uk/1/hi/business/4861024.stm, accessed 4 April 2006.

Brian White, 'Review Essay: Who Are the Real Competitors in the Olympic Games?', 12 *J. Contemp. Legal Issues* 227 (2001).

Carolina Pina and Ana Gil-Roble, 'Sponsorship of Sports Events and Ambush Marketing', *E.I.P.R.* 2005, 27(3), (2005), pp. 93–6.

Carsten Fink and Beata K. Smarzynska, 'Trademarks, Geographical Indications, and Developing Countries' in Bernard Hoekman, Aaditya Mattoo, and Philip English (eds), *Development, Trade and the WTO*, (Washington DC: The World Bank, 2002).

Carsten Fink and Carlos A. Primo Braga, 'How Stronger Protection of Intellectual Property Rights Affects International Trade Flows' in Carsten Fink and Keith E. Maskus (eds), *Intellectual Property and Development* (Washington D.C.: World Band and Oxford University Press, 2005).

Cristina Garrigues, 'Ambush Marketing: Robbery or Smart Advertising', *E.I.P.R.* 2002, 24(11), pp. 505–7.

Edward Vassallo, Kristin Blemaster and Patricia Werner, 'An International Look At Ambush Marketing', 95 *Trademark Rep.* 1338 (2005).

Erinn M. Batcha, 'Who Are the Real Competitors in the Olympic Games? Dual Olympic Battles: Trademark Infringement and Ambush Marketing Harm Corporate Sponsors—Violations Against the USOC and its Corporate Sponsors', 8 *Seton Hall J. Sport L.* 229 (1998).

Geoffrey D. Wilson, 'Internet Pop-Up Ads: Your Days Are Numbered! The Supreme Court of California Announces a Workable Standard for Trespass to Chattels in Electronic Communications', 24 *Loy. L.A. Ent. L. Rev.* 567 (2004).

Geoffrey P. Lantos, 'The Boundaries of Strategic Corporate Social Responsibility', available online at http://faculty.stonehill.edu/glantos/Lantos1/PDF_Folder/Pub_arts_pdf/Strategic%20CSR.pdf.

Glaucio Scremin, 'Impact of Antitrust Laws on American Professional Team Sports', available online at http://www.thesportjournal.org/2005Journal/Vol8-No1/SCJ_04_antitrust.asp.

Gordon V. Smith, 'Brand Valuation: Too Long Neglected', *EIPR* 1990, 12(5), (1990), pp. 159–64.

Graeme Orr, 'Marketing Games: The Regulation of Olympic Indicia and Images in Australia', E.I.P.R. 1997, 19(9), (1997) pp. 504–8.

H. Jackson Knight, 'Intellectual Property "101" ' in Bruce Berman (ed.), *From Ideas to Assets-Investing Wisely in Intellectual Property* (New York: John Wiley and Sons, 2002).

Ignacio De Leon, 'The Enforcement of Competition Policy on Intellectual Property and its Implications on Economic Development: The Latin American Experience', available online at http://papers.ssrn.com/sol3/papers.cfm?abstract_id=270730#PaperDownload.

J. Thomas McCarthy, 'McCarthy on Trademarks and Unfair Competition', Fourth Edition, 4 *McCarthy on Trademarks and Unfair Competition* Â§ 27:66 (4th ed.).

Jacqueline A. Leimer, 'Ambush Marketing: Not Just an Olympic-Sized Problem', 2 NO. 4 *Intell. Prop. Strategist* 1 (1996).

Jamie Carr, 'Get real: Sport Costs', http://www.adfocus.co.za/adfocus2003/b8.htm.

Jason K. Schmitz, 'Ambush Marketing: The Off-Field Competition at the Olympic Games', 3 *Nw. J. Tech. and Intell. Prop.* 203 (2005).

Jeremy Curthoys and Christopher N Kendall, 'Ambush Marketing and the Sydney 2000 Games (Indicia and Images) Protection Act: A Retrospective', Murdoch University Electronic Journal of Law, http://www.murdoch.edu.au/elaw/issues/v8n2/kendall82.html.

Jerry Welsh, 'Ambush Marketing: What it is, What it isn't', available online at http://www.poolonline.com/archive/issue19/iss19fea5.html (2002)

Jodie Sopher, 'Weight-Loss Advertising Too Good To Be True: Are Manufacturers or The Media To Blame?', 22 *Cardozo Arts and Ent. L.J.* 933 (2005).

John A. Fortunato, 'Reconciling Sports Sponsorship Exclusivity With Antitrust Law', 8 Tex. Rev. Ent. & Sports L. 33, (Spring 2007), pp. 40–5.

John Vukelj, 'Post No Bills: Can the NBA Prohibit its Players from Wearing Tattoo Advertisements?', 15 *Fordham Intell. Prop. Media and Ent. L.J.* 507 (2005).

Jonathan Weinberg, 'Constitutional Protection of Commercial Speech', 82 *Colum. L. Rev.* 720 (1982).

Juda Strawczynski, 'Is Canada Ready for the Vancouver Winter Games? An Examination of Canada's Olympic Intellectual Property Protection', 62 *U. Toronto Fac. L. Rev.* 213 (2004).

Kristen M. Beystehner, 'See Ya Later, Gator: Assessing Whether Placing Pop-Up Advertisements on Another Company's Website Violates Trademark Law', 11 *J. Intell. Prop. L.* 87 (2003).

Laura Misener, 'Safeguarding the Olympic Insignia: Protecting the Commercial Integrity of the Canadian Olympic Association', 13 J. *Legal Aspects Sport* 79 (2003).

Lisa A. Delpy and Kathleen B. Costello, 'Lawyering on the Front Lines: On-Site Legal Counsel for Major Sporting Events', 6 *Marq. Sports L.J.* 29 (1995).

Lori L. Bean, 'Ambush Marketing: Sports Sponsorship Confusion and the Lanham Act', 75 *B.U. L. Rev.* 1099 (1995).

Mario Monti, 'Competition and Sport the Rules of the Game', available online at http://europa.eu/rapid/pressReleasesAction.do?reference=SPEECH/01/84&format=HTML&aged=0&language=EN&guiLanguage=en.

Mark Roper-Drimie, 'Sydney 2000 Olympic Games—"The Worst Games Ever" for Ambush Marketers', *Ent. L.R.* 2001, 12(5), (2001), pp. 150–3.

Michael A. Lisi, 'Ambush Marketing: Here to Stay?', 12 No. 1 *Intell. Prop. Strategist* 3 (2005).

Noalle K. Nish, 'How Far Have We Come? A Look at the Olympic And Amateur Sports Act of 1998, The United States Olympic Committee, and the Winter Olympic Games of 2002', 13 *Seton Hall J. Sport L.* 53 (2003).

Owen Dean, 'Legal Aspects of Ambush Marketing', available online at http://www.legalcity.net/Index.cfm?fuseaction=MAGAZINE.article&ArticleID=7631391&TopicID=5051638.

Rachel Montagnon and Joel Smith, 'Intellectual Property: The London Olympics Bill', *E.I.P.R.* 2006, 28(1), N11 (2006).

Rick Kurnit, 'Intellectual Property and Marketing', SJ075 ALI-ABA 607 (2004).

Robert D. Anderson and Alberto Heimler, 'Abuse of Dominant Position-Enforcement Issues and Approaches for Developing Countries' in Vinod Dhall (ed.), *Competition Law Today—Concepts, Issues and the Law in Practice* (New Delhi: Oxford University Press, 2007).

Robert Feinberg, 'Trademarks, Market Power, and Information' in Ruth Towse and Rudi Holzhauer (eds), *The Economics of Intellectual Property—Volume III* (Glos: Edward Elgar Publishing Ltd, 2002).

Robert N. Davis, 'Ambushing The Olympic Games', 3 *Vill. Sports and Ent. L.J.* 423 (1996).

Scott A. Bearby, 'Marketing, Protection and Enforcement of NCAA Marks', 12 *Marq. Sports L. Rev.* 543 (2002).

Scott Bearby and Bruce Siegal, 'From the Stadium Parking Lot to the Information Superhighway: How to Protect Your Trademarks from Infringement', 28 *J.C. and U.L.* 633 (2002).

Stacey H. Wang, 'Great Olympics, New China: Intellectual Property Enforcement Steps up to the Mark', 27 *Loy. L.A. Int'l and Comp. L. Rev.* 291 (2005).

Stephen M. Mckelvey, 'Atlanta '96: Olympic Countdown to Ambush Armageddon?', 4 *Seton Hall J. Sport L.* 397 (1994).

Stephen M. McKelvey, 'Commercial "Branding": The Final Frontier or False Start for Athletes' Use of Temporary Tattoos as Body Billboards', 13 *J. Legal Aspects Sport* 1 (2003).

Steve McKelvey and John Grady, 'Ambush Marketing: The Legal Battleground for Sport Marketers', 21-WTR *Ent. and Sports Law.* 8 (2004).

Steve McKelvey and John Grady, 'An Analysis of the Ongoing Global Efforts to Combat Ambush Marketing: Will Corporate Marketers "Take" the Gold in Greece?', 14 *J. Legal Aspects Sport* 191 (2004).

Sudipta Bhattacharjee, 'Ambush Marketing- The Problem and the Projected Solutions vis-à-vis Intellectual Property Law—A Global Perspective', *Journal of Intellectual Property Rights*, Vol. 8, September 2003, pp. 375–88.

Susan Barty and David Roberts, 'United Kingdom: London 2012 Olympics: Ambush Marketing', www.mondaq.com (2006).

Taran Atwal, 'Canada: Keeping your Competitive Edge', *Mondaq Law Review*, 30 May 2006.

The Deccan Chronicle, 'Beckham Addicted to the Pain of Tattoos', (Hyderabad: 4 April 2006), 20.

The Economist, 'The Good Company', (20 January 2005).

The Economist, 'The Year of the Brand', (24 December 1988).

The Economist, 'War Minus Shooting', (16 February 2006).

Therese Catanzariti, 'The Plot Thickens: Formats, Sequels and Spin-Offs After Goggomobil', *Ent. L.R. 2004*, 15(3), (2004), pp. 85–93.

Thomas J. Arkell, 'National Hockey League Jurisprudence: Past, Present and Future', 8 *Seton Hall J. Sport L.* 135 (1998).

Tony Tollington, 'The Separable Nature of Brands as Assets: The United Kingdom Legal and Accounting Perspective', *E.I.P.R.* 2001, 23(1), (2001), pp. 6–13.

U.S. Department of Justice and Fed. Trade Commission, 'Antitrust Enforcement and Intellectual Property Rights: Promoting Innovation and Competition (2007)', available online at http://www.usdoj.gov/atr/public/hearings/ip/intro.pdf

Valentine Korah, 'Competition Law and Intellectual Property Rights' in Vinod

Dhall (ed.), *Competition Law Today—Concepts, Issues and the Law in Practice* (New Delhi: Oxford University Press, 2007).

Vikrant Rana, 'A Case of Ambush Marketing in India', *INTA Bulletin*—15 August 2003, available online at www.inta.org.

Wanda Jane Rogers, 'Beyond Economic Theory: A Model for Analyzing the Antitrust Implications of Exclusive Dealing Arrangements', 45 *Duke L.J.* 1009 (1996).

William E. Kovacic, 'The Intellectual DNA of Modern U.S. Competition Law for Dominant Firm Conduct: The Chicago/Harvard Double Helix', 2007 *Columbia Bus. L. Rev.* 1 (2007).

William M. Landes and Richard A. Posner, 'The Economics of Trademark Law' in Ruth Towse and Rudi Holzhauer (eds), *The Economics of Intellectual Property—Volume III* (Glos: Edward Elgar Publishing Ltd, 2002).

WEB REFERENCES

http://bwnt.businessweek.com/brand/2006/

http://www.olympic.org/uk/organisation/facts/introduction/index_uk.asp

http://www.macmillandictionary.com/New-Words/050815-ambush-marketing.htm

http://www.olympic.org/uk/organisation/index_uk.asp

http://fifaworldcup.yahoo.com/06/en/partners.html

http://www.tmcnet.com/usubmit/2006/03/31/1524884.htm

http://www.macmillandictionary.com/New-Words/050815-ambush-marketing.htm

http://www.poolonline.com/bios/biojwelsh.html

http://www.olympic.org/uk/organisation/facts/introduction/index_uk.asp

http://www.tmcnet.com/usubmit/2006/03/31/1524884.htm

http://www.onpoint-marketing.com/beverage-marketing.htm

http://www.abc.net.au/goldcoast/stories/s1593547.htm

http://www.icc-cricket.com/icc-cwc/content/story/243734.html

http://barbados.gov.bb/Docs/Act-World%20Cup.pdf

http://www.austlii.edu.au/au/legis/vic/consol_act/meaa2007309/

http://www.opsi.gov.uk/acts/en2006/06en12-a.htm

http://news.xinhuanet.com/english/2007-06/14/content_6242374.htm

http://www.chinadaily.com.cn/2008/2007-06/13/content_893703.htm

http://en.beijing2008.cn/98/69/article211986998.shtml

http://english.ipr.gov.cn/ipr/en/info/Article.jsp?a_no=55149&col_no=926&dir=200702

http://news.xinhuanet.com/english/2007-06/14/content_6242374.htm

www.ipr.gov.cn/ipr/en/info/Article.jsp?a_no=6309&col_no=926&dir=200606
www.ipr.gov.cn/ipr/en/info/Article.jsp?a_no=10472&col_no=99&dir=200608
www.ipr.gov.cn/ipr/en/info/Article.jsp?a_no=8861&col_no=99&dir=200607
http://english.ipr.gov.cn/ipr/en/info/Article.jsp?a_no=3004&col_no=893&dir=200604
http://www.adamsmith.org/smith/won/won-b1-c10-pt-2.html
http://www.olympic.org/uk/organisation/facts/programme/profiles_uk.asp
http://www.fifa.com/aboutfifa/marketingtv/releases/newsid=540450.html#visa+becomes+fifa+partner+period+through+2014

Index